Deeds of John and Manuel
Comnenus

by John Kinnamos

NUMBER XCV OF THE RECORDS OF CIVILIZATION
SOURCES AND STUDIES

Deeds of John and Manuel Comnenus

by
John Kinnamos

Translated by
Charles M. Brand

COLUMBIA UNIVERSITY PRESS
NEW YORK
1976

Library of Congress Cataloging in Publication Data

Cinnamus, Joannes, 12th cent.
  Deeds of John and Manuel Comnenus.

  (Records of civilization, sources and studies;
no. 95)
  Translation of Epitomē tōn katorthōmaton tō makaritē
Vasilei kai porphyrogennētō Kyrō Iōannē tō Komnēnō kai
aphēgēsis tōn prachthentōn tō aoidimō hyiō autou tō
Vasilei kai porphyrogennētō Kyrō Manouēl to Komnēnō.
  Includes bibliographical references and index.
  1. Byzantine Empire—History—John II Comnenus,
1118–1143.   2. Byzantine Empire—History—Manuel I
Comnenus, 1143–1180.   3. Joannes II Comnenus, Emperor
of the East, 1088–1143.   4. Manuel I Comnenus,
Emperor of the East, 1120 (ca.)–1180.   I. Title.
II. Series.
DF606.C5613   949.5′03   76-15317
ISBN 0-231-04080-6

Columbia University Press
New York   Guildford, Surrey

Records of Civilization : Sources and Studies

Edited under the Auspices of the Department of History, Columbia University

IN MEMORY OF
GEORGE SOULIS
1927–1966

Contents

Preface

This work was commenced as a necessary preliminary to a translation of the history of Nicetas Choniates; it is impossible to read Nicetas' account of the same period without comparing it with Kinnamos' version. As I advanced, I became steadily more impressed with the value of Kinnamos as a historian. I have striven to convey something of his lively and vivid narrative style.

Because the existing edition of Kinnamos is unsatisfactory, I have utilized corrections suggested by Moravcsik, Babos, Chalandon, and Wirth. The conventional book and chapter numbers have been preserved, but further paragraphing is my own responsibility. Since the text is usually cited according to pages of the Bonn edition, these have been inserted between virgules. My annotation has been intended to clarify places and dates, and to point out the principal modern studies. An attempt to include every monograph or solve every problem posed by Kinnamos would have been futile.

Proper names have occasioned difficulty and forced some arbitrary decisions. Kinnamos' archaisms ("Persians," "Scyths," etc.) have been rendered as "Turks," "Petchenegs," and the like. Place names have been retained in their Byzantine form, because Adrianople, Laodikeia, and the Lykos are better known than Edirne, Denizli, and the Çürüksu Çay. At their first appearance, and again in the index, the modern equivalent has been added in brackets. For Byzantine personal names, I have used conventional Latin or English first names ("John" or "Andronicus") and a transliteration of surnames, except "Comnenus" and "Angelus." For the spelling of non-Greek names, I have taken K. M. Setton's *A History of the Crusades* as my principal guide and supplemented it with suggestions from Moravcsik, Grumel, and others. Foreign princesses who married into the Byzantine imperial family customarily received new names; their original ones have been noted in brackets, e.g., "[Piroska-]Irene."

This work commenced as a result of a Fulbright Research Fellowship, granted by the United States Educational Foundation in Greece; it was continued during a sabbatical leave from Bryn Mawr College and the tenure of a Fellowship from the John Simon Guggenheim Memorial Foundation. I am deeply grateful to these institutions for their assistance. I am happy to express my thanks to the librarians of Bryn Mawr College, in particular James Tanis, Thomas Song, and Pamilla Reilly, and those of the Gennadius Library, Francis Walton, Sophie Papageorgiou, and Artemis Nikolaides, for their patience and kindness. I am also much in debt to the American School of Classical Studies in Athens for the use of their library, especially their excellent collection of large-scale maps of Asia Minor. Richmond Lattimore, Mabel Lang, and Francis Walton assisted me with difficult passages of Greek, and I am thankful to them. I am particularly indebted to Angeliki Laiou for her detailed criticism, which has saved me from many pitfalls. Finally, I am happy to express my thanks to my wife for her manifold assistance and encouragement.

This book is dedicated to one of the finest of this generation of Byzantine scholars. None who knew his kindness and learning will soon forget him.

Bryn Mawr College   Charles M. Brand
June 1976

Deeds of John and Manuel Comnenus

by John Kinnamos

Introduction

The evolution of the Byzantine Empire, which as its inhabitants knew was really the Roman Empire Christianized, is delineated by a series of outstanding historians. The age of the Comneni and Angeli, 1081–1204, received the attention of three contemporaries whose works surveyed extended periods of time. Long after the death of Alexius I Comnenus (1081–1118), his daughter Anna wrote a biographical epic, fittingly titled *The Alexiad,* with a strong panegyric tone. While it focuses on her father's military activities, its broad canvas touches on myriad aspects of Byzantine life and thought. John Kinnamos took up the task where Anna left off. He proposed to write the history of the reigns of John II (1118–43) and Manuel I (1143–80), but the surviving text breaks off during the year 1176. Kinnamos' work also eulogizes the emperors. Finally, Nicetas Choniates likewise began his narrative with the accession of John II, and, adding to his text from time to time, carried his history through the western conquest of Constantinople in 1204 and into the succeeding events, breaking off in 1206. His work is almost uniformly derogatory of the emperors under whom he lived; he sought to allocate the blame for Byzantium's downfall in 1204. As a historian, he is a major figure; embittered and scarred by the tragedy of his times, he wrote with an acid pen, not unworthy of Thucydides. His lengthy work, which deserves to be better known, is available in a German translation.[1]

Why, then, undertake a translation of Kinnamos, who is the least important of the three? Without him, both our knowledge of Byzantine history and of the Byzantine mentality would be the poorer. For the years 1118 to 1176, he and Nicetas Choniates cover the same ground, yet in fundamentally different ways; this is especially true for the reign of Manuel. Where Kinnamos describes at length, Nicetas is brief, but Nicetas frequently reveals matters concealed by Kinnamos. Thus, neither can be read without the other.

Further, both Anna Comnena and Nicetas are exceptional individuals, educated far beyond the level of most of their contemporaries. Kinnamos is very much an ordinary Byzantine bureaucrat. He was reasonably well-read in the classics, and unquestioningly accepted the outward forms and doctrines of Christianity. But his real religion was the empire and the emperor: the empire as God's vehicle for unifying mankind, the emperor as the chosen leader for His people. These conceptions, which he shared with the population at large, make his work a leading exposition of the simple, straight-forward understanding of the nature and purpose of history entertained by literate Byzantines.

John Kinnamos, as he repeatedly states, was born after the death of emperor John II, in April 1143, but probably not long after.[2] While nothing is known of his family, a Basil Kinnamos was bishop of Paphos on Cyprus about 1165 and thereafter.[3] Seemingly from his early years, there remains an Ethopoiia or rhetorical exercise which attests the influence of Nicephorus Basilakes. The latter, a prominent rhetorician, was probably his teacher.[4] The title of his history specifies that Kinnamos was an imperial secretary;[5] thus he was one of a large body of clerks attached to the imperial court and the emperor's person. They might at times be utilized for diplomatic missions or sent to accompany armies.[6] Secretaries who, like Nicetas Choniates, distinguished themselves might rise to posts in the provincial and central administration, but Kinnamos apparently did not do so. He states that he entered

Manuel's service at a very early age: ". . . before I was even a youth I accompanied many of his expeditions into both continents." [7] To judge from his military interests and what little we know of his career, much of his life during Manuel's reign was passed with the soldiery. [8] It seems possible that he participated in the Italian campaign of 1155–56: his descriptions are vivid and usually geographically precise, although he could have been no more than twelve at the time. [9] Similarly, when he narrates the conduct of the Byzantine embassy in Rome in 1157, he displays a sudden, unprecedented knowledge of Roman city politics, the papal practice of Interdict (unknown to the Eastern Church), and the policy of the Byzantine envoys. If he was not present, he had extremely good information available. Ultimately, he became sufficiently intimate with the emperor, he says, to discuss questions of Aristotelian philosophy with him. [10]

The first occasion on which he specifically states that he was an eyewitness was in 1165 at Manuel's siege of Zeugminon (modern Zemun) in Yugoslavia. [11] Two quotations, taken together, suggest that Kinnamos was present in 1176 at the disastrous battle of Myriokephalon. The first relates to Kinnamos' incredulity in regard to Manuel's personal daring in battle, ". . . until the facts of the matter came to my attention, as I was thus by chance encompassed amidst the foe and observed from close at hand that emperor resisting entire Turkish regiments. But the history will describe this at the right moment. . . ." [12] Later, he says, "For when, after many years had passed, Kilidj Arslan became careless of his engagements toward the emperor, he caused the Romans to attack the Turks in full force. By some chance the army fell into difficult terrain, lost many of the aristocracy, and came near a great disaster, save that in warfare the emperor was there seen to surpass the bounds of human excellence. But, as I have already said, these things will be related later by me." [13] The second text clearly alludes to Myriokephalon, and the reference backwards in it can only indicate the former quotation, which occurs a few pages earlier. Apparently Kinnamos was one of the handful who escaped from that disaster; regrettably his history, as it survives, breaks off at the start of the campaign prior to that battle.

The next stage of Kinnamos' life was closely linked with the composition of his history. He wrote after the death of Manuel, who, he says, ". . . perished, leaving the empire to an adolescent son." Later, he refers to the birth of this heir, Alexius II, in elaborately complimentary terms, and promises a full description of him at the appropriate moment.[14] He gives an extraordinarily favorable account of Louis VII's relations to Manuel during the Second Crusade, an account which ignores numerous disagreements and conflicts between the two rulers.[15] This treatment becomes comprehensible when one considers that Louis VII was Alexius II's father-in-law. The Angelus family is not singled out for eulogy; indeed, Constantine Angelus, grandfather of the later · emperors, is depicted as incompetent for his loss of a fleet to the Normans.[16] Andronicus Comnenus receives somewhat ambiguous treatment: his violent hatred and treachery toward Manuel are described in detail, but his clever escape from prison won Kinnamos' admiration. He is neither lauded, as if he were presently emperor, nor reviled as a fallen tyrant; rather, he is apparently a dangerous rival to the dynasty.[17] All these details point to the period from September 1180 to April 1182, the regency of Marie-Xena and Alexius Comnenus the protosebastos for the young Alexius II, as the time of composition of Kinnamos' history. Alexius II is mentioned as if still alive, and his mother receives favorable consideration; Andronicus is a potential enemy, not regent or emperor. The Angeli have not yet ascended the throne.[18]

Why Kinnamos chose this time to write can be guessed from a few details in his history. He was personally very hostile to Latins, and rarely loses an occasion to attack them; Raymond of Poitiers and Louis VII, grandfather and father-in-law, respectively, of Alexius II, are among the exceptions. The Normans of Sicily, the Germans of Conrad III and Frederick Barbarossa, the Venetians, the papacy, all come in for their share of abuse—save on those rare occasions when they chance to be acting in accord with the emperor's will, as Kinnamos would put it. The regency, however, was extremely favorable to Latins. Such antithetical views would suggest that Kinnamos had been compelled to withdraw from public service. This supposition would explain the reference in his preface to his leisure to write history, ". . . the present favorable opportunity. . . ."[19] as he calls it. It also helps to explain the fact that he had no access to official archives (or at least, made no use of them) while he wrote.[20] In composing his history, with its eulogy of the dynasty, Kinnamos was attempting to regain imperial favor and a place in the government.

Our final glimpse of Kinnamos seems to confirm this view regarding the date of composition of his book. Nicetas Choniates shows him in the spring of 1184, debating theology with Euthymius Malakes, Metropolitan of Neai Patrai, in the emperor's tent at Lopadion. Andronicus Comnenus, now emperor, threatened to pitch both disputants in the river if they did not desist![21] Kinnamos had thus regained a position in the bureaucracy, enjoyed the emperor's confidence, attended him on his campaign against rebels in Bithynia, and frequented the imperial tent. His prejudice against Latins and his seeming dismissal by the regency would have served to recommend him to the usurper.

Of his ultimate fate, little more is known. He survived the downfall of Andronicus (September 1185), and addressed an oration, now lost, to one of the Angeli emperors.[22] The new government, however, may have forced him again into retirement or a monastery.

Kinnamos' sources are far from clear. He quotes neither imperial documents, although he had knowledge of the contents of some of them, nor the records of ecclesiastical synods.[23] In regard to the reign of John II, Nicetas, who deals with the same period, states that he is utilizing oral communications from those who had been alive then and had shared in the emperor's wars. Kinnamos

notes the difficulty of writing about the period, so he chooses to
survey it only ". . . in brief and as if in summary, because as I
said I did not exist in his times." [24] Elsewhere, regarding John's
conquest of Cilicia, he says, "But to record these matters in detail
exceeds, I think, our undertaking. It was my purpose to speak of
the present events in summary, because I was not an eyewitness,
nor did I receive a faithful account of them." [25] His principal materials were certainly oral communications from individuals, and,
from perhaps 1155 on, his own observations. Occasionally it is
possible to detect his source: John Comnenus the protovestiarios
and protosebastos has long been recognized as his informant
regarding Andronicus' plots against the emperor at Pelagonia (ca.
1154).[26] John Kantakouzenos may have given him his account of
the conflict with the Serbs and Hungarians on the Drina and Tara,
John Doukas, of the campaign in Italy (if Kinnamos did not himself participate), Michael Branas, of a campaign to recover Sirmion.[27]

Anna Comnena states that she had available to her narratives composed with great simplicity and artlessness by certain
former soldiers of her father who had subsequently retired to monasteries.[28] It is tempting to look for similar narratives incorporated
into Kinnamos' work. A leading possibility would be the account
of Manuel's attack in 1146 on Ikonion, and the subsequent disastrous retreat.[29] This is the first extended narrative contained in
Kinnamos' book. The geographical details are unusually accurate,
permitting a detailed reconstruction of much of the route. No single individual, apart from the emperor, seems to stand out as a
"hero" (and possible informant). On the other hand, the misconduct of the Byzantine army during the retreat is unsparingly (and,
for Kinnamos, well nigh uniquely) laid bare. These qualities
suggest a narrative by a professional army officer, who ranked
below the aristocracy. The account of the Second Crusade might
have come from the same or a similar source.[30] For the bulk of his
history, however, Kinnamos gathered his information from his
own observations and reports of eyewitnesses.

Like other educated Byzantine laymen, Kinnamos had been nourished on the classical Greek authors. In his preface, he alludes to Xenophon's *Education of Cyrus* and *Anabasis,* and, possibly, to Herodotus; further on, there is an allusion to an exploit described by this author.[31] At one point, he seems to echo Thucydides: "That year ended, having wrought such changes." [32] Procopius, however, seems to have furnished his literary model, and from him he drew an account of Romulus Augustulus, Odovakar, and Theodoric.[33] Other authors, such as Plutarch or Arrian, and Libanius, can be dimly perceived behind his pages.[34] Kinnamos, however, cannot compare with Anna Comnena for extensive reading in the ancient writers, nor with Nicetas in having absorbed them and made their literary style his own.

In common with other Byzantine writers of history, he strove to disguise his material in an antique garb. Thus, so far as possible, medieval peoples are given ancient names. Nearly all eastern, Islamic nations are arbitrarily labeled "Persians"; tribes from north of the Black Sea are "Scyths"; the Hungarians alternate between being "Paionians" (from Herodotus) and "Huns" (from Priscus and Procopius). Confusingly, the French are called "Germans," and the Germans, "Alamanoi." [35] The Byzantines themselves are always designated "Romans," save on the rare occasions when the populace of the capital is meant. This usage, however, genuinely reflects the strong sense of Roman identity entertained by the Byzantine people, expressed even in oral Greek as "Rhomaioi."

From Thucydides, ultimately, derives the conception of the pseudo-speech and pretended letter. Not one of the letters quoted by Kinnamos can be considered anything but a confection of his own. When genuine documents survive (notably the correspondence between Byzantine and German rulers), their content differs widely from Kinnamos' allegations.[36] Thucydides' conception of using an imaginary speech to set forth the position of one party to a dispute has, in Kinnamos, been debased into "a few appropriate words," school-boy exercises, and rhetorical commonplaces. The most elaborate is the speech put into the mouth of the dying John II, and it is also the most false—although Kinnamos was here almost certainly the victim of a conspiracy to conceal the truth about John's death.[37] Otherwise, such speeches and pretended letters are often utilized to conceal a Byzantine withdrawal or defeat.[38]

Apart from the speeches and letters, Kinnamos' style is unusually clear and direct, at least for a Byzantine author. His syntax is rarely involved, and his sentences are usually short; his vocabulary is not extraordinary in its range. These characteristics, which render him palatable to the modern reader, would all have been viewed as defects, signs of an imperfect education, by his fellow Byzantine authors. Elaboration, use of complicated diction, an incessant quest for the rarest possible classical words, characterize Kinnamos' more cultured contemporaries, Michael Choniates, Nicetas Choniates, and Eustathius of Thessalonica. As a result, his narrative, once he reaches the reign of Manuel, flows swiftly and usually smoothly. He is capable of vivid and lively scenes: the Byzantine retreat from Ikonion, the battle with Richard of Andria, the old witch at the siege of Zemun.[39] Andronicus Comnenus is skillfully depicted as a man of great abilities, ruined by insatiable ambition, hereditary enmity to Manuel, and incurable personal vices.[40]

For the modern reader, his style is partially spoilt by his excessive praise for Manuel Comnenus. Every quality of Manuel, his dashing valor in warfare, his shrewd perception of an enemy's strategic dispositions, his horsemanship, his medical skill, and his penetrating intellect all inspire Kinnamos to excesses of enthusiastic admiration. Even less attractive are his protestations that he is merely reporting things he himself has seen or which have been creditably represented to him. While there is undoubtedly some truth behind his accounts of Manuel's achievements—the emperor imitated western knights in their craving for single combat and feats of headlong daring—facts unfavorable to Manuel are suppressed. In particular, the outcome of court intrigues and alleged conspiracies is never reported in a way hostile to Manuel. According to Nicetas, for example, the allegations of intended usurpation brought against Alexius Axouchos were entirely false.[41] Nicetas Choniates' *History* is a valuable corrective to Kinnamos.

In his adulation, however, Kinnamos was in no way exceptional. Indeed, he was simply working within an accepted tradition of historical and courtly literature. To mention only a few examples from among his immediate predecessors, Michael Psellos' famous *Chronographia* concludes with a lengthy eulogy of Michael VII Doukas; Michael Attaleiates addressed his history to Nicephorus III Botaneiates, and even included an irrelevant narrative of the conquest of Crete by Botaneiates' alleged ancestor, Nicephorus II Phokas; Nicephorus Bryennios and Anna Comnena wrote in honor of Alexius I.[42] Learned orations, complimentary to the reigning sovereign, were part of the ceremonial of the Byzantine court, and all well-educated persons were capable of writing them. Neither sincerity nor truth were necessary for such an oration; Nicetas' contemporary addresses contrast strongly with his *History,* composed later.[43] For Kinnamos, given his hope of regaining favor and office, the eulogistic passages were not merely important, but central to the purpose of his book. His repeated declarations of objectivity are merely verbal ornaments and shallow conventionalities.[44]

Kinnamos' narrative is far from perfect. Usually, he follows a reasonably straightforward chronological sequence; this results in some rapid changes of geographic scene, and seemingly irrelevant insertions of segments of ecclesiastical history. Occasionally, the necessity to supply background, and a tendency to proceed by association of ideas, lead him into kaleidoscopic shifts. At one point, within four or five sentences, apropos the conclusion of a treaty with Hungary (1153), Kinnamos refers to a later (1154–55) war stirred up by Andronicus' intrigues, to Andronicus' dispatch "at that time" (1152) to Cilicia to settle the revolt of Toros, and to the latter's escape from Constantinople (ca. 1145) and subsequent activities in Cilicia. Andronicus, however, was accompanied by the caesar John Roger, a candidate for the hand of Constance of Antioch, the cause of whose widowhood (in 1149) is then described at length. Several pages later, the narrative returns to Andronicus in Cilicia (1152). It is the figure of Andronicus and the necessity of sketching his career which is here the connecting link, but Kinnamos has no fear of an excursus.[45]

Some of these irregularities might have been smoothed out if Kinnamos had revised his work, as he presumably intended. The single surviving medieval manuscript breaks off at the bottom of a verso folio in the middle of a sentence; the recto of the next folio commences another work. Whether the historian completed his book, whether leaves are missing from the manuscript, or whether the scribe simply tired of his task is unknown.[46] The primary evidence for lack of revision by Kinnamos is the existence of a number of references backwards ("as has often been said," or similar expressions) for which no corresponding passage exists. The most important examples are mentions of the marriage in 1148 of the emperor's niece Theodora to Henry of Austria, an event omitted in its proper place by Kinnamos.[47] Combining these defects with the beginning of the text-title, "Epitome of the Successes . . . ," which is in turn reflected in the Latin title given by the editor, "Epitome of the Deeds . . . ," the first students of Kinnamos asserted that the existing text is an abridgment by a later hand. This view is no longer maintained: an epitomator would have removed much of the excess rhetorical baggage, while the cases of defective references backward are explained by the author's failure to revise his text. Another proof that Kinnamos left his book imperfect is the frequently sketchy nature of the portion relating to Manuel's last decades. These pages give the impression of being notes awaiting the author's final attentions.[48]

That the book was unpublished is indirectly attested by Nicetas Choniates, who in his preface states that no historian has yet offered an account of the period since Alexius I's death, on which he is about to embark.[49] Yet Nicetas almost certainly utilized Kinnamos' work himself.[50] The explanation must be that the book, being unfinished, was not published and did not circulate outside the group of imperial secretaries to which both belonged.

In the thirteenth century the original text was copied, and so survived: many much greater historians of the epoch came close to being lost. Only a single manuscript of Psellos' *Chronographia* and two manuscripts (both twelfth-century) of the complete text of the *Alexiad* endured into modern times.[51] Compared to classical Greek authors, Byzantine historians had slight value in the eyes of later bookbuyers and scribes. The thirteenth-century copy of Kinnamos' history was still in Constantinople in 1453; somehow, it reached the Vatican Library, where it now reposes. A transcription of it was made in the sixteenth century, and three more in the seventeenth. From one of the latter, Isaac Vossius made a copy, which Cornelius Tollius used as the foundation for the first printed edition, Utrecht, 1652, with an accompanying Latin version. The great Byzantine scholar Charles du Fresne, sieur Du Cange, published another edition, Paris, 1670, with a new Latin translation and notes which are still valuable. For his edition, Bonn, 1836, A. Meineke utilized a collation of the older printed ones with the Vatican manuscript made by Theodor Heyse. A new edition remains one of the fundamental necessities of Byzantine scholarship.[52]

Summary of the Successes of the Late Emperor and Porphyrogennetos Lord John Comnenus. And Description of the Deeds of his Renowned Son the Emperor and Prophyrogennetos Lord Manuel Comnenus. Wrought by the Imperial Secretary John Kinnamos.

First Book of Histories

1. The task of historical writing was not deemed dishonorable by those who of old were wise. Many of them even became highly esteemed thereby. One admitted into history the deeds of the Hellenes, another described the training of Cyrus from childhood and the deeds which / 4 / were achieved by him when he reached manhood. Once what had been revealed by time risked being hidden again, [but] those men who set things down in books as if on imperishable columns bound them over for continuing life. Such indeed is this task.

I think that those who do not entirely unworthily undertake this must be well supplied with knowledge of individual events, and as a general rule must stand apart from affairs which are closely linked to this life. Neither of these things, which I deem necessary, is possible for us. Yet we must not therefore be entirely silent about deeds which indeed happened in our age; rather, since a favorable opportunity is presently at hand, we must take care, lest one should not return again to us. We might succeed if we overlook the narration of all the other things which have pertained to the general life of mankind and set forth the deeds of two emperors. One of them departed this life prior to our advent into the world, the other flourished in our day and perished, leaving the empire to an adolescent son. These were John and Manuel Comnenus.

We who are undertaking [this] need not again set forth how
he fared from whom both were sprung (for one was endowed with
imperial office by relationship to his father [Alexius I Comnenus],
the other, to him as grandfather), and how he managed the Romans' public affairs, as these have I think been sufficiently described by those who recorded his deeds—nor even [need we re-
late] how he revolted against Nicephorus [III Botaneiates] who
then / 5 / ruled the empire, a man who had passed far beyond
youth and was in the decline of life. As I said, all that has been accurately narrated by persons who wrote without any hostility to
him.[1]

John's deeds will be specified by me in brief and as if in
summary, because as I said I did not exist in his times. I do not
know whether anyone would be better able than I to set forth those
of his successor Manuel, because before I was even a youth I accompanied him on many of his expeditions into both continents.
Such is my purpose; were the occasion suitable, we would take our
account back to the beginning and commence our history there.

2. When Alexius concluded his life [1118], John succeeded to the imperial office which had been previously promised
him by his father. After he had devoted himself to civil affairs as
far as time allowed, he set out for Asia [1119]. Close to the
Phrygian rivers Lykos [Çürüksu Çay] and Kapros [Kadiköy Dere]
is situated a city, by name Laodikeia [near Denizli]. It had been
seized some time previously by the Turks, and the emperor intended to regain it for the Romans' land; he directed a notable expedition against it. When he was near the city of Philadelphia
[Alaşehir], he planted a palisade and camped there; he dispatched
one of his favorites, John [Axouchos] who was related to the
Turks by ancestry,[2] with a force to make an attempt on the city.
And a little later coming up on request with his whole army he
took it almost without resistance. / 6 / There was a mass of barbarians there, no less then eight hundred of their most eminent men,
among whom was Alp-qara,[3] a man widely experienced in many

battles. Then, leaving a garrison sufficient for the city and filling it adequately with supplies, he set out for Byzantion.

Campaigning some time later against Sozopolis [Ulubor-lu],[4] he effortlessly placed it under the Romans' sway. How this came about will be related by me. Sozopolis is one of the formerly outstanding cities in Asia; situated on a steep and overhanging site, it is unassailable from every side save one, which offers a single, very narrow approach. It is impossible to drag a war machine up it, nor could any of the materials for siege warfare be prepared. Approach to the city was difficult for men unless they advanced in small groups. The city possessed this situation.

The facts of the undertaking first brought despair to emperor John, then a plan occurred to him which easily yielded the city to the Romans and caused him to be invested with great renown among all men. I shall reveal what it was. Summoning two of his spearmen, one of whom was named Paktiarios, the other, Dekanos, he ordered them together with their force to make straight for the gates of the city and shoot at those on the wall. When those people came forth, they [the Byzantines] should flee unashamed until, when the others sallied forth in pursuit as far as possible, they left the narrow place; then / 7 / gaining the advantage by a sudden about-turn and charge from there, they should occupy the region of the gates. So they set out for the city. When the barbarians saw them approaching, they immediately flung back the gates and rushed forth on them as fast as they could. As they [the Byzantines] turned their backs, the pursuit was pressed far. Then one of the said men turned back, and many Romans followed him. When they came to the gates, they dismounted from their horses and stood there. Subsequently the rest of the Romans' army learned of what they had done and advanced with great speed. The foe, trapped in the middle, ran this way and that in the adjacent plain, and the city was taken.

3. Setting forth from there, the emperor took the fortress of Hierakokoryphite [5] and many others which for the most part

were situated adjacent to Attaleia [Antalya], and so he returned to Byzantion. After he had made a short stay there he set out for Macedonia. The Petchenegs [6] had crossed the Danube with an army and burst into the Romans' boundaries. But as winter [1121–22] overtook him there, he passed the season someplace around the city of Berrhoia [Stara Zagora], partly to make ready for war, but more because he wished to win over some of their chieftains, so that when he had thus divided them, he could easily conquer the others. After he had by embassies induced many to come over to him, he advanced against the rest in spring, wishing to decide matters by battle.

/ 8 / When the armies clashed with one another, the battle was for some while in balance, and then the emperor himself was hit in the leg by an arrow. But since the Romans fought courageously, the Petchenegs were severely defeated: some of them fell, others were taken in captivity. No insignificant portion [of the Petchenegs] who returned to their camp considered it unworthy to flee, but chose to endure peril there with their wives and children. They fought in front of their wagons, which they had overspread with ox hides and neatly fitted together: in them they placed their wives and children. So again a fierce battle occurred and a slaughter ensued on both sides. The Petchenegs treated the carts like a fortress and wrought great harm to the Romans. Perceiving this, the emperor desired to dismount from his horse and continue the struggle on foot with the soldiers. When the Romans did not agree to this, he ordered the ax-bearers around him (this is the British nation, which has been in service to the Romans' emperors from a long time back) to cut apart with their axes the opposing [wagons].[7] Since they at once entered the conflict, the emperor thus became master of the Petchenegs' camp. Of the others who had sought safety in flight, most came voluntarily to the emperor out of affection for the captives; they were trained in the Romans' ways and, after they had been enrolled on the military registers, they served for a long time.

/ 9 / 4. Such was the passage of the Petchenegs into the Romans' land; but the emperor was again occupied with affairs in Asia. As he unexpectedly attacked the barbarians there in winter [1124?],[8] he absolutely took them captive; he converted many of them to the true faith and thereby caused an increase of the Romans' forces. Since they were still untrained in agricultural labors, but gulped milk and devoured meat, like the Petchenegs, and were always encamped in scatterings on the plain, they were ready prey to whoever wished to attack them. Thus the Turks had previously lived.

A war broke out between the Romans and the Hungarians, who dwell in the region beyond the Danube, for the following reason. László [I], king of Hungary, had two sons, Álmos and Stephen [István II].[9] When their father died, Stephen who was the elder received the royal office, and the other came as a fugitive to the emperor. For it is the Hungarians' custom that when their ruler dies leaving children, so long as he who receives lordship over them is not the father of a male child, the brothers shall be associated with one another and enjoy good relationships with each other, but when a son is born to him [the king], he does not grant them any continuance in the land, except when their eyes have been gouged out. On this account Álmos came to the emperor's court. He regarded the man favorably and received him with kindness. For the emperor John had taken to wife [Piroska-]Irene, László's daughter, / 10 / a very chaste woman if one ever was, who in the highest degree attained virtue. Whatever she had been provided by her husband the emperor and the empire, she neither set aside in portions for her children nor did she expend in excess and luxury of adornments. Rather, she passed her whole life benefiting persons who were begging for something or other from her. She established a monastery in the name of the Pantokrator [Christ the Almighty],[10] which is among the most outstanding in beauty and size. Such was this empress.

When the Hungarians' king heard about his brother, he sent

envoys to the emperor and demanded that he [Álmos] be expelled
from the Romans' land. As he [István II] was unable to prevail
upon him, he crossed the Danube, besieged Belgrade [Beograd], a
city situated beside it, and took it [1128]. Destroying it to its foundations, he carried off the stones by boats; thereby he erected
Zeugme [or Zeugminon, modern Zemun],[11] a city in the direction
of Sirmion [Sremska Mitrovica]. It endured for many years, but in
the reign of emperor Manuel it was leveled to its foundations, so
that by a turn [of fortune] all of it served for wall-construction of
the city of Belgrade. But this will be related by me later, when the
advancing narrative reaches those years.

When he heard of this, the emperor rushed with his whole
army to the Danube, taking an allied [i.e., mercenary] force of
Ligurian knights, whom our people call Lombards, and of
Turks.[12] He camped there beside the [Danube's] banks and prepared for battle; / 11 / but Stephen happened to be sickly in body
and was recuperating someplace in the midst of his land. Still he
did not desire to be heedless, but sent forces as quickly as possible, ordering them to oppose the emperor's crossing. The Hungarians did as commanded. So that the opposition should be inef-
fective, the emperor planned as follows. He separated the allied
force and ordered it upstream to a region called Tempon, where a
hill which rose from the Hungarians' land extended to the river, to
cross there. He, with another force of Romans, stayed opposite the
fort of Chramon [Kama] and made a pretense that he would presently cross from there. When this was done, the Romans crossed
without difficulty. The Hungarians were at first unable to oppose
them, and fled full speed. The pursuit was pressed up to a river,
where, as the Hungarians rushed in crowds on a bridge which
spanned the stream, it collapsed; many of them, swept away by the
river, yielded up their souls, but many fell into the Romans'
hands, among whom were Ākuš and Keledi,[13] very notable men
among the Hungarians.

After he had succeeded in this, the emperor won the fort of

Chramon without resistance and at once crossed back to the Romans' territory. After he had strengthened Branitshevo [near Dubravica] with a garrison of soldiers, whom Kourtikios commanded, he / 12 / returned to Byzantion. A short time later the Hungarians besieged Branitshevo and took it; they killed some of the Romans in it and took others captive, but there were some who sought safety in flight. Enraged at this, the emperor convicted Kourtikios of a charge of treason and laid many lashes on his back, although he did not abandon the walls (they say) until the foe rushed into the city in full force and set fire to the houses.

5. At this time [ca. 1129–30] the Serbs, a Dalmatian people, also plotted revolt and subdued the fortress of Rhason [Ra-žanj]. On this account the emperor likewise took vengeance on Kritoplos, who had been entrusted with defense of that fortress; he led him, wearing women's garb, through the marketplace mounted on an ass.

Going to Branitshevo for a second time, he made haste to rebuild it. Since some time elapsed in the task, the army, suffering from winter weather and lack of necessities, was in severe distress. When he learned this, the Hungarians' king decided to cross the Danube as quickly as possible and attack them unexpectedly. In the Hungarians' land, however, there was a woman, a Latin by birth, outstanding in wealth and other distinction. Sending to the emperor, she revealed what was being planned. Since he was unable to engage them with an equivalent force, because as stated his army had already been overcome by disease and lack of necessities, / 13 / he fortified the city where possible and withdrew. Indeed, lest he encounter the Hungarians' army, he made his way through steep and precipitous country, locally called the Evil Stair. There the Hungarians' army unexpectedly fell upon the regiments guarding the rear, but did no harm to the Romans: after they had collected portions of the hangings which composed the imperial tent, left behind for lack of baggage animals, they withdrew, and the Romans' army escaped scatheless.

A little later, the emperor marched to Asia, hastening to take the city of Kastamon [Kastamonu] which is adjacent to Paphlagonia [1132].[14] The Turks who dwelt there used to raid the adjacent area, which was subject to the emperor, and continually maltreated the Romans there. Stunning them by the magnitude of his preparation for war, he constrained them to yield the city and themselves to the Romans. Returning thus to Byzantion, he celebrated a splendid triumph. When a car of silver had been constructed, excessively plastered with gold, he prepared to enter it, yet he did not ride in it, perhaps to avoid arrogance. Instead, he placed an image of the Mother of God in it, and he went ahead with the sign of the Cross, while it followed, a wonder for the Byzantines to see, something I think they had not previously / 14 / witnessed since the Herakleians and Justinians guided the Romans' realm.

6. The people of the Romans were busy with these matters. But [Gümüshtigin Ghāzī ibn] Dānishmend who at that time ruled Cappadocia, encircled and besieged Kastamon with an army.[15] Since fortune prevented the emperor from waging war (for his spouse Irene had departed from mankind, while he had been stricken by illness and was recovering in Byzantion), he [Gümüshtigin Ghāzī] first wore it down by hunger and then took it by siege [1132–33]. This disaster greatly affected the emperor's spirit. Since by some chance [ibn] Dānishmend had in the meantime brought his life to a close [1134/35], Muḥammad [his son] had been established in authority, and was at variance with the chieftain of the city of Ikonion [Konya], whom the Turks, honoring him above the rest, call sultan.[16] He [John] sent envoys to Ikonion, and when he won him to his friendship, he persuaded him to fight alongside the Romans against Muḥammad. So in no long time one of the nobles of his court came with an army to give hostages and join in the war.

Coming to Gangra [Çankiri] with the said men, the emperor pitched camp before its wall, to prepare for an attack on the fortifications in the morning. Muḥammad perceived that he was not equal in battle to the emperor and knew that he had to win over the sultan, who was likewise related to him by descent. Terminating their differences, they both joined in opposition to the Romans, while the auxiliary Turks, recalled by / 15 / the sultan, departed in flight by night. When he noted the treachery, the emperor was in a great rage and planned to set forth from there immediately. But some monks who chanced to be present hindered him from the undertaking, contending that he only needed to be brave for Gangra's conquest. Persuaded by them, he attacked the wall on the morrow; but being beaten back from it, he moved to the Rhyndakene [17] and passed the winter there with the whole army. The Romans, who spent a long time there, were greatly pressed by hunger, since there was nowhere to get supplies for winter.

Setting out from there, he went to Kastamon, and after he had taken it by agreement, he led the army over to Gangra. The Turks who held the city had learned that [Turkish] forces had again been assembled at Rhyndakene, and at first hesitated to yield the city to the emperor, being buoyed up by hopes of reinforcement. But since the said forces, which were still not gathered in the same place, then dispersed (for they were unable to campaign in the winter season, as stated by me in the foregoing), they yielded under necessity and surrendered the city to him, on condition that they and those who had been captured by the Romans while [Gümüshtigin Ghāzī ibn] Dānishmend still lived should depart unharmed from Roman power. But the Turks who instead of the freedom available preferred voluntary obedience enjoyed the emperor's favor and formed no ignoble supplement to the Romans' power.

/ 16 / 7. Thereafter the matter of the Romans' Isaurian wars had its origin. For an Armenian, Leon,[18] seized many Isaurian [i.e., Cilician] cities obedient to the Romans, and in particular undertook to invest Seleukeia [Silifke]. When he learned this, the emperor assembled his forces and hastened to it with great

speed [1136–37]. On this account, and also for one I shall now set
forth, the emperor marched to Cilicia. When Bohemond,[19] who
had ruled Antioch, departed from mankind [1130], the principal
personages in the land sent to the emperor and said that if it were
according to his will for Bohemond's daughter to wed Manuel, the
youngest of his sons, immediately after the marriage the Antiochenes' realm would be in his power. But he had not even
reached the Cilicians' land when they [the Antiochenes] altered
their intention and in place of friends and allies became very hostile to him. Aware that they were unequal in might to the Romans'
army, they decided that they must win over Leon to themselves.
Indeed they drew the fellow forth from prison, where since they
had overcome him in war they had kept him shut up; after they had
received pledges from him that he would be their friend and ally
against the emperor, they kindly released him. Arriving in Cilicia,
the emperor took Mopsuestia [medieval Mamistra, modern Misis];
after he had subdued Tarsus and Adana, he pitched camp before
Anazarbos ['Ain Zarbâ, south of Sis].

In the meantime, something as follows had occurred. The
count of Poitou, which is situated around the Ionian Gulf [sic], had
two sons. When the father died, one of them was established in the
ancestral / 17 / office, the other arrived at the church [of the Holy
Sepulcher] in Jerusalem in the guise of a poor man. When the cus-
todian saw him, struck by his handsome appearance and size, he
approached and asked him to reveal who he was; the other answered by what he thought should at the very least be made clear,
but being unable to persuade him, he [the stranger] then made
known facts about himself. When the other heard this, he went
running to the king and immediately informed him about the man.
After he [the king] had summoned Raymond (for this name was
applied to him) to himself, he induced him to wed Bohemond's
daughter, who had not yet come of age.[20] So he [Raymond] set
out to journey to Antioch, and by chance he fell in with Roman
scouts and came close to being captured. One of the soldiers who

encountered him as he advanced struck him on the helm, and had he not prevented a fall by seizing the horse's neck with both hands, and many of his followers then joined him, he would forthwith have been rolled on his back. Having thus avoided danger, he reached Antioch.

The emperor, however, was occupied with the siege of Anazarbos. Those inside, who were scheming to render the undertaking fruitless, heated irons sufficiently in the fire and hurled them by mechanisms at the stone-throwers. Immediately, when they came close, they set afire the wooden uprights in front of them. This, which happened often, put the emperor into a rage. Approaching him as he was distraught, Isaac [the sebastokrator, his son] said, "Come, Father, order the woodwork to be encased with bricks." When / 18 / this was done, those inside were unable to resist the frequent assaults; opening their gates, they admitted the Romans' commander.

8. In this fashion, Anazarbos fell under the Romans' sway. But Raymond and Baldwin, who at that time was lord of Marash [Maraş], as the peril did not yet stand at their doors, gathered a sufficient force and hastened to Palestine to rescue the king there from danger [1137]. As the Saracens who lived near Palestine had prevailed in war over him, they were besieging him where he had taken refuge, in the castle of Montferrand [Ba'rīn].

When the emperor conquered Anazarbos he went to the fortress of Vahka [Feke]; in fear for Antioch, they [Raymond and Baldwin] quickly returned to it. Meanwhile, deferring the siege of Vahka, the Romans' army pitched camp about the river which flows past the city [Antioch]. At first the Antiochenes were fearless, trusting in the strength of their walls and other security. So when the siege had been protracted for a considerable time, some of those from the register [of Byzantine infantry], as usually happens in a large army, ran into the gardens in front of the city to gather fruit. They [the Antiochenes] attacked them by surprise and killed many. After knowledge of this became general and the

Romans' soldiers eagerly rushed to the rescue, they [the An-
tiochenes] ran fleeing to the gates and lost many of their own men
in the flight. When the Romans then vigorously prosecuted siege
operations, they fell into great terror. Therefore / 19 / Raymond
often went to the emperor and warmly begged to yield him the
city, on condition that the emperor should be and be proclaimed its
lord, but he [Raymond] should lawfully be guardian of it by his
[John's] authority. Failing in what he [Raymond] sought, he returned unsuccessful. But a few days later when the Romans' council had made a determination about this, he was received on the
stated terms, and the other Latin troops yielded to the emperor,
those called by them Frères [Hospitallers and Templars] and those
who inhabited that region. Matters went thus.

Emperor John was loath to cast aside such a fortunate occasion; with the said forces he attacked upper Syria, took by right
of war the fortress of Buzā'ah, and seized an immense quantity of
booty from it [1138]. He sent it together with a crowd of captives
to Antioch, after he had put Thomas in charge of them, a man
sprung from unimportant origins, but enrolled since childhood, I
think, among the emperor's secretaries. He himself went on toward Aleppo, an old and noteworthy city. But since the enemy
soon attacked by surprise, Thomas lost the booty and the throng of
captives which he was leading and scarcely escaped from danger.
When the emperor reached Aleppo, he perceived that the country
around it was entirely waterless, and passed it by. Having overcome the fortresses of Hama and Kafarṭāb by assault, he moved on
to Shaizar, a prosperous and populous city. / 20 / He besieged and
took the city, but as he advanced against the citadel, he was beaten
back. As he was about to launch a second attempt on it, envoys
came promising money which they would supply at once and to
furnish annually a fixed payment to the Romans. Such was the
content of their offer. The emperor rejected it, as he hoped to
overcome them by war. But after he had often assaulted them, he
perceived he was attempting the impossible; having received their
embassy he departed on terms.[21]

They furnished him plenty of money, and a cross was added, something remarkable and a gift worthy of emperors. It was a reddish stone of good size, and when it was carved in the form of a cross, it had lost little of the natural color in cutting. They say the apostle among the emperors, Constantine [I], had caused it to be made, but in some fashion it had come into the Saracens' hands. After he had received this and had taken pledges regarding future tribute, he set out for Cilicia again. Once he had overcome the strong fortresses Vahka and Kapniskerti, he remained in the region but separated off a section of the army and sent it to harry the rest. But to record these matters in detail exceeds, I think, our undertaking. It was my purpose to speak of the present events in summary, because I was not an eyewitness, nor did I receive a faithful account of them. / 21 / Yet with fortune looking on favorably, so much had I think been achieved in two years [1137–38].

9. Thus emperor John won renown in wars in Asia, save that matters regarding Nea Kaisareia [Neocaesarea, modern Niksar] did not fall out according to his plan. For it was already around the winter solstice [December 1139] when he camped not far from it, and thought to subdue it by siege. But since the Turks who held the city were very active in waging war fiercely against him, and an unusually severe winter oppressed the soldiery, he departed from the city.[22] Marching into the adjacent territory of the Turks, he drove off immense booty, and restored to the Romans' land a crowd of men who had been enslaved to the Turks for a long time.

In this expedition, I mean when he still occupied quarters at Nea Kaisareia, something happened worthy of mention and of hearing. When a fierce engagement between Romans and Turks occurred, by chance the Turks had the uppermost; observing what had happened, Manuel, who as often [sic] stated by me was the youngest child of emperor John, without his father's knowing, fell upon the enemy's midst, along with his attendants. He thrust them back and revived the courage of the Romans' soldiers, which had waned. His father was reasonably angry at this and abused his rashness, but internally admiration gripped him and he was astonished only that, when he [Manuel] was not yet eighteen, he dared hurl himself into such great perils, and publicly called him savior of the Romans' / 22 / army. Thus courage is incapable of being limited by any age at all. From this war well nigh none of the Romans returned on horseback.

10. Thus the matter of Nea Kaisareia was concluded. As the emperor learned that the Turks again waged war on Sozopolis, he hastened there in full strength [1142]. When he failed to encounter any enemy (for once they learned that the Romans were approaching them, they departed in flight), he led the army to the lake called Pousgouse [Beyşehir Gölü].[23] It stretches to immense length and width, and possesses islands which rise separately from each other in the midst of the water; from of old, forts have been erected on them. The men who dwell on them consider the water as a moat. It is possible for them to go to Ikonion and return in a single day.[24] On this account in particular the emperor attributed great importance to possession of the lake. When the Romans on it would not yield it to him (for by long time and usage they were united in their views with the Turks), he planned something as follows. After he had assembled as many skiffs and small boats as possible, he joined them together by planks on top; placing his war-machines on them, he led them straight for the said forts. When the lake was disturbed by a dry wind, many of the Romans' soldiers were lost; yet with difficulty and extreme violence he took them.

When he learned that Raymond prince of Antioch had rebelled, he marched straight / 23 / back to Cilicia [1142]; he intended that Cilicia and Antioch along with Attaleia and Cyprus should be granted to Manuel for his portion. I am going to relate why he came to this intention. From a long time back he had promised the Romans' scepter to Alexius, who was the eldest of his children.[25] While Manuel was his last-born, stories became current and symbols of rulership were revealed to the youth, one or two of which seem to me not inopportune to recall. Once when Manuel was asleep, a woman appeared to him in a dream, venerable in visage, dark in garb, in her hands the [purple] buskins which law allows emperors. She offered them to Manuel, urging him to use them and take off those, and she pointed at his usual [sebastokrator's] blue ones.[26] Awaking full of fear, since he could not find the ones which had appeared [to him], he burst into tears like a child and thought that they had been taken by someone in the household. Such was this, but something else was no less significant to him. There was one of the monks whose homeland was Galilee, whose way of life was remote and mountain-dwelling; once when he stood before emperor John to preach, he observed the sons approaching him and treated the others like private citizens, but approaching Manuel he addressed him with humility. When the emperor inquired why he did this, the monk said in reply, "Because of them all, Manuel alone seems to me an emperor." From these and other such things, / 24 / the emperor passed into limitless designs; but being unable to undo what had seemed right to him at the beginning, he turned his attention to the aforesaid plan.

But seemingly none of all these matters depended on human planning. He had not yet reached Cilicia when he was deprived of the two sons who came first in age [Alexius and Andronicus], while one [Isaac] of the two remaining, since he was physically unwell, returned to Byzantion escorting the bodies.[27] The emperor reached the end of his life in Cilicia, and Manuel then advanced to the empire's throne.

It is worth while to describe the manner of his [John's] end. As he was going hunting, a boar encountered him, a big one, such as Cilicia and the Tauric Mountains produce in great numbers. Wielding a spear, as they say, he encountered it as it rushed on; when the point was buried in its chest, infuriated at the blow, it tried still more pressure. Thereby the emperor's arm, which was

turned aside from the straight by its violent resistance, twisted the
wrong way a quiver full of arrows with which he was equipped.
His wrist was scraped by the points and a wound immediately ensued. A bloody foam seeped forth, but a thin membrane, which
the multitude vulgarly call *ekdera,*[28] was applied, seemingly to
bind together what had been divided and heal the wound, lest it
become inflamed and stir up pain. It, however, was later the cause
of inflammation. For it transferred to the rest of the body the
poison from the barb which had been introduced into its thickness.
But this was later.

Then, as he still had no sensation of pain, / 25 / a table was
spread for him, and a couch supported him to dine.[29] As the meal
went on, the physicians stood around to observe the bandage; they
inquired the cause of the wound, and when they learned it, they
complained about the table and asked that it [the bandage] straightway be removed from his arm. He, however, maintained stoutly
that the wound had closed up and that he suspected nothing dire
regarding future swelling and inflammation. But after he had dined
and just as he lay down to sleep, severe pains suddenly mounted
and swelling attacked the arm. The whole group of doctors gathered and discussion arose about what should be done. To some it
seemed best to lance the swelling, but its unripeness disquieted the
others, and they preferred that it be relieved in some other way.
But as it seems that he had to fare ill, the opinion for surgery
carried the day. When it was lanced, the swelling mounted still
more and the arm was swollen.

The emperor commenced to be shaken in his soul by antici-
pations of death, especially because he had not brought to completion the plan which he had previously striven toward regarding a
visit to Palestine. On this account he had had made a lampstand of
twenty talents of gold, which he had prepared as an offering to the
church there. Since he was then in an incurable situation, he sent
for a holy man, a monk from Pamphylia, and asked him to propitiate the Divinity by night-long prayer. Allegedly as he [the monk]

was devoting himself to prayer he heard the sound of voices singing. A light raised on high was seen, / 26 / and a divine Youth
who checked their tumult of spirit. Such was this matter.

Sensing that he was already in a perilous state, the emperor
commanded that the nobles and whoever was otherwise highly
regarded among the grandees and generals be present. He spoke as
follows: "Romans who have assembled for this audience with me:
that it has seemed proper to many other of our emperors to transfer
the office of ruler to their sons like an ancestral inheritance, I
myself know, since I received authority from my father the emperor, and each of you know that the same [was done] by me in
this case. So you imagine that I also, who have reached as you see
the end of the present life, have transmitted the office and throne
to the elder of the two sons who remain to me, as is mankind's
custom. But I care so much about you that, if the thing belonged
to neither of the two by right of virtue, I would choose whoever
would not seem contrary to your and my opinion. For I think it
will benefit neither donor nor recipient, should the steersman sink
the ship by ignorance, even if he should perish along with the gift
and make no valid accusation against the giver. I deem this tastelessness and ignorance of making gifts and entirely unsound.

"So I myself have a preference in regard to you. Here is
proof: behold, for your benefit, as is speedily required, I am ready
to do injustice to nature. Both my sons are excellent, and one of
them has precedence in age. / 27 / But good sense rejects the elder
and pursues the better, and teaches that excellence corresponds to
excellence. Of all things this struggle is difficult, to try to obtain
the best. Since one must assign the better part to the best person
(for what else would one esteem more honorable than empire?), I
would wish, fellow soldiers, that perfection of excellence rather
belonged to the elder. But the decision looks toward the youngest,
and the empire's standard of excellence points rather to the latest-
born. I am not forced to fear my vision infected by favoritism. I
love both sons absolutely equally, and neither has precedence in

partiality. This decision in regard to both must therefore be trusted by me more than by yourselves.

"This must be thoroughly investigated together, I mean whether, when a son has excelled his brother and been placed on the throne, he has ever proven inferior. I do not feel confidence in myself in this, that favoritism has been absolutely excluded in my planning; whenever it is not repulsed by equity, it is sufficient to corrupt a decision. So do you desire that I recite his qualities for you, and yourselves decide? It is evident to everyone how much strength and might and valor in warfare he possesses. The events at Nea Kaisareia attest my words, where the affairs of the Romans, manifestly sinking, were restored and recovered by him. If what / 28 / bears witness for him were from his father alone, then hearken. Very frequently, when the rest were at a loss, he seemed to me outstanding in councils, as I toiled in the immeasurable difficulties of affairs: capable of foreseeing the coming storm, skilled in avoiding the gale and opposing the winds' force. We would also be justified in considering him before the rest, as God's decision falls upon the youth. Consider how: Alexius had been summoned to the throne by me, and the decision was published some years previously. But God has just revealed to me the final moment at which he died and has carried away that young man from our midst. I would also tell you some of the tokens which revealed the present fate to him [Manuel], except that I am aware that these things are deemed irrational by the multitude; for nothing leads more easily to slander by people than stories of dreams and prophecies of the future. Whatever I have been able to know of my son has been related by me. Now it should be your part to add your own opinion."

The emperor said this; the others agreed with joy and tears. The youth (more than anyone else, he loved his father) reverencing the laws of nature bent down and casting his head on his chest bathed the floor in tears. After he had been garbed in a general's cloak and wreathed with the diadem, he was acclaimed emperor by the whole army. After emperor John had survived a few days further, / 29 / he passed to his end; he had ruled the Romans for twenty-five years and seven months [sic] altogether, [and died] on the eighth of the month which the Greeks call Xanthikos, the Romans, April [1143].[30]

Second Book of Roman History

1. Let my [narrative of] the deeds of emperor John have an end there. Emperor Manuel, who had already received the scepter, still a youth, just growing his first beard, was not perplexed at the burden of power, nor did he permit anything ignoble. As Isaac [his brother] was at that time living in Byzantion, the multitude entertained a suspicion that he could not then be restrained from creating a revolution. Since he was naturally quarrelsome and usually guided by passion, he would seize an excuse for this; yet he [Manuel] paid it slight attention. He stayed thirty whole days in that place after his father's death and did not depart until he had suitably completed the rites for his father (in addition to other things, he established a monastery on the spot where he had rendered up his spirit), and had securely arranged the affairs of Cilicia.

/ 30 / Beforehand, while emperor John was still alive, the Antiochenes had commenced to slip away from his authority; they sent to emperor Manuel to demand that he depart from the bounds of the land which they declared belonged to their city, but now was forcibly and unjustly held by the Romans. They said this, but the emperor opposed them and spoke as follows in his defense. "It is clear to everyone, envoys, that the Antiochenes have not experienced any ill from us. If someone has robbed something from others, then it would be just that it be returned to the others' possession; so why did you not earlier yield Antioch to the Romans, but by force and violence stole it from my father? Did the Turks not first take it when it belonged to us? Otherwise, of what did you once ask to receive possession from us? Of the city of Antioch? It first belonged to our state.[1] If you are not ashamed to transgress your own agreements, why do you come charging us with slighting your rights, while we should justly demand correction from you? But there will be an occasion suitable to dispose of matters in this regard. Now I command you to depart from what does not belong to you. I would increase, not diminish what came to my hands from my father." He said this to the ambassadors.

Bearing the coffin on his shoulder, along with the nobles, he conducted the body in procession to the ships which were anchored in the Pyramos [Ceyhan] River, which passes through Mopsuestia / 31 / and makes its outlet in the sea. When the dromonds [warships] had already put out to sea from there, he broke camp and himself led the army, marching unheralded through the midst of the Turks' territory.[2] Astonished thereat and admiring his excess of rashness, the Turks did not dare to oppose the Romans: they passed through a foreign country as if through their own. In no long time he reached the Romans' land. The triremes which conveyed the emperor's ashes came to land at Byzantion; the Romans' senate [3] magnificently received them and conveyed them to the holy monastery which, as stated, the empress Irene had previously constructed in the name of the Pantokrator.

As emperor Manuel was still occupied in his return, and since he could learn nothing in regard to the sebastokrator [Isaac, his brother], those who had previously been entrusted with the emperor's affairs trapped him by a trick, on the ground that he was planning usurpation, and made him a prisoner in the precincts of the Pantokrator; the plan came about lest, bearing ill will to some of those with him [Manuel] and especially to those who administered the highest offices, he [Isaac] should also do something unpleasant to their households in Byzantion. He [Manuel] indeed considered how he might cleverly divert him from that attempt. So it seemed right to him to dispatch decrees to Byzantion, charging these men [Manuel's supporters] with alleged treason and therefore punishing them by confiscation of money and / 32 / property. For thus (he said) the sebastokrator would suppose these men had made a plot in behalf of himself as emperor, and would watch over their affairs better, so that he might be able to win them still more to favor him.

2. But the decrees of Providence were entirely unalterable, not to be opposed by men's calculations. For he [Manuel] intended these things and had already revealed the plan to those about him. Yet as to both Isaacs [his brother and his uncle], the monastery as we said already guarded the one, iron fetters held the other, the emperor's uncle on his father's side, I mean, imprisoned at Pontic Herakleia [Ereğli].[4] There he used to live honorably, after he had been made an exile by his brother the emperor while he still lived, because of the plots which from desire of the throne he did not leave off implanting here and there. Then he came to this pitch of fortune [imprisonment] by decision of those who were then in charge in Byzantion, since they had learned that he again intended a revolution. But as I said, Providence made smooth the emperor's path to power. When he [Manuel] heard of these things concerning the sebastokrators, on reaching Byzantion, he immediately summoned his brother, embraced him and greeted him in brotherly fashion. He recalled his uncle from exile, annulled the charges for which his father had previously punished him with exile, and asked his pardon. / 33 / After he had presented the army with money, he sent it home; to each household in Byzantion he offered two gold pieces.

Since Constantinople lacked a shepherd, he raised to the [patriarchal] throne Michael [II Kourkouas], who had governed a monastery on the island which they call Oxeia ["'Sharp," modern Sivri Ada] on account of its appearance.[5] He had as they say sampled general education and secular learning with the tip of his finger, but in propriety of character and study of Holy Scripture he was inferior to none of those who were particularly noted for excellence in that era. By his hands he [Manuel] was later wreathed with the imperial diadem in the church. Then after he had deposited a hundredweight of gold coin on the holy altar, he departed, leaving [the fame of] his generosity and splendor in everyone's mouth. Henceforth he ordered an annual gift of two hundredweight [of silver] from the palace for the clergy; they call this the additional money.

3. Such were his beginnings in office. Being eager to take vengeance on prince Raymond of Antioch for his crime against his father (for he had not yet imposed the penalty due him, since natural obligation had hindered his advance), he dispatched a force against him by land and sea [ca. 1144].[6] Andronicus and John who traced their ancestry to the Kontostephanoi commanded it, along with Prosouch [Borsuq][7] who was competent in warfare. The naval force was led by Demetrius, surnamed Branas. Prosouch and the two Kontostephanoi, when they reached the borders of Cilicia, / 34 / in a short time recovered the forts which the Romans had been deprived of by the Antiochenes. Coming to grips with Raymond, they drove him back and killed many of his followers. How this came about, I will reveal.

When the Romans overcame the said forts, they approached the city of Antioch without opposition, treating all before them as spoil from the Mysians.[8] When Raymond saw the Romans approaching, he kept quietly within the walls. After they had made preparation, they advanced from there (for no one had come forth against them); then he secretly pursued them, intending to attack them in the rear. Coming to a certain spot where it seemed right to spend the night, the Romans pitched camp. After he [Raymond] had positioned his army in the appropriate place, he advanced with a few men to spy out the foe. His approach did not escape the Romans' notice. Some of those who had gone out to forage encountered him not far from the camp and hastily notified the generals. Since it was already night, they posted guards and waited.

The next day had not yet come when, drawn up in order, they returned, planning to fall upon those who were still camped with Raymond. Not that Raymond was careless, but at early dawn, after he had enjoined what seemed proper to his followers, he left them there, while he advanced to scout. Unexpectedly falling in with the Romans he turned and fled, and sent to the rest of his army to order it to set out from there at full speed. / 35 / But coming up at equal speed, the Romans' force routed them and wrought a great slaughter; the pursuit lasted up to the gates of Antioch. Circling around the enemy with difficulty, Raymond himself entered the city by night.

Those with Prosouch accomplished this against Raymond and set out for Cilicia, but Demetrius [Branas] arriving with the fleet plundered the region adjoining the sea, took captive a multitude of men, and burned many of the natives' ships which were drawn up on the seashore. Even someone who was collecting public revenue for them became captive to the Romans. When Raymond heard this, he came in great wrath, but as he observed that the Roman ships had already set sail from land, he departed unsuccessful. Since the sea did not favor them, the Romans cruised off that region for ten days; when they ran short of water, they unexpectedly ran ashore on the mainland, drove back the foe, plundered two coastal forts, and filled their ships with as much wine and riverwater as possible. Meeting with a favorable breeze, they set sail for Cyprus.

These disasters constrained Raymond to travel the road to Byzantion [1145]. When he arrived the emperor was at first unwilling to pay attention to him, until he approached the monument of his father the emperor and thereby gained his forgiveness; then he [Raymond] became his vassal.[9]

/ 36 / 4. At this time [January 1146] the emperor wedded [Bertha-]Irene [of Sulzbach], who had been affianced to him when he was not yet emperor, a maiden related to kings, who was not inferior to any of those of that time in propriety of character and spiritual virtue.[10] The following is reported about her. When she first arrived at Byzantion [1142], some women distinguished for nobility met her, as well as she who was wedded to the emperor Alexius [John's eldest son]; she wore a garment of linen, and for the rest was adorned in gold and purple. But the dark purple of the linen caused her to be noticed by the newcomer. She at once inquired of the bystanders who the nun was who was speaking magnificently. This omen did not seem at all good to the listeners, and the end followed in no long time.[11]

The region of Asia across the straits [Bosporos] occupied the emperor, who was investigating how the frontiers of Bithynia might cease to be points of entry for the nation of Turks. Since in earlier times the fortifications which opposed the barbarians' incursions had been negligently overlooked, the regions there became easy approaches for the Turks. But in later years this was most ambitiously made good by the emperor, who constructed many cities there; at this moment he decided to erect a fort in so-called Melangeia [or Malagina, on the Sakarya east of Iznik].[12] While this task was proceeding, it was reported to him that an advancing disease indicated ineluctable peril to [Maria] the eldest daughter of the emperor John, whom the caesar [John] Roger [13] had wedded. / 37 / Having stayed in the place long enough to bring the work to completion, he took the road to Byzantion.

But in the meantime she had accomplished her fate, an especially high-hearted woman, who had a very masculine outlook. Reaching this point in my narrative, I come to a recollection of this woman's deed which is still worthy of admiration. For they say that the caesar Roger had his eye on the empire at the moment when, after the death of emperor John, Constantinople had not yet received the new emperor; he surrounded himself with many other partisans, and in particular he won over one of the Italians who was his compatriot on his father's side, together with his followers, who amounted to four hundred. This Italian was distinguished and renowned by birth, [Robert] prince of Capua, a very populous and prosperous Italian city. The occasion of his residence in Byzantion was as follows: Roger [II] who then tyrannized over Sicily, of whom we shall make much account in the following books when we write of the Italian wars, was greedy for the principality of Capua and pressed the man hard in war. Having yielded to this, he took the road to Byzantion. So this was accomplished by the caesar [John Roger]. When after many exhortations his wife perceived that he was stubborn and really eager for usurpation and would not be stirred from his purpose whatever happened, she summoned to herself those in charge of public affairs and communicated the matter, and "Either," she said, "you yourselves hand over my husband to me, / 38 / or you must take heed to preserve the realm for my brother." She said this, but by reason of some seeming business they absolutely beguiled the caesar and brought him forth to one of the suburbs near Byzantion. When they came to the place, they let him stay there, but they returned to the city.

5. Such was Maria. When her suffering was reported to him, the emperor went to Byzantion. Some time later [1146], he encamped on the plains by the Rhyndakos [Orhaneli], where a fort had been newly erected by emperor John, called Lopadion [Uluabat, near Karacabey] by the commonality.[14] There he gathered an army, as he intended to invade Turkish [territory]. For in the meantime the Turks had broken their truce with the Romans, pillaged and taken Prakana, an Isaurian city [west of Silifke],[15] and wrought much other injury to the Romans. After he had prepared as well as possible, he set out from there and hastily moved forward, intending to destroy them from youth upwards as he came upon them suddenly, unawares. He did not, however, entirely fail in his plan. He did not indeed utilize [his own] hands in that conflict. For after he had quickly traversed the Mysian Olympus [Uludağ] and had come as far as Pithekas,[16] where he had constructed a strong fort, he marched by night through the mountains there, which rise high and are really overgrown;[17] when his head

was stuffed up by the mists rising over the trees, he suddenly / 39 / collapsed, so that he was unable to rise again. Then until about midnight it kept him unconscious, but as he recovered after a little and became better on the morrow, he remained quiet. Detaching a suitable portion of the army, however, he dispatched it with the generals to its task; when they encountered the enemy's forces not far off, as they were superior in battle, they carried off a great quantity of booty and returned from there with signs of victory. The emperor achieved this.

The Turks, who had meanwhile prepared a great expedition, fell upon the Thrakesians' land [the Thrakesian Theme, west-central Asia Minor], with no one opposing them (for Theodore, whose surname was Kontostephanos, who had been sent by the emperor on this account, had not yet gathered the army to hold it), and went ravaging as far as one of the regions near the sea, whose name is Kelbianon [the Cayster valley].[18] They returned driving a very large spoil. When the emperor heard of this, he was unable to restrain himself. After he had quickly made ready, he set out at full speed for Ikonion, once he had informed the sultan [Mas'ūd] of this by letter. The letter ran thus: "We wish you to know that you have undertaken things which provoke our attack on you. You yourself have robbed us of Prakana, which did not belong to you, and you lately assailed the Romans' land. You also did not desist from fighting in some fashion with Yaghi-Basan [ibn Dānishmend],[19] who is the Romans' ally, and with many other chieftains there. / 40 / You who are an intelligent man must understand that the Romans would never permit themselves to overlook this, and it remains, with God's aid, that you should pay the penalty for this many times over. Either abstain from irrationalities, or be ready to resist the Romans at once." In such terms was the letter. After he [the sultan] had read the letter when it was brought to him, he responded thus: "We have received your letter, mighty emperor. And we have prepared as you commanded. Then you should order your advance, not delay us by lengthy communications. The rest, as to how matters go, will be God's concern, and ours. Let this Philomilion [Philomelion, modern Akşehir] be the place for our encounter, where we are presently encamped.''

In such terms the sultan very vulgarly responded to the emperor; he [the sultan] remained with the greatest part of the Turks' army there at Philomilion where he had first been camped, but detaching a portion of them, he sent them to intercept the advancing Romans. Near the city of Akrounos [Akroenos, modern Afyonkarahisar] they [the Turks] shortly encountered the emperor who was at a place whose name is the hill of Kalograia; they suffered a severe defeat and returned as fugitives to the sultan. Along with many others, Haïrī,[20] renowned among the Turks, became a victim of the Roman blade. The other [the sultan], stricken in spirit at the disaster, did not remain in the place to prepare anything nor attend to anything necessary, but departed in flight from there. Learning of these things, the emperor / 41 / intended to mock him for both his previous rashness and immoderate trepidation thereafter, and wrote him as follows: ''You, noble sir, must understand this well, that however shameful cowardice is, it becomes more shameful when bravado preceded it; nor should it be uncorrected by others in battle. Since, as if entirely forgetful of your earlier pride, and making no account of what you recently wrote to our empire [Byzantine form for Our Majesty], you fled I know not where, behold, we offer you a reminder thereof. If you will not await our coming at Philomilion, as you formerly announced to us, it yet remains that your noble and generous self should quickly overcome your base cowardice.'' Such words were in it.

Reaching Philomilion, the emperor took it by storm and burned the whole of it. Finding there some Romans who had been for a long time confined under guard, he released the wretches from their bonds and allowed them to see the light of freedom. For, as the emperor approached, the Turks were at first confident in their own strength and decided not to transfer them elsewhere in the land; but when fear impelled them, they not only paid them [the captives] no heed, but thought their own property of less account.

When the letter was brought to the sultan, either feeling the rebuke therein or planning something else, he retreated. Swiftly reaching a place / 42 / called in Turkish Andrachman,[21] he camped there. When the emperor heard this, he arrayed his army at once, passed by the city of Adrianople (for that name passed also into Lykaonia itself), and made camp in a place called Gaïta [Akait].[22] On the next day (for both armies had camped not far apart) he drew up the troops and advanced, and, when he came in contact with the Turks, commenced battle. Not enduring the Romans at the first onslaught, the Turks turned to retreat. Following behind them, they [the Byzantines] destroyed some and took others captive.

The sultan did not cease fleeing until, coming in disorder to Ikonion, he rushed within the walls; once he was in safety, he conceived a plan as follows. He did not at all dare remain within, lest, being shut up by the besieging Romans, he should render himself unable to emerge. In general, not knowing the war's conclusion, to what point of fortune it would come round, he deemed it unprofitable to be beleaguered in a confined place. He set part of his army to garrison the city, and dividing the rest in two, he placed one part on the slope behind the city, and keeping the other himself he drew it up on the right, as he relied particularly on the strength of the mountain which extended between Ikonion and the fortress of Kaballa.[23]

6. The Turks were in this situation. When the emperor arrived at Kaballa, aroused to wonderful zeal, / 43 / he chafed to attack the sultan. Being unable to guess immediately where he [Mas'ūd] might be, he [Manuel] held back briefly from the assault, but by military experience he observed that he [Mas'ūd] was in command of the regiment on the right of the city (for at such matters he [Manuel] was keener than anyone), and at once seizing the standard-bearer he pulled him by the rein and turned

him toward that division. When the Romans' army hesitated and considered the maneuver in great astonishment, as to why he should wish to venture so incautiously against such an insuperable force (for the lack of appearance of that army astonished them, and so they thought these would be an advance guard of the regiment with the sultan which was probably concealed in the mountain's undergrowth), and as they were astonished, he relaxed his countenance a little and said, "Romans, do not let barbarian trickery turn your shrewdness to fear: while there is a lack of standards in the army visible in front of us, you should not imagine that they are elsewhere with another force. For I think no other division of troops remains to the Turks, and their standards have been placed in concealment over there in the thicket, so that they might frighten us by the appearance of a multitude. Be not astonished at the barbarian for his number, but rather despise his weakness. Truth does not naturally associate with imagination. I, however, shall set out with the foremost companies to engage them immediately, / 44 / and you, drawn up in order, must follow me with the rest of the army, lest you encounter the enemy's ambushes."

Speaking thus, the emperor rushed upon the foe, himself appropriating the position on the left, since this faced the center of the opponents' army, where the most numerous and best Turks were. The Turks I think were deprived of courage by the preceding battles; when they saw the Roman blade, they broke formation and dashed off in disorder, each one eager to escape from there first. Rumor had reported that the sultan was present there. Busied with the pursuit of the fleeing, the Romans wasted much time. So they were occupied with this.

The other army of Romans, which as stated had been placed in the rear, advanced, fell unexpectedly into ambushes, and was turned back; then others assailed them, who formed the garrison in Ikonion (these took courage because the emperor was making a lengthy pursuit far from Ikonion, and sallied out), and those who as stated had been posted on the slope behind the city. They [the Byzantines] commenced to fall into confusion. As soon as the emperor heard of this, he sent forces of his attendants to them by the quickest route; Pyrrhogeorgios, a very active man, commanded them, he who was later honored with the rank of primikerios of the court,[24] and also Chouroup, who belonged to the emperor's servants, even the ones with the purple robe. Even when they had come to help, however, / 45 / the utterly exhausted force was again in no less panic.

The emperor, who was very acute in finding what was needed and very clever in inferring what had to be done, decided the matter required shrewdness rather than force. He summoned one of the soldiers, Bempitziotes by name, who sprang from Adrianople, and ordered him to remove the helmet from his head and with his hand to wave it around in every direction in the air, to proclaim the sultan's seeming capture to the army. When this was done the Roman [force] at once recovered courage and thrust back the foe who were strongly pressing them. Frequently thus a single clever plan succeeds over manifold strength, and the excellence of one man is mightier than many shields.

As night then came swiftly on, they camped there; setting out from there at dawn, he camped at Ikonion. Making a circuit around it, he [Manuel] perceived that it was inaccessible. Also there increased daily a rumor which warned that the nations to the west, rebelling by ancestral custom, would invade the Romans' land in full force. So he gave up the siege, thinking he required more time and greater preparation than [he had] at that [moment]; after he had ravaged and destroyed what was nearby, he departed from there.[25]

Reportedly, while the Roman [army] was abusing the Turks' tombs outside the city and ejecting as many of the bodies as possible, not even in the press of the moment / 46 / did he wish the splendor of the sultan's mother to be insulted, but ordered her dust to be preserved undisturbed. He stated briefly that wise men must rather be ashamed at distressed nobility. Writing a letter which was not far from mildness, he sent it to the sultan's wife. The letter went thus: "We wish you to know that the child of our empire,[26] the sultan, lives and still survives, since he has fled the forces of war." She, however, had in readiness around two thousand sheep and a vast quantity of oxen and many other sorts of edibles, to welcome the emperor with them; but since as stated the Roman [army] burned the dwellings outside the city, she did not accomplish her intention. Such was this matter.

When the emperor commenced his withdrawal, he again sent a letter to the sultan. The text went thus: "We have repeatedly sought you, but we have not encountered you. You continually flee and slip away like a shadow. Lest we seem to battle with shadows, we are presently departing on our way home; in spring we shall come to you with greater preparation. You should take care not to flee altogether, in a way so unworthy of yourself."

7. This letter was in such terms. Very numerous forces of the Turks who dwell far beyond Ikonion, where the late [ibn] Dānishmend [27] used to rule, arrived in alliance with the sultan and joined him. Spurred on by them, / 47 / he did not wish to flee as before, but once he was in good array he hastened to attack the Romans who had reached a place named in the barbarian tongue Tzibrelitzemani.[28] The place is more difficult of access than any [other], not only for men drawn up in array, but it is not easily passable even for travelers in small groups. The one army of Romans was already suffering difficulties around the camp, but the emperor, impelled by his youth, and having not long since wedded a wife, himself desired to achieve something in battle, according to their custom. For to the Latin who has just taken a wife, not to appear noble brings no common disgrace. So in two ravines on either hand he placed parties in ambush, one consisting of those nearest him in blood, among whom were many of his most intimate associates and those who had wedded his sisters,[29] the other [consisting] of two military regiments, whom Nicholas surnamed Angelus [30] commanded, a man valiant in action and well supplied

with courage; he ordered them to remain there quiet, until they saw him charging against the foe.

Unwillingly yielding to the demands of his brother Isaac and John [Axouchos] the *domestikos* of the eastern and western [troops],[31] he went with them to a spot where he saw some of the Romans going in groups to forage; cloaking his weapons there, lest he be known to the Turks by their superlative quality, he waited for some of the Turks who would probably come to do damage. But as no one / 48 / was visible to him in any direction, he sent for one of the Romans' soldiers named Poupakes [Abū-Bakr],[32] a Turk by birth, who possessed great courage and activity, and ordered him to advance and investigate carefully as to whether he could see any Turks approaching. So he set out, and when a little later he returned, he asserted he had seen no more than eight Turks. Leaving the others in the ambushes, as aforesaid, the emperor along with his brother and the *domestikos* went toward them with such speed as was possible, while Poupakes showed them the way. His brothers-in-law, who had been overlooked, became so annoyed that each and all of them bound and tied themselves with fearful oaths, that truly he would join the emperor (who did not desire it) in this battle, if it could be so.

The emperor had not yet clashed with those Turks who had been observed, and it transpired that they numbered some eighteen. He longed and chafed to attack them; lest, because they were better equipped, they might be able to flee (as he still stood far off he was unable to charge them from close by), he contrived as follows. He ordered Poupakes to go very close to them, and when he perceived them approaching, to flee with all his might until he came near himself. So he [Poupakes] did as commanded, and when he commenced to be pursued by the barbarians, he fled. He did not entirely outrun the foe, but while continually offering them a hope of capturing him, he escaped / 49 / and thus drew them on up to the emperor.

Yet the emperor did not entirely succeed in his plan. For

once they saw him, they departed, riding quicker than thought; when they met some fifty others coming up behind them, they took courage from the number, and reckoned they could resist him as he attacked. Albeit those with him [Manuel] strongly opposed the undertaking (for they said they were already very far from the army), yet without losing time he pursued at full speed. For some distance the sebastokrator [his brother Isaac] accompanied him and rode beside him; but when he was unable to go further, as his horse was exhausted, he was left behind, and despairing of safety he strongly pleaded with his brother in behalf of his wife and children. The other [Manuel] reproached him and blamed his slight opinion [of Manuel], saying, "Well, dearest brother, did you suspect that so long as I lived I would leave you in the enemy's hands? Not you? Think and speak not thus unworthily of yourself." When the other [Isaac] added these words, "But remain here, so that I shall join you as you attack the barbarians," he [Manuel] said, "After the engagement if God grants, I will come swiftly to you; now I intend other things, and a yearning for valiant deeds absolutely draws me to itself." Saying this to his brother, he rushed at the foe. So matters went there in regard to the emperor.

Those who as stated were placed in ambushes hastily sent one of the nobles, Kotertzes by name, to learn / 50 / what situation the emperor's affairs were in. The emperor sent him back to them, ordering them to come as swiftly as possible. Just as he [Manuel] reached an adjacent hill he encountered an entire Turkish force totaling some five hundred, and not far behind it the sultan marched with his whole army. As soon as he saw them he immediately aimed his lance and rushed at them; he speared many and cast them to earth. But they, as if stricken speechless, stood quiet. When this happened, the aforementioned forces of Romans who formed the ambushes appeared near the emperor, who as stated had sent for them; understanding this, the Turks separated a part of their force and ordered those who were at the rear to oppose the approaching Romans. They thought that enveloping him [Manuel], they already had him in nets. So they acted thus.

But he stood leaning on his spear, upright on the ground, and directed Poupakes (for he still accompanied him) to observe closely lest the Roman [force] should be shut off from the nearest hill by the Turks, whereby he would be entirely bottled up. But Poupakes, behaving in the opposite fashion from what he wanted, said, "Cease, really cease, master. Don't you see how much trouble we're in? Consider your own safety." After he said so much and more, yet was unable to persuade him, he did as ordered. The emperor paid no attention to what was said (it was impossible for him to flee except with future disgrace), but again charging the foe / 51 / and slaying one of them, he threw the rest into confusion; thus seizing the opportunity he went and stood on a little hill, where other Romans joined him, before all [the rest] John, whom because he was his nephew he later enrolled in the rank of the protosebastoi.[33] In this fashion the emperor escaped from there, since his horse was absolutely covered with sweat and really blown.

While the emperor was engaged with the enemy, the *domestikos* John [Axouchos] had been left behind, and feared lest he fall into [the enemies'] hands, since the foe was continually appearing here and there in groups, while he was bereft of aid. He composed some feeble excuses for his own benefit, saying that the place where he stood was a very suitable one, and they must rather assemble there to make a rallying-point for the emperor. In this way he was able to detain near him many of those who as stated were going out from the camp to the emperor; after he had been saved by them, he reached the emperor. Then John [Axouchos] himself and many other Romans reproached his [Manuel's] bravery and maintained that such things were not far from rashness. It causes me, as I consider this, to be astonished that, when on that day he was in the midst of so many perils, he was neither wounded nor hit. I dare not say whether on account of his repeated bold deeds against those barbarians he furnished them experience of his nobility and became well nigh unapproachable for them, or whether [it was] by Providence caring for him in ways which It understood. / 52 / I myself do not consider what he did among things worthy of commendation. Nor can I approve Alexander's boldness, when I systematically review the facts about the man, unless one grants something to the prime of youth: for youth is irresistible, and combined with strength and might it becomes invincible. But let each person think and say what he likes on this matter.

When as stated he was being reproached by his followers, the emperor said, "At present we do not need such [words]; but we must take council as well as possible lest more Romans be lost on this day; for many are coming who have been left behind us." It seemed right to place an ambush in the nearest ravine, to help those who were following, while the rest went quietly to the camp. This was done. With a few of his attendants, the emperor went forward, and Nicholas [Angelus] as well, who as has already been mentioned had been left behind in ambush with the two regiments which, when he attacked the Turks, the emperor had placed under his command. The emperor had not proceeded far when he reached a ravine, saw Turks approaching, and acted as follows. With a few of his men, he stood on one side of the valley; he ordered the others who were ascending to make straight for the foe. As they encountered the barbarians, those in the ambushes, hearing of it, came up at a run. The aforesaid Nicholas struck with a spear at a Turk, yet was unable to tumble him from his seat, as a strong thrust could not be made because of the terrain's steepness. / 53 / Contriving lest he thrust them back too far, he [Manuel] ordered his attendants to go to the ravine at seemingly full speed, but not to ascend it. When they observed this, the Turks quietly withdrew. At this moment, the bowmen with Kotertzes, whom as stated the emperor had sent to come to the aid of those Romans left behind, encountered the emperor, and again he attacked the foe. They suddenly turned their horses' heads and commenced to flee; perceiving this, the emperor said to his followers, "Take courage: a force is coming to us from the camp." When they failed to approach, some stated the reason: "The Turks, without any fear urging them (for we were not equal in strength to them), suddenly turned their backs and left because they were able to see something still hidden from us, since they were looking down from an elevation." And this proved to be very accurate truth. For they were Romans from the camp who had learned that the emperor was involved in a really tight place and had quickly hastened to aid him.

Then allegedly the emperor's paternal uncle Isaac the sebastokrator, who was then present in the camp, as he learned that the emperor was in desperate peril, approached the imperial tent, went into a chapel outfitted with furnishings, and awaited what was going to happen, intending to usurp the throne. From a long time back, as stated, longing for it / 54 / had possessed that man, flourished, and not only grown up, but even like an ancestral inheritance had passed to his children. The advancing narrative, however, will speak about this later.

8. When the forces from the camp, as I said (I am returning to where I made an excursus), joined him, the emperor was encouraged by their number, again charged the foe, and became the hero of valiant deeds; then he returned to camp in good order. Rising at dawn, he took the road. The Turks (who had encamped very near at hand) attacked the Romans' force, which was again in rough country, from both sides and galled it severely; many of those from the infantry regiments fell for the following reason. In the Romans' army was an excellent warrior, Kritoples by name. This man then commanded the infantry forces. Turning aside his formation, he came to grips with the Turks who were following close, and when he was overcome by their multitude, he looked toward undisguised flight; in this way, after he had lost many of those with him, he escaped with difficulty. When he learned this, the emperor entrusted the regiment with him to his brother and

many other of the most noble persons, but with a few men himself hastened to rescue the suffering [part] of that force. Arriving at their midst, he ordered them to stand bravely, and himself attacked the Turks. The latter, recognizing him, did not fight the Romans hand-to-hand.

The emperor took thought as to how / 55 / the Roman [force] could recover its courage; already, due to what had as stated happened to the infantry troops, their valor had commenced to slip away a little, since nothing is so capable of shaking the spirit as observing close at hand the effusion of one's fellows' blood. Drawing forth a roll which he had in his bosom on which was each of the regiments by name, he directed what each must do in so acute a crisis of affairs. Many of the units had refused all day to face the enemy, broke formation, and moved to the army's baggage train; they disregarded the emperor's orders to such an extent that, although on that day many of them were therefore bodily punished by him, the rest paid almost no heed to what was being done. Excessive cowardice made them utterly forgetful of their courage.

While in this fashion the rear guard was mixed with the van, the enemy's whole remaining force surrounded the emperor and pressed him severely; but he opposed the foe with his martial experience and so was able to survive unharmed. Then it seemed proper to others to camp there and proceed no further; but this displeased the emperor, lest the Romans as they hurried in confusion and disorder were defeated either immediately or on the morrow when they were packing up for departure; [34] rather, he said they must attack, so that if somehow they repelled the enemy / 56 / they might without hindrance plant a stockade and camp when they were not confined in a limited space. After he had said this, when he saw that not all of them accepted the advice, he placed Tzikandyles [35] and Sinopites, as well as Kritoples and many of the other generals, in charge of the camp.

Taking the imperial standard, he charged the enemy at full

speed with his followers. Astonishing them by the suddenness of his onset, he constrained them to look to flight. When a splendid chase developed, the pursuing Romans slew many but took some alive; among them was Pharkousas,[36] an outstanding man among the Turks, who with his own hands offered the cup to the sultan as he dined—the Romans call this [personage] the "cupbearer." In the barbarians' army was someone who was related to the Romans by birth, but as he had been nurtured and reared among the Turks, he held by chance an emirate among them: Gabras was his name.[37] When on that day the Romans slew him, they went about the camp parading his head. The emperor gave up pursuit (as it was already far into night) and returned with symbols of victory. Finding the Romans still in great confusion and disorder (the pack animals had not even been relieved of the burden on their backs), he quickly made the rounds of the whole camp and allotted the appropriate space to each of the regiments. But no few of the soldiers passed the night on horseback, as by the excess of / 57 / crowding they were unable to dismount from their beasts. So they camped for that night.

When the sun had just ascended to a view of the earth, he went into the center of the army, mounted, as is customary for those who command military units, and spoke as follows: "Noble sirs, I do not come exhorting you to be brave because I perceive your cowardice or any other weakness; not thus ignobly do Romans conduct themselves, not thus shame their ancestral glory. But as I fulfill this military custom, I am also persuading you to safer courses for the future. For there is a moment when an unforeseen danger occurs and throws valiant determination into confusion. Know then, fellow soldiers, that today we face conflict greater than the previous ones; this is as it were the last and final struggle. We must be well prepared on account of our prior efforts, lest we now disgrace the previous excellence of our deeds and be the cause of great misfortunes to ourselves. Just as a concluding piece of good fortune naturally rectifies prior ill luck, so later disaster ruins previous success. Lest this should happen to ourselves, best of men, each must keep formation as much as possible, since we are well aware that if we maintain absolutely unbroken ranks and each contributes his share to the rest, there will remain for us [the possibility] of winning and preserving for ourselves fame which will endure to men in after time. / 58 / If, however, the opposite happens, that we be divided from each other, know that we shall at once be easy prey for the enemy. Just as when a city is besieged the walls breaking down make entry easy for the foe, so it goes in armies. On this account companies and regiments, rear and front ranks, right and left wings, parallel ranks and forms of marshaling were devised by the ancients. For the army is also a city. It requires gates, walls, moats, and every other appurtenance similar to cities. Thus we must prepare ourselves. For we are still in the midst of enemy country, and we have wandered far from the bounds of Romania.'' [38]

After he had said this and had arranged the army in order, he set out straight for the lake which people formerly called "of Skleros," but now, "of Pousgouse." [39] When the army reached the plains from that narrow place and came into open country, he ordered one of the soldiers to shout very loudly and summon one of the Turks. He did as ordered. To the Turk who approached, the emperor said, "Report this to your sultan. 'The great emperor communicates this through me. We have come up to Ikonion itself. We have scoured your land since we particularly desired to prosecute your crime against our empire [i.e., Our Majesty]. You, however, fled continually, like / 59 / runaway slaves, shifting from one place to another and heretofore not remaining to oppose us face to face. Therefore we are departing to our own land, but you must get ready, knowing well that when spring comes we shall again return to you with greater preparation.' '' After he had communicated this to the Turk and had presented him with the breastplate of one of the nobles, so that it would be evident that he had been sent by the emperor, he was dismissed. When the sultan heard this, he dispatched envoys a little later to ask about peace. The emperor, however, esteemed the matter of great and not negligible importance; on pretexts he went from one place to another and repeatedly postponed to the morrow the conclusion of the embassy, until, I think, it should be possible to learn something definite regarding those who, as stated, were expected from the west.

9. When he reached a certain place where the Maeander [Büyükmenderes] had its springs, thinking that he was already outside enemy territories and observing that the country was well watered and offered much that was pleasant to men's eyes, he desired to seek recreation from the labors of battle in the relaxation of hunting. Observing some movement far off in the undergrowth, since by reason of the distance he was unable to identify what he saw, he sent some of his attendants to scout. He heard that many tents were assembled there, and the movements in the grove were the horses of those in the tents, grazing on grass with unbridled mouths. He immediately recognized who these Turks were, naming them according to their tribe, / 60 / reckoning that a certain Raman was their chief, and that they had come according to their custom to pillage some of the neighboring Romans and now were well stocked with booty.[40]

After he had chosen some of the soldiers with him, he quickly sent them off in pursuit. Hastening to a place which offered a good view, he stood there looking out with a few men. In the meantime the Turks had packed up and set out from there. Because they speedily commenced to be overtaken by the Romans, and saw them rushing along in clusters, they turned around and stood facing them. When the Romans overtook them, they again turned their backs; the fact that they did this often caused many of the Romans to falter; so, giving up pursuit, they bethought themselves of their return.

Observing this, the emperor (for as stated he stood high up looking out) at once went to them as swiftly as he could, without his breastplate. When the Turks saw many of the Romans ex-

hausted as aforesaid by the pursuit and separated from one another, and observed exactly how few the others were, they caused
them [the Byzantines] to be attacked on both sides and came close
to working great and irremediable harm, save that the emperor
unexpectedly appeared to them and rescued them from danger. He
spent a long time continually pursuing the fleeing Turks. So when
he perceived his horse exhausted, he stayed there waiting to be
furnished one of the particularly swift horses which, in allusion to
their speed, are called Wild. He directed the Romans, as they continually came individually and in groups and caught up with him
from behind, to pursue still further / 61 / and not abandon their
zeal. Others after a very lengthy pursuit, since they were unable to
achieve anything and observed the place where for the most part
they had come as they sallied forth to be deserted and really inaccessible, turned back. He [Manuel] chanced on his cousin Andronicus,[41] of whom we made a long account in the foregoing [sic],
who was rushing at the foe, and under constraint he gave up his
horse to him [Manuel]. Mounting, he allowed him [Andronicus] to
wait there, directing him to take the aforesaid Wild horse which
would immediately be brought and so to join him in battle; but he
[Manuel] rushed against the foe.

The Turks' army was divided in two. One part went in
front bringing the whole herd of horses, which followed them in a
bunch without saddles; the rest came behind to hold off the approaching Romans. As none of the Romans appeared anywhere,
they took courage for the future, joined together, and planned to
assemble in one place the herd which as stated was rushing about
uncontrolled. When they observed the emperor alone of all the
Romans attacking them without his breastplate, they poured down
on him in crowds, drawing their bows and cheering each other on.
Adopting a heroic stance which was beyond courage, since he perceived that encirclement by the enemy was impossible there (the
locale, which extended far on either hand, hindered them in that),

he took the encounter on himself, brought many of them low, and constrained the rest to seek flight.

Then / 62 / one of the barbarians who was unable to endure the emperor's point was cast prone on the earth; once he observed him [Manuel] charging onwards, he shot an arrow and hit the end of his leg from the back, where on the heel below the ankle nature turns back and forms a prominence. He [the Turk] hurried to shoot again, but in advance of his attempt the emperor took him captive by the hair; as he returned with him to the army, he encountered Andronicus. For when the imperial horse had been brought to him, he had mounted and charged the Turks. He [Manuel] vigorously dissuaded him from going further, as he was absolutely without arms; since he was unable to persuade him (for he [Andronicus] continued the pursuit courageously and limitlessly, and snorted for battle, handling spear and shield fairly well, not using his own but what he had taken from one of the nobles), he let him go. He [Manuel] proceeded on the road and joined the rest of the Romans' army. He did not reply at all to those who inquired how matters had fared for him in battle when he had gone entirely alone against the foe, nor about the slaughter of the enemy whom as stated he had killed, averting suspicion of ignoble boasting. For a deed which does not occur in sight of persons willing to hear about it favorably easily leads to denial.

He ordered his wound to be cared for at once, lest it become inflamed and incurable. Then something happened worthy of mention. Since they did not know how to treat it, one of the soldiers / 63 / drew a dagger and himself intended to remove a portion of his own flesh, so that, applying it still warm to the wound, it might prevent inflammation. While the emperor accepted the man's good will, he forbade this; ordering a piece of the flesh of one of the horses which had perished of exhaustion on the route to be cut off, he applied it directly to the wound.

Sustaining a long march through the middle of the night, he

reached the camp situated at the springs of the Maeander. There a measureless amount of water flows from the rocks below the mountains as if emitted from myriad mouths; it overspreads the adjacent region and first collects in a lake, then, advancing, cuts a deep channel and forms a river from there.[42] Andronicus, who as stated had proceeded forward, achieved nothing else except to drive to the camp many horses which those of the enemy killed by the emperor had been riding. So much for this. The emperor took the road to Byzantion, but when he reached Bithynia he settled there those Romans rescued from Philomilion, as previously stated; he obtained a property for them by exchange from one of the holy monasteries. He erected there a fort and called it Pylai.[43]

10. About that time Kosmas, who was then in charge of ecclesiastical affairs, a man decorous [kosmios] in life and speech, / 64 / was deposed from the [patriarchal] throne for the following reason.[44] There was a man who had assumed the monastic life, Nephon by name, who had not proceeded to the temptation of general education and the secular sciences, but had devoted himself from childhood to the Holy Scriptures. While Michael, a holy man outstanding in virtue, held the ecclesiastical throne, this Nephon gave invalid teaching to many around him regarding the Christians' doctrines; he was condemned on this account by a synodal decision, his beard shorn, and he was committed to prison fettered at the ankles. But when that Michael was lost to mankind, and Kosmas adorned the throne in his stead, Nephon straightway received greater freedom of speech and was much in meetings and marketplaces; he did nothing except circulate his teaching everywhere and reject the God of the Hebrews.[45] He desired to benefit by such things. Kosmas liked him excessively, and made the fellow his associate; he called what had previously been decreed against him injustice, and hastily repealed the former penalties on the man. He reverenced his virtue, and attributed something to his words, because much earlier he had foretold his elevation to the patriarchal throne.

The multitude was displeased at this. So some of those who cared for Kosmas approached him as he was at leisure and said, "Why, holy shepherd, do you entrust yourself to a wolf? Don't you know that the flock views you askance on this account? Break away from the corrupter's companionship. / 65 / To associate with an outcast man is a sufficient accusation." So they spoke. Those who were hostile to the prelate openly clamored against him and accused him before the eyes of God and the emperor. But he continued heedless of everything, clung tightly to Nephon, and was unwilling to be parted from him, whatever happened. By his excessive simplicity he scarcely escaped being immoderately punished. After the emperor commanded that the fellow be recommitted to prison, when the men had come to take him [Nephon] away, he [Kosmas] was at first almost struck dumb, then gathering himself together and going on foot into the church's courtyard, he endeavored to tear the fellow away from the men taking him. As they did not yield, he desired to be taken with him to prison. Strife gripped the church on this account, and Kosmas was involved in accusations. It was not released from these troubles until, when the emperor reached Byzantion (for he was still toiling in martial activities), he [Kosmas] was cast down from the throne in the fashion I am about to relate.

Receiving each of the bishops individually, he [Manuel] inquired how Nephon's piety seemed to him. After each of them had truly declared the situation to him, he finally referred the question to Kosmas. As usual, he heedlessly set forth an intensely laudatory view of Nephon, openly calling him pious and unrivaled in virtue. The matter was brought to trial, and the emperor consulted the bishops, not again individually, / 66 / but asked them all together what their opinion of Nephon was. They expressly charged the man with impiety. They were of this opinion, but the emperor directed the question to Kosmas, "But you, master, what do you think of the man?" When he with simplicity again freely maintained the same views, the multitude cried out against him

and deemed him unworthy to remain on the throne. So he was removed from their midst on this account; apart from his simplicity,
he was I think a man enriched with all virtues.

11. A little later the emperor returned to deal with the
Turks [1147]. After he reached the Rhyndakos River he was busy
in preparations to besiege Ikonion and overrun everything around
it. The army had not yet moved from there, however, when
envoys came from the sultan requesting peace. A very powerful
man among the Turks, Suleimān by name,[46] was at the head of the
embassy; he was experienced in many wars and had made proof of
the emperor's might when, as narrated by me, he had encountered
the Romans' army around the so-called hill of Kalograia and had
been severely defeated. The purport of the embassy was as follows: they restored Prakana to the emperor and whatever else had
previously been taken from the Romans. So they agreed there
would be peace in the future / 67 / between Turks and Romans.
Accepting these [terms], the emperor concluded the war and returned to Byzantion.

12. From this point affairs of the west had their outset.
Normans and French and the nation of Gauls and whoever lived
around old Rome, and British and Bretons and simply the whole
western array had been set in motion, on the handy excuse that
they were going to cross from Europe to Asia to fight the Turks en
route and recover the church in Palestine and seek the holy places,
but truly to gain possession of the Romans' land by assault and
trample down everything in front of them.[47] Their army was
beyond count. When the emperor learned that they were close to
the Hungarian boundaries, he dispatched envoys, Demetrius
Makrembolites and Alexander, an Italian by birth who had been
count of Gravina, an Italian city, but who had along with many
others been driven from the realm by the tyrant of Sicily [Roger II]
and consequently had become the emperor's voluntary subject.[48]
He directed them to investigate their [the westerners'] intent, and

if they had not come for the Romans' ill, to confirm the matter by oaths.

When they came before the barbarians' leaders, they spoke as follows: "To conduct undeclared war against those who have committed no offense is neither pious nor otherwise suitable for men who outstandingly possess distinction of birth and excess of strength. For, being victorious, should it go thus, they win without bravery, and being worsted, / 68 / they will not have endangered themselves for the sake of distinction. Neither is commendable. It will be impossible for you to traverse the Romans' soil without first giving the emperor pledges to do no harm. Unless you are going to falsify your oaths, why do you covertly wage war? It will be difficult for you to fight the Romans immediately. But it will be much more difficult if you perjuredly make war on them. For [in that case] it remains that you fight God and the Romans' might. If, however, your friendship is genuine and no treachery lies in wait, by means of oaths confirming the matter you will be able to pass through the great emperor's land as if through friendly country, reasonably enjoying hospitality and other kindness." So said the ambassadors.

The others [Crusaders] assembled together at the tent of the Germans' king, Conrad, because he possessed the principal position among the nations of the West, and stated that they had not come for the Romans' ill; should the matter need to be guaranteed by oath, they asserted they would very readily do so. Behold, their expedition was to Palestine and the Turks who plundered Asia. So it seemed proper to the Romans that they should put their words into action, those who were close to the kings and whoever else was outstanding among them, dukes, I mean, and counts. Their offices are peculiar and like distinctions descending from the height of the empire, since it is something most noble and surpasses [all] others. A duke outranks a count, / 69 / a king, a duke, and the emperor, a king. The inferior naturally yields to the superior, supports him in war, and obeys in such matters. Therefore the Latins customarily call the emperor "Imperator," alluding to his superior rank, but "kings" those who take the second rank. Be this so.

When what they had come to the barbarians for had been achieved by the envoys, they returned to Byzantion, while the kings continued on the road. The armies did not indeed mix with each other, but the German went first, and behind it the French; I know not why they did this, whether each boasted he was separately battle-worthy, or whether they were taking care lest supplies be deficient for them. They advanced, innumerable and beyond the sands of the shore. Xerxes, when he bridged the Hellespont with boats, did not boast so many myriads. For when they came to the Danube, there where the emperor had appointed preparations for their crossing, he directed the greatest part of the secretaries who were stationed on each bank of the river to write down each ship's cargo. After they had ennumerated up to ninety myriads [900,000], they could not count further.[49]

13. So great was this multitude. When they came near the city of Naissos [Niš], which is the capital of Dacia,[50] / 70 / Michael surnamed Branas, who had been entrusted with governance of that region by the emperor, provided necessities for them, as commanded. Thereby they came to Sardika [Sofia], where two men from the aristocracy met them, to welcome them suitably and furnish them necessities. One was the sebastos Michael, of the Palaiologoi, a very clever man, experienced of many affairs; he had earlier been expelled by the emperor John, I know not why, and become an exile, but was recalled by emperor Manuel and became his favorite and especially devoted to the Romans' state. Such was he. The other had been designated *chartoularios* by both emperors. He stood so high in emperor John's favor that when Alexius the eldest of his sons died, the emperor relied on him to summon Manuel to the sceptor after his death and transmit to him the imperial office.[51] For this reason they went to Sardika.

Hitherto the barbarians had been in difficult country (for from the Danube river up to Sardika many mountains rise, high and really inaccessible), and they had advanced quietly and done nothing contrary to the Romans' wishes. But when they entered the plains which succeed to the difficulties of the regions in Dacia, they began to manifest their evil intent: they applied unjust force on those who were offering them goods for sale in the market. / 71 / If one resisted their seizure, they made him a victim of their sword. King Conrad was entirely heedless of what was happening: he either paid no attention to the accusers, or if he paid attention, he ascribed everything to the folly of the multitude.

When the emperor heard this he sent an army under Prosouch, a war-hardened man,[52] against them as quickly as possible. After he met them around Adrianople [Edirne], he followed them for a time at a distance, reining in the multitude's disorderly outbreaks. Because he saw them becoming still more outrageous, he then openly engaged in martial encounters, for the following reason. A certain monastery at Adrianople housed one of the distinguished Germans who was suffering bodily illness, together with his money and all his equipment. Some of the Romans from the infantry regiments pillaged this; they set fire to his abode, and after they had thus destroyed the man, they possessed his goods. Once what had happened came to the ears of Conrad's nephew Frederick, a man ungovernable in passion and really presumptuous on account of his immoderate willfulness, he turned back, albeit he had pursued Conrad's route for two days, and hastily returned to Adrianople. He burned the monastery where the German had previously perished, and thereby afforded this occasion of war to the Romans and themselves. Coming to grips on this account, Prosouch drove Frederick back / 72 / and made a great slaughter of barbarians. It was this Frederick who ruled the Germans after Conrad, for a reason which will be related in the subsequent narrative.[53] From then on the Germans abandoned their prior boasting, having been taught the Romans' might by action.

14. So this was done there. Andronicus, whom they call Opos, who had been sent by the emperor on this account, reminded them of their oaths, frequently put before them what they had previously sworn about doing no harm to the Romans, and upbraided their faithlessness; should they not wish to fall into evident peril, he advised them to proceed to the ferry-crossing at Abydos [Çanakkale] and cross there. Since, after he had said this much, he was unable to persuade them, Andronicus returned unsuccessful to Byzantion.

Assembled in council, the others [Germans] considered the matter at hand. As it seemed right to keep the road to Byzantion, they set forth and advanced on their way. They were again no less boastful, even after their defeat. They slaughtered cattle mercilessly and slew many Romans who resisted them. Yet open warfare did not develop.

When the emperor heard this, he decided he himself had to make preparations. So troops at once garrisoned Constantinople, some camped in front of the walls, others having their station within the gates. He dispatched Basil whom people surname Tzikandyles,[54] who had gained glory in many conflicts in the regions toward the rising / 73 / sun and in fights with the barbarians there, together with the aforementioned Prosouch, a Turk by birth but one who had enjoyed a Roman upbringing and education, to lie in wait with their forces at a place called Longoi. He directed them that whenever the Germans again attempted to commence unjust violence, they should oppose them insofar as possible.

When they reached the spot, they observed the number of Germans and carefully scouted how their formations were in order or disorder. They perceived that their physiques were excessively large and totally armored, but their cavalry was not at all swift; observing that they practiced great disorder on the march, and supposing that their force would be very easily overcome by Romans who engaged scientifically, they sent to the emperor, reported these things, and inquired what should be done. Being still cautious about the barbarians' ostensible purpose, I mean their alleged expedition to Palestine, he therefore shrank from an undertaking [against them], waiting until they more openly attempted violence. So the emperor held to this decision.

The barbarians continued on their way, and when they reached the plains at Choirobacchoi [55] (for the country there spreads out and offers especially abundant grass for horses' pasture), they camped there. / 74 / A disaster beyond description allegedly happened to them there, from which one might reasonably guess that the Divinity was angry at them, who had falsified their oaths and who practiced great inhumanity toward people who were of the same religion and who had done them no wrong. When an unexpected storm suddenly burst, the rivers which flow past that place, one of which is called Melas [Karasu] by the natives, the other, Athyras, rose far beyond the usual level and flooded the greatest part of the plain. They swept away a large portion of the Germans' army with the horses, weapons, and the very tents; rushing along, they spewed them forth from land to sea.

When the emperor learned this, his spirit was moved to compassion toward the men; he sent members of the aristocracy to console Conrad for the disaster, and invited him to participate in discussion and plan with him regarding important affairs. The other [Conrad], still unwilling to abandon his pride, demanded that the emperor meet him as he approached Byzantion, and esteemed his own conversation worthy of other such things. Since the emperor thereby perceived that his pretension was limitless, he overlooked the rest. With his whole force, Conrad hastened to Byzantion; when he reached the imperial dwelling opposite the walls which people call Philopation—I know not whether hinting at its pleasant habitation (for it offers relaxation and release from cares to people who escape thither from urban turbulence), or whether that it is overgrown with leaves / 75 / and produces rich grass (the place is extensive and bears everywhere a green appearance) [56]—he gave his attention to the city's wall from there. As he observed the towers mounting to considerable height and saw the great size of the deep moat which encircled it, he became very astonished. When he perceived a crowd of women and the populace standing unarmed and idle on the outwork (for of all those who were used to martial toil, some were placed on guard on the inner walls, the rest stood in front of the city's fortifications, waiting for the Germans to commence battle)—when he observed these things, he straightway determined that the city remained impregnable from its excess of strength, which was true; he set out from there and swiftly crossed the bridge which yokes what one might call the adjacent "river-sea" [the Golden Horn], and arrived at one of the suburbs opposite Byzantion, which is called Pikridion [Hasköy].[57] Here is the rationale of the crossing there. The Euxine [Black] Sea creates a backwater by turning to the right as it proceeds westwards, forming a spacious port for the Byzantines. A certain river which arises someplace higher up runs down through the plains there, then reaching the head of the harbor a little above Byzantion, it comes to the place where the bridge stands.

15. Such is this. When he reached there, Conrad sent a letter to the emperor which was really not far from extreme conceit. / 76 / The statement ran thus. "One who possesses intelligence, emperor, must consider not merely a problem in itself, but particularly inquire the reason whence it arose. Whoever depends on a prejudice frequently fails to commend what is good, and does not naturally blame what appears base. And, contrary to general opinion, one sometimes meets with good from enemies, but again experiences something ill from friends. Do not impute to us the causes of the damages lately wrought by the commonality of our army in your land, nor be wroth on that account, since we ourselves have not been causes of such things, but the mob's impulse, recklessly hastening onwards, was capable of doing this of its own will. For when a foreign and outland army is everywhere wandering and roving about, partly to investigate the land, partly to gather necessaries, I think it not unreasonable that such injuries occur on every hand." Such the Germans said.

The emperor, who reckoned the matter a piece of sarcasm, answered as follows. "The inclination of the multitude, perpetually unmanageable and uncontrollable, has not escaped our empire. Indeed, it was our care that you, foreign strangers, should pass uninjured through our [realm] without alleging or really experiencing any harm from us, lest we gain an ill repute among mankind for acting contrary to hospitality. Since, however, such things apparently seem unworthy of blame to you, inasmuch as you are very clever and well skilled in accurately investigating / 77 / the nature of affairs, we owe you thanks. We shall not then consider how we should rein in the mass impulse of our people, but we shall attribute it to the mob's folly, as you have kindly instructed us. So it will no longer profit you to take the road in groups, nor thus to wander in a foreign land. Since this has seemed right, and the commonality are allowed to exercise their passions on every hand, foreigners are likely to suffer much from natives." So saying, he sent them back.

Knowing the Romans' army to be much less in number than the barbarians, but that it was equally superior in military science and perseverance in battle, he planned as follows. He commanded Prosouch and [Basil] Tzikandyles and many other Roman generals to lead out a sufficient force and take a stand confronting the Germans. They were arrayed thus: the least warlike, common part of the army stood far forward, in four units; thereafter, the well-armed and armored; then those who rode swift horses; and finally, behind the line of battle, the Cumans with the Turks and the Romans' archer force. The Romans acted thus; as soon as the Germans saw this, seized by great eagerness and disorder, they advanced at a run. A fierce battle developed, and a great slaughter of Germans occurred. As they attacked, the Romans scientifically resisted and slew them.

Conrad, who had not yet learned / 78 / what had happened, still remained insolent and was driven on by great hopes. The emperor, who wished to mock at him for his previous arrogance, wrote to him thus. "We must be well aware that a horse which does not abide the bridle does not benefit his rider, even if perhaps it did not carry him over a cliff, and that army which fails to harken to its commanders generally involves its leaders in perils; they should not allow their own troops to be carried along separately according to their impulses. But since, I know not what ails you, you despised this and persuaded our majesty, as it was treating you in friendly fashion, to be of the same opinion as yours, now consider what the mob's license has contrived for you. For I learn that a minute army of Romans which encountered an immense number of Germans manhandled them. The native and local [army] is as a rule apt to be superior to foreign strangers. Nor will it be possible for us to chastise the mob's irreverence. How [could we]? We have allowed them absolutely to be swept along by their own violition. If it seems right to you, we must both hold back both sides with official rein and restrain the soldiers' impulses. If it does not seem so, let matters abide in the present situation. So reveal to us clearly what has been done.''

16. The emperor's words concluded in such terms. As Conrad had not yet heard what had befallen the Germans, / 79 / he did not think it at all proper to pay attention to any of this. He rather demanded that the imperial dromond and the usual triremes be sent him by the emperor, to use for the crossing. Should they not speedily come to him, he threatened to encompass the city with many thousands on the morrow. Angered thereby, the emperor was still unwilling to answer the braggart to the extent of false modesty. Therefore, writing to him, he attacked him with bitter words as follows: ''For those able to examine minutely, affairs are not customarily judged by quantity, but by quality and by superiorities and defects therein. So one must distinguish contestants in war not by number, but by their excellence and exercises and skill therein. Even should a large army follow you, it yet exceeds the native one by little, although the greatest portion [of the native army] is divided among many parts of the Romans' realm, and it [Conrad's force] is also a common herd and largely unwarlike.

Flocks of sheep might vainly be reckoned in entire myriads if they suffered a [single] lion leaping at them. Or were you unaware that you are like a sparrow under our power? Should we desire it, would you not straightway perish? Consider that they possess this country whose ancestors passed through the whole earth with arms, and became masters of yourselves and every other race under the sun. You must also consider that you will never embark on the imperial gallery nor fulfill amongst us what you seek, but / 80 / your horses' legs will bear you back on the same road. And you must not blame us, if we make ourselves very unpleasant to those who wish to act wrongfully. For to do wrong and to take vengeance are not the same: the first stems from defective judgment, while caution guides the other. Previous subjection owes us whatever [lands] will presently be regained from the neighboring Turks; indeed the Romans will possess these without difficulty. What we have not endured our own people demanding [i.e., attack the Germans], we now risk doing at once by your urging.''

When Conrad heard this and learned simultaneously what late misfortune had befallen the Germans, he boarded a wretched skiff which was pulled up someplace on the seashore there, crossed the strait of Damalis,[58] and quickly reached the opposite shore, because a certain barbaric heedlessness drove the man. For in prosperity the barbarian is likely to be exalted and boast beyond measure, but in disaster he is downcast more than is suitable and is immoderately humbled. As the emperor was minded to humiliate him still further, he acted as follows. Sending some Romans to the rear of the Germans' army, he corrupted with money some, reputed innumerable, to withhold their allegiance to Conrad.

Observing this, Conrad was no longer the previous supercilious fellow. Writing to the emperor, he asked that one of the Romans be sent to him to guide him on the road and conduct him in security. He who then filled the office of *akolouthos* [59] was sent. / 81 / He had also been directed to discuss an alliance with Conrad. Since the Romans and Germans had combatted in long debate, he [Conrad] should grant it [alliance] to the emperor, but receive far more in exchange, if he were willing to join the emperor in battle with the Turks. Since two roads lay before him, he should select whichever he wished to proceed on. So Stephen [the *akolouthos*] reported this to Conrad. After he had taken counsel with his followers, he rejected the alliance, but chose the road which led to Philomilion.

As far as Melangeia and Dorylaion [Eskişehir], nothing unpleasant blocked the Germans. When they reached there, a Turk by the name of Mamplanes [60] with a small force attacked their vanguard, to test their strength and learn what kind of formation they kept. When the Turks first appeared before them, the Germans advanced in disorder; seized by great eagerness and confusion, they rushed at them. Since the Germans were not far from their own camp, the Turks turned tail and pretended flight; but when their [the Germans'] cavalry was exhausted and they were far from camp, they [the Turks] made rapid charges and slew horses and men. This same thing which happened frequently cast them into immeasurable terror. Then it was possible to observe those who were formerly rash braggarts, who attacked in the fashion of irresistible brutes, cowardly and ignoble and incapable of either doing / 82 / or planning anything. Then Conrad (for he was courageous in warfare) rushed against the Turks, lost the particularly swift horses which the emperor had presented to him, and came close to being captured by those barbarians.

17. The Germans were in such straits. The king of the French [Louis VII] (for reportedly he had crossed the Danube and advanced further) had determined not to become unnecessarily presumptuous like Conrad. He welcomed those who had come to him from the emperor, I mean the sebastos Michael Palaiologos and Michael to whom the surname Branas was applied, and promised his favors to the emperor; he was observed doing no harm to the Romans thereafter. I am unable to say whether he was instructed by the previous misfortunes of Conrad, or whether the

man's character was naturally such. Therefore he ended by enjoying a very great reception from the emperor. When he drew near Byzantion, he sent envoys to the emperor, promised still further friendship, and agreed to cooperate with him in important matters; should it be advisable for them to meet each other and join in discussion in the palace, he did not wish to neglect this. The emperor harkened to these messages not unfavorably, and directed him to come confidently.

When he arrived, there met him men close to the emperor in family and station, who then controlled the more important offices, to conduct him in splendor to the emperor and accord him appropriate honors. / 83 / When he came inside the palace, the emperor was seated on high, and a lowly seat, which people who speak Latin call a chair, was offered to him. After he had been seated on it, he said and heard what was proper, and then departed to the suburb outside the wall which as stated is termed Philopation by the multitude, to be lodged there. A little later, along with the emperor, he went to the palace [Blachernai] south of the city,[61] to investigate the things there worthy of awe and behold the holy things in the church there: I mean those things which, having been close to Christ's body, are signs of divine protection for Christians. After he had accomplished this in Byzantion and had given pledges on oath to be friend and ally to the emperor so long as he lived, he also crossed to Asia.[62]

18. So this was done there. The emperor promoted a certain Nicholas, by surname Mouzalon, to the patriarchal throne; [63] he had previously belonged to the priestly order, but after he had possessed the throne of the Cypriots' church he then voluntarily resigned from it. But no sooner did he take up administration than every mouth was roused against him. They claimed he had unlawfully mounted the throne, because he had previously abandoned the priesthood along with the church assigned to him. At first he was stubborn and unwilling to resign the throne. / 84 / But once the emperor had made a determination on the matter, he

[Mouzalon] perceived that he had been allotted the losing side; without waiting to be examined again, he abandoned the throne and continued to live as an individual. In his stead was designated Theodotos, who was thoroughly practiced in ascetic discipline.[64]

As stated, the Germans had been frequently defeated by the Turks and lost many of their men; once they abandoned passage through Philomilion, they hastened back. Coming to Nikaia [Iznik], they met there the French who were marching on the road, and the other kings who were bringing with them large forces: one of these ruled the Czechs' nation, and had seemingly been appointed king by Conrad; the other, that of the Poles, who are a Scythic people and dwell beside the western Hungarians.[65]

When the armies united together, a certain byword which from of old used to be uttered by the French to the Germans was then openly applied, which verbally runs something like "Budge, German." [66] Whence such a thing takes its origin I will immediately reveal. These nations' fashion of waging battle is not the same. The French are particularly capable of riding horseback in good order and attacking with the spear, and their cavalry surpasses that of the Germans in speed. The Germans, however, are able to fight on foot better than the French and excel in using the great sword. So whenever the Germans campaign against the French, they feel doubtful / 85 / of their cavalry and determine to wage war on foot. Encountering their undisciplined cavalry, the French defeat it; charging the more expert part of the Germans, they drive back those who go on foot, although they are greatly inferior to them in number; they mock them with the said expression, because while it is possible to fight with horses, they choose warfare on foot. As stated, this was then repeatedly applied by the French to the Germans and greatly vexed them.

Therefore, and because the risk of taking second place to the French on the roads threatened them, they marched as far as Philadelphia together; [67] from there Conrad, unable to endure being slighted by the French, determined to return: he wrote to the emperor and revealed his plan. As he [Manuel] desired to separate the kings from each other, and sympathized with the man, he replied thus: "Men who claim to grow a little wise customarily observe matters not according to turns of fortune, but individually, apart from any sudden alteration. So when you were prospering we decided not to treat you beyond your worth, and now that you are in a moderately bad situation, we do not hesitate to welcome you back with those same things which we were eager to do in honor of a relative, the ruler of such nations, and to take counsel together regarding the present circumstances, on account of the said [reasons] as well as of being of the same religion. But you, I know not how, / 86 / carelessly held in less esteem what would be profitable to you, and selected something inferior. But since it is impossible to undo what has once happened, come over at length to us, and let us consider as well as possible what is still available to us, what has not yet passed away. Fortune has this quality, to change continuously, never to stand still; should one first gain something, he then has the whole, but when it has gone past, it is equally impossible to be recalled. So long as your affairs have some manner of cure, hasten to seize on what will be profitable."

19. The letter concluded in such terms. Conrad had previously perceived his own folly, but not knowing what he should do, he had unwillingly followed the French. When the emperor's letter reached him, believing the thing a piece of luck, he received the advice with pleasure and speedily returned; reaching the Hellespont, he crossed to Thrace by the ferry there. He encountered the emperor who was making a stay there and returned to Byzantion with him [winter 1147–48]. There amusements succeeded one another: imperial residences, varied spectacles, horse races, and splendid receptions, whereby his exhausted body recuperated.

Furnished with sufficient funds, he set out for Palestine with triremes; Nicephorus Dasiotes commanded his ship and provided other service. / 87 / There he met the other kings and performed appropriate rites at the life-giving tomb of Christ; while the others set out for their individual homelands as best they might, he left there with the said ships and landed at Thessalonica. He saw the emperor there for a second time and again joined in discussions and conversations with him. The emperor reminded him of what had been previously agreed; this was, that Italy [i.e., Apulia and Calabria] should be restored to the empress [Bertha-] Irene for her marriage-gift, as she was his [Conrad's] relative and he had betrothed her to the emperor. After he and Frederick had pledged their agreements with additional oaths, they departed from the Romans' land. So Conrad's affairs had their conclusion there [winter 1148–49].[68]

Something as follows happened to the French king as he returned from Palestine [1149] with ships which, lying at anchor in great numbers there, offered a crossing for hire to persons who wished it. Sicilian ships, which had previously set forth on a raid in the Romans' land, were afloat on the sea thereabouts. A fleet of the Romans, led by Chouroup, met them and offered battle. As both fleets were fighting, the king by some chance sailed into their midst. Since the Romans were then superior in battle, he came close to being captured, for the following reason. When as stated he encountered the Sicilians' ships, he disembarked from his own and boarded a Sicilian vessel; save that when he perceived the peril, the banner of one of the Romans' allies was displayed on it, / 88 / he would quickly have fallen into the Romans' power. After he had lost many of his followers who became prizes of war, he was himself rescued with difficulty. Once he had petitioned the emperor, he won the captives' release and regained all that had been taken. The incursion of the western nations into the Romans' land concluded there.[69]

20. Having returned to his native land, Conrad soon ended his life [1152], without having completed anything which he had promised the emperor. After him Frederick held power.[70] Why after Conrad the Germans' realm devolved upon Frederick, the fol-

lowing account will relate. The king of the Germans, Henry [V],
who had imprisoned his father [Henry IV] while he was still alive
and who had beset the bishop of Rome [Pope Paschal II] with war,
held office very lawlessly. On this account the Germans took vengeance on him: when he died, they determined not to grant sovereignty to his children (his sons were this Conrad and Frederick's
father),[71] but they invited to the office a very old man, Lothar
[II],[72] and granted him supremacy over the Germans. But as the
others [Conrad and the elder Frederick] could not endure being
driven from their hereditary office, they determined to attempt
revolts. When he perceived this, Lothar, who was really old and
far gone in age, but who possessed a noble nature and did not
know how to speak and act save with simplicity, agreed to pass on
his office to them, / 89 / when his fate overtook him. When he
died soon after, although the inheritance fell to the eldest of the
brothers, I mean Frederick's father, he who had been injured in
one eye chose his brother Conrad in his stead; [Conrad] first
agreed on oath that when he died he would transfer power to the
younger Frederick. So, as stated, when Conrad was dying, he
placed the crown on Frederick. Those matters went somewhat like
that. Thereafter, the Sicilians' wars had their beginning.

Book III

1. Roger was a man who at first ranked among the counts; [1] but he was in general an active and vigorous man, skilled in contriving matters and clever at setting in motion what had been settled. He loaned money to William, duke of Longibardia [i.e., Apulia], under whose authority he was placed, who was setting forth for Palestine, and on that account received the rule of Longibardia as security; [2] after he had exercised compulsion on the bishop of Rome in a fashion which is going to be related, he was consecrated king by him.

When he who then held the [papal] throne of Rome heard that Longibardia was possessed by Roger, he was vexed at this bold act, / 90 / pretending that from a long time back it had belonged to his own church. [3] Complaining thereat, and not suffering the pope's rank to be despised, Lothar invaded Longibardia with a great army [1137]. He seized no small part of it and came close to driving Roger out of the whole country, save that Roger, as usual, contrived treacherous schemes and without battle expelled Lothar from there. How, the narrative will next relate. Lothar had a certain relative-in-law who was very powerful in his court and was esteemed by the Germans next after Lothar. Without Lothar's knowledge, Roger approached him, corrupted him with money, and persuaded him to give the usual signal of a war's conclusion to the Germans' army. This is not a blast of a trumpet or anything similar, but a barbarous and foolish custom. By tradition, once a certain tune has been played in the camp, it does not permit the soldiery to remain, but as soon as he hears it, each one scatters to prepare for return. Lothar's relative treacherously contrived to have this tune played by surprise, and caused the army to set forth straightway. Angered thereby, Lothar attempted to check the mob's impulse, impaling upwards of five hundred men, but without success. The Germans slipped away none the less, ignoring penalties and prohibitions alike. / 91 / Seized by despair and therefore gripped by severe fevers, Lothar soon after departed from mankind. As stated, Conrad succeeded to his authority.[4]

2. This happened there. Roger seized firm possession of Longibardia again. Unable to endure this, the bishop of Rome established an alliance of the Germans with himself and hastened against Roger with great zeal [1139]. But Roger appeared before him by surprise as he camped, drove off his followers, and took him captive. When he had him in his power, he pitched a tent of linen and caused the bishop to be seated in it; throwing himself face downwards on the ground and crawling on hands and feet, he went toward him, seemingly did penance for his crime, and asked to be designated king. The other received him as he approached (what else could he do?) and then named him king. From that time on the ruler of Longibardia is customarily titled king.[5]

When Roger succeeded in this plan, he sent envoys to emperor John who was still alive and asked to obtain a bride of imperial blood for his son. The embassy had not achieved its goal when John died. Some time later he communicated with Manuel who then governed the empire and made the same requests [ca. 1143–44]. Therefore Basil, by surname Xeros, went to Sicily to discuss this with Roger. But / 92 / seduced by gold, he promised him some unwelcome things, chief of which was that in the future the emperor and Roger were to be on an equal plane of greatness. Major conflicts arose thence. When Xeros died as he was returning to Byzantion, without paying the penalty of his rash deed, the em-

peror treated as jokes his embassy and dismissed Roger himself
from his mind.[6] He [Roger] was angry and deemed the matter
some deceit; constructing a fleet, he held it in readiness, waiting
for the moment somehow to be avenged on the Romans.

The barbarian succeeded in his scheme. At the height of
the western nations' incursion into the Romans' lands, he pillaged
Corinth and Euboea and Boeotian Thebes [1147–48]. Since at that
time the Romans' army was occupied with matters close at hand,
the barbarians attacked the said cities utterly unhindered and filled
their ships with spoils. Crossing from there to Kerkyra [Corfu],
they took it by storm, claimed it as their own, and absolutely ruled
it.[7] When he learned this, the emperor was enraged; he considered
how he might be avenged on Roger and impose the penalty
required by such bold acts. He prepared a fleet of upwards of five
hundred triremes, as well as an entire thousand horse-transports
and supply ships; while he went by land, the fleet sailed around as
swiftly as possible.

/ 93 / 3. Just as the emperor reached Philippopolis [Plov-
div], a rumor flew around that Cuman armies had crossed the
Danube and were ravaging and pillaging all before them; they had
even taken a notable city situated on the Danube's shore [1148]. In
such terms were the contents of the rumor. Turning aside from
there, the emperor hastened to the Danube; he directed ships to be
brought from Byzantion to the Danube through Anchialos [Po-
morie]. As they had not arrived, in the meantime he went about
the plains there hunting. For a great quantity of wild beasts dwell
in herds on those [plains], since they have lain entirely deserted
and uninhabited from a long time back.

While he was thus occupied, it was reported to him that
Cumans driving booty back from the Romans' land had just
crossed the Danube and were camped nearby. When he heard this,
he hastened to the river as quickly as possible. Chancing on a skiff
there, of the sort made of a single log which customarily lie by the
banks there, he ordered it brought to him. But the ferryman was

stubborn; hearing that the emperor had summoned him, he said, "If the emperor were concerned about our affairs, Demnitzikos [8] (for so the fortress seized, as stated, by the Cumans was named) would not have been taken, nor our property carried off and driven away by the barbarians without hindrance." Reportedly the emperor was indignant at this, and declared, "Verily, may I not be he to whom the Romans' affairs have been entrusted by God, if / 94 / the Cumans do not forthwith pay the penalty of their rash acts."

Therefore he left the rest of the army to make camp there on the banks, and since as stated the ships had not yet arrived, he bound together and combined boats with each other, and crossed the Danube with five hundred followers. As he was going to march forward, he encountered two other navigable rivers. Because no skiff was to be seen there which one could use to cross, he ordered those with him to fasten the boats on the Danube to their horses' tails and convey them to the said rivers. When this was done, they easily crossed; having traversed a lengthy region, they reached the mountain of Teli-orman,[9] which extends near the boundaries of Russia. Finding the Cumans' camp absolutely bereft of men (for they had set out in departure not long before), they proceeded onward.

Since it was about midday and none of the enemy had appeared at all, the emperor chose those Cumans who fought alongside the Romans, with Giphardos as their commander, a man experienced in many battles, and sent them to follow the enemy, to track them and to combat them wherever possible; he, however, marched behind at a more leisurely pace. So not far on Giphardos encountered the foe; since he did not dare an engagement (the barbarians' number appeared to him beyond count), he sent for the emperor and begged him to come as speedily as possible. When the emperor heard this, he went / 95 / straight for his weapons, and the whole force armed itself. Pursuing the Cumans, they came to grips with them. The Cumans at first stood firm to receive them;

drawn up in formation, they wished to fight for their own defense
and for the booty which they were driving off. The conflict developed with shoving and violence from either side. Many of the
Romans were then valiant, but the emperor most of all. When the
enemy pressed closest, very strongly, he rushed with his spear and
broke their shield-wall, slaying not merely individuals, but many
in pairs. When they were repulsed by the emperor's irresistible
onset, the Romans thrust at them in full force and made a splendid
charge. Many of the barbarians fell, and upwards of a hundred
were captured, among whom was Lazaros, a man who had attained the highest degree of valor and was respected by the chiefs
among them. The excellence of their horses and the undergrowth
of the mountains, which extend around there in great numbers,
preserved the rest. Recovering all of their plunder, the Romans
then returned; at this time, too, that Sotas, who as aforesaid [sic]
excelled in wealth and family and had been captured by the Cumans, grasped his freedom and returned to the [Roman] camp as a
fugitive.

/ 96 / 4. Having in this wise quickly succeeded, the emperor marched forth to prepare for the war with the Sicilians. For
in regard to martial toils he was so tireless that I think he was not
inferior to any of the common soldiery, nor even to emperors or
generals. He advanced, contriving cleverly about Sicily and all of
Italy, but as it seemed fate rejected his honest expectation and well
understood how to end scientific generalship in the complete opposite, effortlessly. For although the Cumans had in the meantime
been turned back, he yet reached in a seasonable time the region
where the voyage over [to Kerkyra] had to be made. The fleet,
however, whether detained by unfavorable winds or by the *doux's*
[admiral's] ignorance of the matter, came late after the proper
time. It had set out from the Byzantines' harbors in spring, but
reached the emperor in the autumn; therefore the Romans' affairs
were in a bad way. The emperor boarded a bireme and the whole
fleet set to the oars to cross over at once, but a fierce storm and the

strength of the winds which unexpectedly broke forth hindered him from the enterprise. The sea there stretches vastly, and voyaging is really dangerous, especially in winter. Wherefore he set out for a place near Berrhoia [Veroia, west of Thessalonica] and spent the winter there [1148–49].

/ 97 / He sent his relative-in-law Stephen, whom people, speaking I think disparagingly, call Kontostephanos ["Short-Stephen"] (for he was short in size), with the whole fleet to Kerkyra which was as stated held at that time by the Sicilians, to recover it for the Romans. After he had reached the city and conducted every sort of attack on the wall, while affairs were still in suspense he lost his life there in a manner I am going to relate. He had constructed an extremely large ladder which extended far above the outer walls, and by its means led the army against the city. A great mass of stone flung from the citadel by an engine struck the ladder; shattered by the shock, it hurled fragments everywhere; one of them reached the *doux* and struck him a mortal blow.

Although sensing he was going to die shortly, he took much forethought lest, when knowledge of it reached both sides, it should probably bring discouragement to the Romans, but courage to the Sicilians who were already yielding. So he ordered them to lay him quietly on the ship's decks, and to return to battle, but summoning Andronicus, who was youngest of his sons, and the chief of the ax-bearers, he offered them advice that the Romans should not abandon courage, but now should be especially active, since they stood not far off from their hopes of taking the city. These I think were expressions of a spirit manly and wholly warlike and patriotic. / 98 / But as soon as the business had been completed and became known to the commonality, everything proceeded in the opposite fashion. The Sicilians thrust back the Romans, albeit they had already come over the walls, and confusion and tumult seized everything.

5. The affairs of the Romans were in this state. The em-

peror was probably grieved at hearing of this, but appointing an admiral in his stead, he ordered him to maintain the siege unremittingly. Since he produced nothing worthy of note (for a broil which unexpectedly broke out between Romans and Venetians, who fought as their allies, deprived the Romans' army of success), the emperor himself finally was constrained to go there to engage in the siege. After he had terminated the disagreements between the Venetians and the Romans' force and had applied punishments appropriate to the guilty on both sides, he very strongly assaulted the wall. So he was engaged in this [1149].

But the tyrant of the Sicilians, Roger, learned that the emperor was spending his time in Kerkyra, and sent a fleet against the Romans' land, intending to constrain him to abandon the siege by a diversion thither. The emperor, however, set aside a portion of the ships with him and quickly dispatched them, under command of Chouroup, to oppose the Sicilians when they, as stated, assailed the Romans' land; he himself pressed the siege of the Sicilians still more fiercely. He propped against the walls extremely large ladders from the ships, / 99 / and led the army up, with difficulty and exertion. One of the ladders broke under the weight of those ascending and cast many into the sea, where the wretches breathed forth their souls and left to the Romans a great account of their valor. Although the Sicilians saw that the Romans had come within the walls, they were unwilling to yield the city to the emperor. And so rushing to the citadel as quickly as they were able, they defended themselves from there, throwing down on them stones and arrows and everything handy, like a shower from heaven. For the castle ascended to such height that it was not easily possible to inspect the structure with a craned neck.

Then allegedly the emperor, boiling with rage at that evil turn of fortune, stood up on the bireme which bore him and ordered those at the oars to head the ship straight for the walls, to attempt the assault himself, I think.[10] But some of the generals and those related to him by blood forbade this with all their might, very much against his wishes, I believe. For he was extremely steadfast in valor. I myself heard some people impute the charge of rashness to him; he always nurtured a wonderful audacity beyond [ordinary] courage. Indeed, at sixteen he often produced [many] barbarians, captive by his own hands. Therefore, the lady from among the Germans who had married him [Bertha-Irene] once said in full / 100 / senate that she drew her descent from a great and warlike race, but out of all of them she had never heard of any who boasted so many feats in a single year.

Then one of the ships of the Roman fleet approached the Kerkyrans' wall, not one of the lightly-laden ones nor such as are low and long, but one which possessed sufficient height and width, and was entirely full of horses and stuffed with arms; by force of wind it was carried to a certain portion of the wall where headlands of shore piled with stones made the place very difficult of approach, and it was really stricken. Wagon-size rocks and arrows and everything handy poured down on it, so that those in it gave way at what had happened, and, thoroughly frightened, crept cowering under the ship's decks. Observing this, the emperor took in one hand a shield, not one of the usual ones nor of those with which a single body is defended, but a particularly broad one which was not easy for a man to lift. In the other [hand] he grasped and skillfully wielded the implement customarily furnished on the imperial bireme, so that thereby he might ward off shots from the wall, lest one strike him, and hastened to the ship. After he had made it fast with ropes, he was able to pull it off and rescue it from danger.

Then allegedly the man entrusted by Roger with the wardship of Kerkyra, / 101 / since the people from the city were flinging many stones at the emperor, said, "By your salvation, fellow soldiers, don't, don't shoot another arrow at such a physique. Should it be necessary to render account for this, I myself will endure the [king's] wrath."

So matters went there. When the Sicilian fleet came to

grips with Chouroup, most of it was overcome, but forty of their ships avoided peril and reached Byzantion. After they had come to land there, they achieved nothing worthy of account. When they had striven to set fire to the wharves around the region of Damalis [part of Üsküdar] across [from Constantinople], they shamefully departed, having lost many of their own men. Nor did those who fled danger entirely escape. For encountering the ships which convoyed the public revenue from Crete, many of them became the spoil of battle.

By famine and siegecraft the emperor overcame the city [of Kerkyra], and set forth from there. Regarding Sicily and the Italians' land, he made plans to recover them in the future for the Romans.

6. Discovering that, when the Germans and Serbs and Hungarians had learned that he had prepared for war on Sicily, they had joined in alliance with one another to attack the Romans from the west, and that Yaghi-Basan, the Turks' chieftain, had decided to plunder Asia together with the sultan [of Ikonion], he himself hastened against the Serbs, as he was eager to ward off their grand župan,[11] / 102 / who had meanwhile commenced action. He entrusted the whole fleet to John [Axouchos] the *domestikos* of the eastern and western [armies], and ordered him to put in at Ancona (Ancona is a port of Italy) and to harry Italy from there as base. When, however, he reached the river Vijosë [in Albania], John decided to go no further. Either the *domestikos* failed by inexperience in naval affairs, or by the counsels of the Venetians' leader, lest the Romans become possessed of Italy and then, being established as neighbors to their land, would probably be able to despise them and would desire their alliance very little. So, whether for this or that reason, the *domestikos* accomplished nothing of what the emperor had commanded him, but vainly wasted his time. So when a great storm suddenly arose (for it was about the autumn equinox), many of the ships, overlooked by the general's negligence, were smashed. While all those landed at the

river could possibly have been drawn up on either side, he, however, left them high up on the sea-beach.[12]

Attacking Serbia, the emperor subdued the fortress of Rhason and pillaged everything in its neighborhood [1149].[13] After he had placed an innumerable multitude in the captives' brigade, he left them there with troops under the sebastohypertatos Constantine, whom people surname Angelus.[14] He himself advanced further and seized the region of Nikava which belonged to the grand župan and effortlessly subdued all the fortresses which had been constructed there. Coming to Galitza,[15] / 103 / since he found the barbarians, trusting in their multitude and in the terrain's difficulty, would not yield the fortress to him, he pitched camp and ordered [his men], without losing time, to hit those on the outworks with arrows and stones from slings. Thus on the third day he took it by storm. Finding there a multitude of barbarians who belonged partly to the knightly class, otherwise to the commonality, he led them away captive.

When on his return he reached Rhason, he sent them to be settled in Sardika and the Romans' other lands; but, informed by Angelus that the župan had waited an opportunity after his withdrawal, commenced to attack the Romans, and forthwith prevailed in battle, he [Manuel] returned as swiftly as possible, eager to surprise him. Hearing of the Romans approaching, however, he [the župan] rushed to the mountain passes and fled danger with equal speed. The emperor entered the land, and in the absence of a defender he pillaged it all. As he passed by, he burned the dwellings set apart by the grand župan for a palace.

7. Once a fierce winter [1149–50] had set in, because when in a living creature bodily heat is concentrated around the heart, in many cases injury attacks the extremities, he [Manuel] then thought of the road to Byzantion. In the following year [1150], when the season was already becoming autumnal, at which time the [roads] in Serbia are particularly accessible to an enemy / 104 / because the greenery has then left the trees, he assembled the army at Naissos.

When he learned there that forces had been sent from Hungary to the Serbs in alliance, he made haste to conduct the army through the so-called Longomeros region,[16] so that the Romans' army might encounter the Hungarians, who were marching on the right. When he approached the Sava, he crossed from it to another river, by name Drina, which takes its origin somewhat higher up and divides Bosnia from the rest of Serbia. Bosnia itself is not subject to the Serbs' grand župan, but is a tribe which lives and is ruled separately.

I shall at once show why the Hungarians clashed with the Romans. Among the Serbs was one whose name I know not, but whose brother was Beluš; both were notable among the Serbs. He was wedded to the grand župan's sister, but as he happened to be injured in an eye in some fashion which I am unable to relate, he departed to Hungary. After he spent a long time there, he became particularly esteemed by king Géza,[17] since he had participated in his nurture and education from childhood. Owing favors for this, he undertook to make Serbia a subject-ally to Géza; having discussed this on every possible occasion, he was able to persuade the man by persistent requests. So when Géza heard of the Romans' attack on Serbia, he dispatched forces in alliance with the Serbs. This was the occasion of the Romans' ill will toward the Hungarians.

As the Romans' army advanced further, / 105 / those going out to forage encountered the Hungarians as they marched along, and came to grips with them. When news of this reached him, the emperor sent the protosebastos John [Comnenus] [18] with a force to aid them. Once the engagement occurred, the Hungarians, defeated by the Romans, fled and reached the course of the river Strymon [sic].[19] There, casting aside moderation, they fled straight on, but the Romans continually followed at the fugitives' back; coming to the river Tara,[20] since they [the Romans] observed no one opposing them, they thought of returning. The emperor, however, pitched camp in the midst of the [route] leading to Setzenitza,[21] and, unable to learn where the grand župan was, remained some time in doubt. When he heard from captured Serbs that their forces awaited the allied Hungarian ones which had almost arrived, he moved his army forward. No opponent appeared to the Romans from any direction until they reached the river Tara.

When they came there, while the sun had not yet passed the western horizon, an immense crowd of Serbs, fully armed, was visible. The Romans, gripped by anguish and fear, came and reported what they had seen. The emperor accurately judged that this visible force was that of Hungarians which was expected to reach the Serbs, and at once predicted about this to the scout Chouroup, "Now the Serbs intend suddenly to fall upon the Romans." / 106 / For they were not far off, making camp. Since night was swiftly falling, he planned something as follows. It is customary for Romans going to war, if the army must make a halt someplace, to sound a trumpet late in the day, and for the multitudes this was the signal that they should from then on remain in that spot. So that he might deceive those there who also knew the Romans' custom, he ordered the trumpet to be blown at once, but secretly he advised the generals individually of what had been planned: that when the sun rose, out of the regiment under each one's command, whoever was clad in full armor and was suitable to be among the picked troops should stand quiet and await an order from him. Lest they be revealed, he ordered the weaponry to be wrapped with cheap cloth.

8. So they did thus. When day was at hand, he set forth with them from camp, as if going out to forage. Therefore he ordered some entirely unarmed men to go in the van with mattocks and shovels, with which it is customary for those who provide supplies to the army to search out underground food stores. Whenever they saw the enemy advancing against them, he directed them to flee until, joining the Romans coming up from behind, they should be safe. In order that knowledge of what was happening should quickly reach the general, he ordered two to go first, not far behind them four, / 107 / then six and again ten and more thereaf-

ter; having positioned another regiment of archers, he directed it to
attack the enemy from another side. Should the Serbs commence
battle, those who were inferior in number should flee, but if no
one attacked them, they should stay quiet in front of the camp. He
did this so that if, while he stayed with the other force, they put
the Serbian one to flight, the defeated might be slain by these
light-armed troops.

Thus advancing, they had not gone far, when some of
those scouting came running to the emperor, lamenting aloud and
absolutely pallid, and said that an innumerable army stood in formation on the other side of the river, not merely a native one, but
a countless allied force of Hungarian cavalry as well as of the heterodox Chalisioi among them. For while the Hungarians reverence
the Christians' [doctrine], they follow the Mosaïc laws, even
though these still are not altogether pure.[22] They [the scouts] reported that these as well as Petchenegs fought alongside the Serbs.
When the emperor heard this, he took care lest the few Romans
who marched in the van should be encircled and overpowered by
numbers; he proceeded very eagerly, urging them to follow the
standard-bearer. Since that individual, as his horse was exhausted,
advanced slowly, the emperor himself seized the banner and raced
onward. When he reached a certain vantage point, he allowed the
enemy to recognize who he was, and the banner.

/ 108 / Meanwhile the archers who had reached the river
stood face to face with the Serbs; but as neither commenced battle,
they mostly remained quiet. When the emperor's banner appeared
to them, the Serbs abandoned the bridge and gave the Romans an
opportunity for skirmishing. Perceiving this, the emperor (for as
stated he stood a little higher up, observing what happened) advanced to cross the river himself with them. For, as has often been
said by me, he was always stirred up in battle in a superhuman
fashion, even beyond [mere] courage.

Although pursued only by an insignificant number of soldiers, the Serbs fled until they were in rough country. Turning

back from there, however, they came to close quarters, and when battle was joined, a few from both sides fell. Learning of the emperor's presence, the Serbs again broke off; continually pursuing, the Romans slew many of the Hungarians and of them [Serbs]. At that time Grdeša and Vlcin,[23] distinguished men among the Serbs, fell into the Romans' hands. For the rest, the emperor deemed it very important to put on his armor. When he had wasted some time on this (for those who were bringing it were not close by), some of the Romans' generals, among whom were Giphardos and Michael, surnamed Branas, and many other men capable of acting independently and skilled in generalship, had reached an impenetrable and / 109 / steep thicket in the course of pursuit. They were in distress because they had advanced into evident danger. For, perceiving that they had come far from the other Romans, the Serbs turned about and stood facing them.

9. They were in these straits. Having donned his armor, the emperor followed at full speed and overtook them. Finding them assembled close to one another in a single spot, openly and bitterly he accused and berated them, reproaching them for cowardice and ignorance of military tactics. When they alluded to the nature of the locale and the excess of snow, he himself led the way and commanded them to follow. Already another crowd of Romans had joined them. While they took their road, an ambush of enemy leapt out of concealment and attacked the Romans on the left. But since the emperor observed that it was of scanty size, he did not deem it necessary to turn back. He pursued unremittingly, in order to lay hands either on the grand župan himself or on him who that day commanded among the Hungarians, someone well-endowed with courage. Since they had achieved nothing worth mentioning, those from the ambush slipped away again.

After he had pursued a little way, when the emperor observed that his followers were in sore straits, he outstripped them; taking two of his own relatives, one of whom was John Doukas,[24] the other, by name John and by surname Kantakouzenos, who had married a daughter [Maria] of the sebastokrator Andronicus [Manuel's brother],[25] he advanced with them against the foe. They recognized him by his armament / 110 / (for it was all decorated with gold) and also knew him by the height and shapeliness of his body (he was really like unto [ancient] heroes, inasmuch as he was distinguished by the extreme unusualness of his horsemanship and of his ambidextrous manipulation of weapons). They were not ashamed to turn their backs. As he attacked the fugitives, he reportedly hurled fifteen of the foe to the ground with a single thrust of his lance. For swept along in the confusion and turmoil, they struck against one another in disorder. After he had laid low forty, he drove off the others; following the fugitives he smote them continually, using sword and lance.

Then something as follows happened. One of those who had been previously speared by him (he had not been hit mortally) recovered from his fall; considering himself finished, he got out of the trail. When he saw that the emperor had come near, he drew his sword and rushed to smite him. But the other, kicking his chest with a foot, threw him to earth and passed on, after he had taken note of him by a visible injury about one eye.

While he [Manuel] sensed that his horse was exhausted by the weight of his weapons, he did not yet desire to turn back. He ordered Kantakouzenos (out of the emperor's men he happened then to be riding along) to advance further and engage the barbarians, so that by means of their occupation with him, it should be possible for himself to overtake them. And he succeeded in his purpose. When John [Kantakouzenos] speedily came near the foe, he struck the grand župan Bakchinos [Bagin] [26] on the back, as he was eager to thrust the spear through him; yet he was / 111 / unable to succeed because the armor resisted. Turning around, the other saw that he was pursued by two men. As aforesaid, the other John accompanied the emperor. Collecting seven of his followers, he engaged Kantakouzenos, and the fight became hand-to-hand. At this time, when one barbarian was coming up from one direction, another from another, Kantakouzenos was in extreme peril; save that the emperor appeared nearby and rescued him from danger, I think the man would not have failed to become a victim of a barbarian sword. Nor was the emperor himself entirely out of danger. For reckoning that if he opposed the seven who still surrounded John, it would be possible for others numbering upwards of three hundred to attack on both sides, he decided that he had to engage the main body first. When they gave way, it was likely that those surrounding John would also withdraw. Spurring his horse he rushed into their midst. Intending to strike one of them with his spear, however, he missed him. For as the barbarian twisted his hips, the spear passed vainly by his side. Then he engaged him hand-to-hand.

Observing this, Bakchinos himself and his followers left John there and assailed the emperor at a run. The event was laden with horror. The emperor, however, let go his lance and drew the sword with which he was equipped; continually striking and being struck, he turned about among them, until when the rest were scattered, the result of the whole battle devolved on himself and Bakchinos, who excelled in bravery and possessed an immense frame. / 112 / After a long engagement, Bakchinos struck, bringing down his sword on the emperor's jaw, yet was unable to cut the screen [of chain mail] which hung from the helmet over the eyes. The blow, however, had enough force that the rings placed next to the flesh were deeply impressed on it. The emperor, having deprived the barbarian of a hand with his sword, hastily turned him over to his cousin [John Kantakouzenos], while he himself was impatient to attack the foe again; but both Johns and the barbarian Bakchinos labored to withhold him from the assault. For already the latter, reduced to obedience, pretended friendship. Displaying the hair of his head, he thereby signaled [his surrender] to the mob which was coming to meet him. In this struggle Kantakouzenos was deprived of two fingers of one hand. Leading about forty of the enemy captive, the emperor returned to camp. Then there came to mind the

one whom he had overthrown and left behind, after he had taken
note of a mark on his eye; he sought him in the camp, mentioning
the sign. So he came upon him, recognized the defeated man, and
was recognized.

No long time later, envoys from the grand župan [Per-
voslav Uroš II] reached the camp, requesting forgiveness for his ill
deeds. And since the emperor ordered it, the man came a little
later, offering himself as a pitiable suppliant. Accepting the suppliant, the emperor forgave his error. / 113 / Having raised himself a
little from the earth, where he [the grand župan] lay after casting
himself down before the emperor's feet, he pledged his agreements
with oaths, declaring that for eternity he would be subject to the
Romans. Should he [Manuel] campaign in the west, he agreed to
attend him with two thousand men; for fighting in Asia, he would
send two hundred in addition to the previously customary three
hundred.

Having succeeded in these things, the emperor returned to
Constantinople. Meanwhile the fleet, which had achieved nothing
in Italy, returned to Byzantion. Thus the Serbs preserved their subjection to the Romans; many years later, after they had dismissed
Uroš [II] from office, without the emperor's consent they con-
ferred it on one of his brothers. They feared lest, as was likely, he
[Manuel] would be angry with them, and came conducting Desa
and Uroš into his presence, saying they necessarily had to obey
whomever he would appoint. When the case had been unfolded by
them, Uroš had his office again as an award from the emperor. But
this was later [ca. 1155].

10. The emperor marched on Hungary, considering as
stated their prior alliance with the Serbs as an excuse for war on
them. He did not attack them by surprise, but first by letter he
showed them their misconduct toward him and advised them of the
Romans' imminent attack. When he reached the Danube's shore
[autumn 1151], the ships which he had prepared in Byzantion were
not at hand. / 114 / Lest he throw away the moment of opportu-

nity, something which in such affairs is particularly likely to make for success, he boarded a skiff, such as the wooden ones which lie by the shores there, and hastened to the farther shore [of the Sava]; he himself held his horse towed by the bridle. Thereafter, when the Romans' army had crossed in the same fashion, they trod Hungary under foot; advancing inward they mercilessly pillaged everything in their path.

There was a certain fortress situated on one bank of the river there, Zeugminon [or Zeugme, modern Zemun] by name, which was well provided with strong walls and other defenses. Since he could not take it on the spur of the moment, he left there his brother-in-law Theodore Batatzes with an army; sweeping through the villages there, he carried absolutely everyone off captive. Then an army of Hungarians advanced to oppose the Romans; since it realized it was going to attempt impossibilities, it went over to the emperor, and thereafter he managed and carried on everything without interference. Then it was possible to see a whole generation marching in captivity and entire nations moving and emigrating, and the whole island [sic], which the rivers Danube and Sava form as they flow from the Alps to Hungary, dividing apart high up and after an extensive circuit joining together again, emptied and bereft of inhabitants. The Romans then tore down the royal habitation, something worthy to be recorded among the Romans' greatest feats.

Successful in this, the emperor returned to Zeugminon, where as stated Batatzes had been left and had maintained a blockade. But those / 115 / who had its warding firmly kept possession so long as it was hoped that the king would in no long time come to their aid. But since he was not reported anywhere near, and the Romans were ready to assault the wall, dismayed at the impending peril, they asked the emperor if they could yield the fortress to him and depart with their bodies unmaimed. When he refused this, they bound their necks with ropes, removed the coverings from their heads, and submitted themselves to the emperor in disgrace.

He forbade any of them to be put to death by the Romans, but plundered the fortress, which was filled with numerous supplies.

11. After they had achieved this, the Romans hastened to cross the Sava, leading a generation of Hungarians captive, much greater than their own army. But they had not yet crossed when rumor reported that the Hungarians' king, who had already successfully concluded a war in Galicia, a Russian province, was coming in great haste against the Romans, leading a strong force. On this account in particular the emperor was punishing him, because contrary to his [Manuel's] will he [Géza] was attacking Vladimirko (for this name was applied to the prince of Galicia), who was the Romans' ally.[27] Hearing of this, the emperor ordered the rest of the army, whoever was in the baggage train, and the great masses of captives who were beyond count, who had crossed, to remain on the further bank. Taking the pick of the army, / 116 / he hastened to engage him [Géza] as quickly as possible, although the generals strongly disapproved his plans. He [Manuel] declared that to attack a flock of sheep was the work of wolves, not lions, but when shepherds or dogs appeared from somewhere they were not ashamed to flee; by this means alone they were scarcely and with difficulty capable of saving their prey.

Then something is reported which, if it seemed good to him who chose it outright, I cannot approve, but if [it was] as I think on account of a certain foresight and so that the Romans around him might exert themselves very courageously, I deem it a worthy example of martial inventiveness. For when he was prepared to set out from the Sava's course to encounter the Hungarians, he directed the person entrusted with command of the fleet to stay in harbor with his ships on the further bank of the river; should any of the Romans come as a fugitive to the other shore and demand to be ferried across, he should pretend not to see the fellow. "Should I myself," he said, "be there and as emperor desire something other than the present commands, you must reject those words, or else, if you do not act thus, you will not avoid

immediate impalement.'' He arranged things in this way, opening
thereby, I think, the gate of courage for his soldiers, as I have already stated. For when there exists no profit from fear, it necessarily becomes a prop to courage.

As he was about to march forth, one of the captive Romans
came to him as a fugitive from the Hungarians, and reported the
king's imminent approach. When he heard this, the emperor became unable to restrain himself, / 117 / lest the Hungarian force,
arriving too soon, should appear to attack fleeing Romans. So, arraying [his troops] in order, he withdrew. As the king, however,
was not at hand, but Beluš who bore the highest rank among them
(the Hungarians call this office ''Ban'') [28] was reported to be not
far off, he [Manuel] quickly hastened toward him. Since darkness
had set in, he dismounted from his horse and himself slept with his
weapons on his upturned shield, and the whole army passed the
night in the same state. On the morrow Beluš learned of the emperor's approach and departed with his whole force, after he had
concocted some feeble excuses. Contriving a pretext for flight, he
[Beluš] declared that he had been directed by the king to turn aside
from the prescribed route and go to the city of Branitshevo, so that
he might be better able to attack the Romans from there.

Abstaining from pursuing him, the emperor crossed the
river [Sava], went to Branitshevo, and camped there. Somewhat
later, intending to plunder another part of Hungary, where there is
the mountain called Temises [29] by the natives, he sent Boris with
an army, who himself is said to have sprung from the same parent-
age as Géza, but who on account of some quarrel had long before
come to emperor John as a fugitive.[30] He [John] accorded him sufficient honor and united him in marriage with a bride of his own
family. Reaching the region, this Boris went around ruining the
towns there, which were almost jammed by numbers of inhabitants
and / 118 / were burdened with every sort of valuable thing. Then
coming to grips with three Hungarian regiments, he severely defeated those who imagined that the emperor was at hand, and on

withdrawing returned to the Romans' camp laden with spoil from there. Knowing that Boris, not the Romans' emperor, had wrought these frightful things on Hungary, the king pursued him, eager for battle. Yet he was unable to encounter Boris, who had crossed [the Danube] at night, by the light of torches which the emperor had lit for him in great numbers from camp. Then two members of the regiment of infantry, who had been left on the further shore when the Hungarians arrived, crept under the brush there and succeeded in escaping.

After this success, the emperor stayed there to strengthen as far as possible the Paristrian cities [those alongside the Danube or "Ister"]; he intended to cross the Danube again and engage the king, who himself was encamped on the Danube's opposite bank. Learning of this and terrified at fortune's [possible] outcome, lest if he [Géza] were defeated at this time he involve the remaining Hungarian force in destruction, he communicated with the emperor and discussed peace terms. Thereafter the emperor returned to Byzantion, celebrated in triumph, and offered splendid thanks to God.

About this time a daughter, outstanding in beauty, was first born to him by the Augusta [Bertha-]Irene; she was named Maria and was hailed as empress.[31]

12. The Romans were occupied with these affairs. Roger [II], tyrant of the Sicilians, reached the end of his life [1154]; his son William [I] / 119 / who took up rule was well aware of his father's many crimes against the Romans' realm, and recognized that he had to send envoys to the emperor to resolve their differences. So men came, each invested with episcopal office. The purport of the embassy was as follows. He promised to restore all the property and persons which, as narrated by me, Roger had [in 1147] carried off in ships from Euboea, Thebes in Greece, and Corinth, and agreed to serve the emperor readily in whatever he willed.[32]

But the emperor rejected the envoys; having assembled a

fleet of ships and embarked an army on it, under command of
Constantine surnamed Angelus, who was his uncle, he ordered it
to make port someplace around Laconia and await the rest of the
fleet which was yet to arrive. So setting forth from Byzantion and
enjoying a favorable breeze, he landed at the promontory of Laconia, which is called by the commonality Monembasia [i.e.,
"Single Entrance"] from the shape of the place.

The emperor, however, learned that the Hungarians' king
Géza, who was aggrieved at what had previously happened, intended unexpectedly to attack the Paristrian cities; he hastened to
anticipate the attempt [1152]. Returning to the Danube's shores as
quickly as he could, he settled down opposite the Hungarian army,
camped on the other side. For some time neither desired to join
battle, especially because the Romans' ships were not yet at hand.
/ 120 / When a few days later the Romans had constructed as
many light boats as possible out of available materials and dragged
them to the river, the Hungarians' king recognized what had happened, and as stated feared lest being defeated a second time he
imperil his realm; he proceeded to negotiations. Sending envoys,
he requested that Hungary should not be punitively deprived of
more than ten thousand persons, but should regain the remaining
throng of captives. Thus he declared he would remain friendly to
the Romans throughout his life and would be enrolled among their
allies forever. After peace had been concluded on these terms, the
Romans' army started back from there.[33]

13. Affairs on land were in this situation. But by sea,
because of the commander's folly, they ended in the opposite way
[1154]. Angelus, learning that William's fleet was returning from
Egypt's land and the river Nile, filled with booty and riches from
there, intended to achieve a great feat. Therefore he put to sea as
quickly as he could, eager to encounter it, without awaiting the
rest of the fleet from Byzantion—although the emperor had
frequently objected to this and had advised him by letter that with
an inferior force he should not contend against a much larger

power. For he asserted that nothing hindered Angelus himself from
being captured by the barbarians, and not even a messenger
[*"angelos"*] would return from there, as people say. But paying
scant heed to this, he joined battle with the Sicilian fleet the moment it appeared.

The Sicilians at first / 121 / backed water and withdrew in
good order. But when they perceived that the Romans were in
great disorder and the inferior number of their ships was evident,
they turned back quickly and rushed against him, while the wind,
which had been steady on the Romans' stern, by some chance
swung round to a head wind. The Romans' other ships, commanded by an Angelus who was brother to the principal admiral
(but he headed few ships), took to disordered flight. Constantine
[Angelus], who had remained in the midst of the foe, fell into their
hands, thus profiting by his folly. After it had wrought such
changes, that year ended.[34]

14. The emperor heard that the Hungarian ruler was again
in revolt (he could not endure such affronts), and he took the road
leading back to the Danube. Since the other was frightened at his
approach and again opened negotiations about peace, their war
was concluded, and the benefits of peace smiled [1153].[35] A little
later, however, when the emperor's cousin Andronicus furnished
occasion, he [Géza] again made war on the Romans. But that was
later.

At that time [1152] the emperor sent this Andronicus to
Cilicia and Isauria, having named him commander-in-chief of the
war there. For the Armenian Ṭoros, a man of outstanding rank,
had long before been taken captive by emperor John, when he
[John] campaigned on the Isaurians' [i.e., Armenians'] borders.
He [Ṭoros] had returned to Cilicia as a fugitive from Byzantion
[ca. 1145], and after he had rebelled, he attempted to make the cities there revolt from the Romans' authority.[36] / 122 / On this account the emperor sent Andronicus, as well as the caesar [John
Roger] in order to join in marriage with Constance the wife of

prince Raymond [of Antioch], who had departed from mankind in a way which I will now relate.

The barbarians who dwelt around there had attempted to gain by siege a certain fortress situated near Aleppo which was tributary to the Antiochenes, since they knew it was deficient in supplies [1149]. Raymond, who was more active than anyone else in martial affairs, heard of this and with his attendant force went in great haste to the fortress. Since the enemy had not waited, once he had furnished supplies to the fortress he set forth. While it was late afternoon, it seemed right to go further, because no place was yet at hand in which it was safe for them to unharness. Those with him who were worn out by the exhaustion of the journey wanted to camp somewhere there; they showed him a place largely surrounded by marshes, with the rest shut in by hills and ridges which rose there. But he was stubborn and declared that, pointing to the hill, ''he feared lest when the enemy attacks by night, it will prove a place without exit for us, and then, incapable of defending ourselves, we would be slaughtered like sheep penned up inside.'' But one of those with him cast rash words at the man and declared these [hesitations] were from cowardice, not prudence. Yielding to wrath at this, Raymond said, ''I know, noble sir, that if we depart from here / 123 / you would never leave off accusing us of this; therefore we shall camp there, since it seems good to you, but look you lest you be incapable of displaying in deeds the valor which you have unnecessarily proclaimed, when an army of foes falls upon us from the place I have mentioned and does frightful deeds.'' So saying, Raymond entered the place, which was so situated as to enclose him completely. When it was late at night, the Turks attacked from the direction whence he had said and slew their horses and themselves, without their being able to defend or otherwise preserve themselves.[37]

But as we said, in these circumstances the caesar John went to Antioch [1152], but achieved nothing of what he had come for (because he was aged, Constance regarded him with displeasure),

and returned to Byzantion; when sickness beset him, he tonsured
his locks and donned the black garb [of a monk].[38]

15. When Andronicus came into Cilicia [1152], since
Toros was staying at Mopsuestia, he settled down to its siege with
his whole army. And he would speedily have accomplished something noble and have gotten the rebel into his hands with great
ease, except that he devoted himself to indolence and sports in his
tent, and thus the Romans' affairs collapsed. For when Toros
comprehended Andronicus' effeminacy and observed the licen-
tiousness which needlessly preoccupied him, he waited for a
moonless night, on which it rained ceaselessly, threw down many
parts of Mopsuestia's wall, and unexpectedly led forth his whole
force. He attacked / 124 / the totally unprepared Romans and severely defeated them. Too late, Andronicus learned of this (as stated, he practiced extreme negligence), mounted a horse, and
charging with his lance displayed marvelous deeds of might (as I
have often [sic] said, he yielded to none of the great in reckoning
of valor); but, being unable to accomplish anything, he fled with
difficulty and reached Antioch. In this fight Theodore Kontostephanos, who had risen to the sebastoi's rank, lost his horse to an
arrow shot and was deprived of his head by one of the Romans'
mercenaries, because of his enmity toward him. For allegedly
Theodore had driven this wretch from the imperial court long
before on account of his bad character.[39]

16. This was what happened in Cilicia at that time. When
Andronicus returned from Antioch to Byzantion, he was no less
esteemed in the palace and contrary to expectation enjoyed his
previous license of tongue. But allegedly, receiving him in private,
the emperor bitterly abused him, blaming the man for negligence
in martial affairs and condemning his untimely slackness. In public, however, he presented him with splendid gifts and honored
him above the rest. Indeed, he then appointed him *doux* [governor]
of Naissos and Branitshevo, and in addition granted him Kastoria
[1153].

Whether he [Andronicus] toiled for revolt from the very outset and had that yearning in him, I am / 125 / unable to affirm: but commencing from when his ill will became evident, I shall narrate from there. When emperor Manuel took over the imperial office, he became concerned as to how the Romans might improve their armament for the future. It had previously been customary for them to be armed with round shields and for the most part to carry quivers and decide battles by bows, but he taught them to hold ones [shields] reaching to their feet, and trained them to wield long lances and skillfully practice horsemanship. Desiring to make respites from war preparation for war, he was frequently accustomed to practice riding; making a pretence of battle, he placed formations opposite one another. Thus charging with blunted lances, they practiced maneuvering in arms. So in a brief time the Roman excelled the mettle of French and Italians. Nor did the emperor himself hold aloof from these conflicts, but he was arrayed in the front ranks, wielding a lance incomparable in length and size. For in addition to what has been said, a great length of banner was fastened to it, which, as it is divided in eight parts, is customarily called an "eight-footer." Indeed they say that Raymond, a man like the legendary Herakleis, when he came to Byzantion, was astonished and thought the matter some trick. Approaching the emperor, he asked for the very spear and shield; taking them, he realized the truth and announced his discovery with surprise.

/ 126 / 17. When the emperor was engaged in this [mock] strife at the former Herakleia of the Mysians [Pelagonia, modern Bitola],[40] John the son of the sebastokrator Andronicus [Manuel's brother], a handsome, statuesque youth, was wounded directly in one of his eyes by the thrust of an Italian lance. Desiring therefore to compensate him for this injury, he [Manuel] promoted him to protovestiarios and elevated him to the rank of the protosebastoi.[41] This, they say, greatly affected Andronicus' spirit. From that time on he continually worked at and plotted treachery: when he was subsequently in command in Cilicia, he won over the king of Palestine and the Turks' sultan. Entrusted as aforesaid with the government of Naissos and Branitshevo, he pledged by letter to the Hungarians' king that if he would take part in his attempt to carry out his intended usurpation, when he succeeded in his purpose, he would give up all claim to Branitshevo and Naissos in his favor. So that these things, being discovered, should not make him suspect for the future, he decided to turn elsewhere. So he revealed to the emperor that, treacherously deceiving some of the powerful men in Hungary who had commenced to have friendly relations with him, he meant to place them easily under his power. The emperor, however, was aware of the deception: already the letter had reached his hand in which Andronicus had agreed on the aforesaid terms with the Hungarian ruler. Desiring to test him, he [Manuel] allowed him to act in this without dissimulation. Confidently imagining that every sort of suspicion had been removed from him for the future, / 127 / he [Andronicus] sent envoys to the Hungarians and to the Germans' king, luring even him to his aid at the proper moment.

After he had contrived this, Andronicus returned to Byzantion [1154], having apparently brought to completion the treaty between Romans and Hungarians. The emperor, I know not whether caring for the fellow (for he liked him exceedingly, because he was the same age as himself and had shared his upbringing and education, indeed had exercised along with him in races and wrestling and many other contests) or having something else in mind, still abstained from doing him harm.

When he was also once at Herakleia of the Mysians, which, following some native tongue, the Romans now call Pelagonia, the emperor went on an overnight hunting trip, as was frequently his custom [1154]. The nobility of his physique sent him forth against bears and armed him very frequently to combat wild boars on foot with a spear.

Allegedly he was in the first place wearing his breastplate and almost continually in arms, guarding as is reported against the plots of the sebastokrator and grand stratarchos Isaac [his brother],[42] even if ultimately he [Isaac] did him no other harm than steal the imperial seals, with which the emperor customarily approved grants. Nor indeed [did he take] them without excuse, but for a reason which I am about to relate. While he was staying in Melangeia at a place called Metabole, speeches were offered to the emperor at dinner. While all the others there unanimously / 128 / extolled the emperor's deeds, Isaac rather praised and greatly preferred those of their father. The emperor was pleased at what was said and liked being inferior to his father. While Isaac seemed wearisome to others, yet he did not stay his speech at this. For it would seem proper to utter these things in demonstration of loyalty to the departed emperor, something which I think many men know how to do; praise by the living toward those who no longer survive is sure proof of kindly feeling toward them. But to this he added something more biting, and spoke ill of the son. Then, with a quarrel inflamed, this Andronicus hurled an insult at the sebastokrator and came within a little of being deprived of his head by his sword, save that the emperor extended his arm, and John Doukas, who was himself the emperor's cousin, interposed under the descending sword the whip with which he customarily spurred on horses, and caused the enfeebled blow to strike Andronicus' jaw. In this way he was rescued; extending his arm over Andronicus, as stated, the emperor was struck, not indeed a deadly wound, but so as to divide the flesh a little: throughout his life he bore its scar on his wrist. So his quarrelsomeness which had advanced so far was silenced. The emperor banished Isaac from himself for some days; yielding John to judgment, he imposed on him a penalty much less than that specified by law.[43] But let the narrative return to its previous subject.

/ 129 / 18. Since Andronicus knew that the emperor was going out on a night-long hunting expedition, he armed a sufficient number of his Isaurian followers, who had previously given pledges to fight at his side against everyone; taking the swiftest of his horses, he went with them to the spot. He placed them rather far off in a thicket, holding the horse, while he approached the emperor's tent with a mule, and dismounting he went quietly forward at a walk, gripping a dagger in his right hand. Lest he be detected by anyone, he wore an Italian cloak in place of his usual one. But as he noticed that he had been observed (for already those who surrounded the sleeping emperor had bared their swords; among them was the emperor's nephew John [the protosebastos], who they say first saw Andronicus advancing), as Andronicus perceived this, bending down he pretended to make an evacuation of his belly, and so in a short while he departed. Thus that plot was broken up there.

But a little later, with more Isaurians, he set forth by night fully equipped against the emperor. When this was reported to the empress [Bertha-Irene] by Alexius, who was then in charge of stabling in the palace (the Romans call this office "protostrator"),[44] one of the guardsmen was straightway dispatched to warn the emperor of the plot. Then also Ishāq,[45] a man of barbarian descent who was a particular favorite of the emperor, was sent with three hundred armed men. But Ishāq had not yet reached the spot, / 130 / when the emperor learned of the affair; while the rest were anxious and perplexed in regard to themselves (for most happened to be mounted on mules), he declared that they must avoid the direct route which led to camp and the imperial tent, but, pointing with his hand, go on this unusual and untrodden one. Nor should they make the journey openly, but individually and separately. "For thus," he said, "we would seem to be some persons returning from foraging and going to the tents visible there." Thus the emperor fearlessly went to his tent. But a boar which encountered the aforementioned John [the protosebastos] rent him with its tusks. As soon as he learned of this, the emperor went back to him; after he had taken appropriate care of him, he departed.

He behaved himself so generously in this matter that he did not even reprove Andronicus by as much as a look. As if he knew nothing of the affair, he [Andronicus] took excessive care of the horse which I have mentioned and was much in evidence speaking and counseling against John. When the emperor once inquired of him why he preferred the care of this horse, he said, "So that when I deprive the bitterest of my enemies of his head, I shall flee and escape," seemingingly hinting thereby at the protosebastos [John]. Because he [Manuel] perceived that the man was sick with folly, he separated him from his fellowship and made him a prisoner in the palace [ca. 1155–56].[46]

19. So he was out of the way. But as he had learned nothing of what had befallen Andronicus, the king of Hungary / 131 / had assembled forces of Czechs and Saxons and many other nations, and settled down for a siege of Branitshevo [1155]; he had been stirred up I think by what Andronicus had promised him. Hearing of this, the emperor was stunned by the report and wondered at the Hungarians' faithlessness, why for no reason they should disregard what had been lately pledged by them. He resolved that the affair should inspire fear by its rapidity, and hastened straight for the Danube. Aware that his followers were not equal in battle to the Hungarians' army (for, since no one had opposed them from any direction for so long, the Romans' forces each remained in its region), he contrived as follows. There is a place, Smeles by name,[47] which possesses considerable defensive strength. He decided to seize this and make it the base for his expedition against the Hungarians.

In order that in the meantime the people of Branitshevo should guard their city for him, he wrote a letter to advise them that he would come to them shortly. He entrusted it to one of the soldiers, ordering him to shoot it into the city tied to an arrow. He did as directed. But, shot further than was necessary, the arrow fell into the Hungarians' hands. Forthwith a great disquiet overtook them; they set fire to their battering rams and whatever else had been made ready for the siege, and went to the Danube's crossing point. They found it swollen (for a storm drove it on out of the higher reaches), and hastened to Belgrade.

Perceiving this, and learning that Borić, the ruler of Bosnia, a Serbian region,[48] who was enrolled among the Hungarian ruler's allies, / 132 / had returned to his own land, the emperor selected the most valiant part of the army with him and sent it to come to grips with Borić. Basil, who has already been mentioned, commanded this army; he came of an undistinguished family, but had been designated *chartoularios* by the emperor.[49] The emperor with the rest of the Romans' army followed more leisurely. Basil, however, was as I think forgetful of why and with whom the emperor had sent him to wage war, for, advancing at full speed, he approached the Hungarians' army. He encountered the scouts, whereupon he drove them back, and then fell upon the center of the Hungarians' force; he planned to achieve a great success, attack them as they were thus in alarm, and throw them into confusion. Speedily he accomplished something [which was] not at all according to his calculation.

For, as the Hungarians at first deemed that the emperor was in command of this battle, they fled in disorder, and many of them who were crowded together on boats drowned in the river. But as soon as they observed that the emperor was coming along behind, and that Basil led the army, they took courage, turned about, and opposed the Romans. Although the Romans were greatly inferior in number to the enemy, yet they resisted them. There was a great slaughter on both sides, until the Hungarians who attended Stephen the son of Géza,[50] who were fighting in alliance with the Romans, first commenced flight. In the course of the route which then ensued, well nigh all the Hungarians with Stephen and many of the Romans fell. / 133 / Others saved themselves by flight, among whom was the commander Basil.

When this had been reported to the emperor, and in addition that its inhabitants were minded to make Belgrade revolt from the Romans, he felt great anxiety. He dispatched John Kantakouzenos partly to settle the city, which as stated was troubled by thoughts of rebellion, partly to entomb the bodies of the Romans and to recall the rest from flight, wherever in that region they were concealed. He [Manuel], however, was excessively angered at what had befallen; he chafed and longed to follow the Hungarians. When the Romans did not approve this, he said, "But, sirs, it is shameful for me, as I strive for the Romans' prosperity, to withdraw in the face of disasters." When he heard that the Hungarians' force was far away, he abandoned the attempt. Already Kantakouzenos had brought to completion the business for which he was sent; he returned, keeping in chains those people of Belgrade who as stated had attempted a revolution. Then setting out from there, he [Manuel] passed the winter near the city of Berrhoia [Stara Zagora].

In spring [1156], after he had assembled forces from every hand, he returned to Hungary, since he had an eager desire to penetrate to the very innermost parts of that land. So he stayed camped on the Danube's very shores with his whole force, and the ships which had set out from Byzantion anchored there in great numbers, waiting to carry the armed force across. Since the Hungarians' king recognized that his affairs were really in a difficult situation, he then turned to an embassy. Sending to the emperor men who were outstanding at his court, / 134 / he promised to restore at once the captive Romans and thereafter to obey him in everything he wished. At first the emperor seemed likely absolutely to reject and refuse the terms for peace, then he acceded to their requests and concluded the embassage on the said terms. So the captives taken as stated in the foregoing battle were led back to the Romans' camp, as well as the weapons and horses and anything else which was spoil of battle. For the fallen horses and oxen, they were furnished substitute animals from those native among the Hungarians. Having thus concluded the war, they returned home.

And from that moment the Italian wars, which had had the beginning I have already spoken of, commenced to be magnificently set in motion. But turning back a little, let us narrate.

Book IV

1. Frederick, nephew of Conrad who ruled the Germans, of whom we have made sufficient mention in the foregoing narrative, held office after Conrad fulfilled his fate.[1] As he esteemed nobility highly (for in marrying it was of the greatest importance to him that a noble bride be preferred beyond anyone else), / 135 / and he heard that Maria, daughter of the sebastokrator Isaac [Manuel's brother], who was outstanding in birth and superiority of beauty, was growing up in Byzantion, he was immediately captivated by the girl. Sending envoys to the emperor, he asked that she be betrothed to him in marriage. He promised to fulfill everything which his uncle Conrad and he, when they returned from Palestine, had promised toward assisting the Romans in the acquisition of Italy [1153]. Frederick's embassage was in these terms.[2]

Accepting these expressions, the emperor himself sent envoys to Frederick, ordering them to confirm the agreement. But, when they came to speech with him, they observed that he intended nothing concrete, and returned unsuccessful, after having induced him to try a second embassy to the emperor. When it also was rejected by the emperor, men from the aristocracy were dispatched [1155], Michael Palaiologos and John Doukas, both of whom had reached the rank of sebastoi; among them also was Alexander [of Conversano], who had ruled Gravina, an Italian city, but when Roger had driven him out, he had come to the emperor as a refugee.[3] A great amount of money was entrusted to them by the emperor as they traveled; if they heard that Frederick was residing south of the Alps, they should all go to meet him. Should he be further off, Michael should go to Italy with the funds, and the others were sent to Frederick; should he disregard the agreement, / 136 / they should then lay claim to Italy by themselves. This indeed happened.

2. Roger [II] tyrant of Sicily had a nephew, by name [Robert of] Bassonville.[4] While Roger lived, he managed the government of Italy [i.e., Apulia]; when he died and authority passed to his son William [I], he [Bassonville] was constrained to continue as an assistant governor, while another controlled Italy. Refusing to endure the affront, he contemplated revolt. So, writing to Frederick, he promised to place the whole of Italy and Sicily in his hands. While Frederick was seized by hesitation at the difficulty, the envoys of Bassonville who were returning unsuccessful happened to encounter Alexander. For, as he had achieved nothing which he had come to Frederick's court for, he was returning from there with [John] Doukas. As Alexander and Bassonville's envoys talked with one another, and Alexander learned wherefore they had gone to Frederick's court, he said to them, "Dear friends, nearby is someone who will grant success to your embassy." When they desired to know who, Alexander said in reply, "The emperor of the Romans." He related everything in order, adding that Palaiologos, who was a member of the Romans' council and who had been [elevated] [5] to the rank of the sebastoi, was at hand with large sums of money; / 137 / he had come there to subdue Italy for the emperor.

When Bassonville's envoys heard this, they communicated the facts to him by letter. He desired to discuss matters with the Romans at Pescara. On learning this, Palaiologos without delay sailed to Pescara with ten ships; en route, he took possession of Viesti, a city which had gone over to the emperor. But as it seemed proper to Bassonville to meet him at Viesti, he sailed back, encountered him there, and having taken and received oaths about the matter at hand, he then joined in the conflict.[6]

Doukas, having already assembled a force, undertook to besiege a certain well-defended fortress, which an Italian, Prountzos, commanded. When they made an attack there, the Romans drove the enemy within walls and fell upon the fugitives; the rest first mounted to the citadel, but as the Romans applied fire to the dwellings and plundered property in the houses, they commenced to descend and hail the great emperor as their lord. So they [the Byzantines] became possessed of it. When they reached a city which was called by the same name as the saint honored there, San Flaviano,[7] the whole populace poured out across the fields, begging to suffer nothing unpleasant from the Romans' soldiers, and they agreed to be subject to the emperor and do everything which the Romans desired. Responding to them with kindness, the general advanced as if through friendly country. As he was setting out from there, / 138 / Bassonville's brother William, who himself was already friendly to the Romans, came carrying a letter from his brother exhorting him [Doukas] to be of good heart for the future, because from then on the region lying before him was subject to himself.[8]

3. When as stated Palaiologos took Viesti by treaty, he went on to Trani. When the people of Trani saw the Romans' army, since they were unwilling to surrender the city to them, they sent envoys to the general and demanded that he depart. For it would be impossible for him to take Trani if he had not first occupied Bari. So, taking no more than ten ships, he left there and went to Bari, not so much persuaded by the soldiers' advice (for he was clever and inferior to none in martial experience), but being well aware that Trani was not easily assailable, he thought it useless to waste time in vain.

Yet Bari seemed entirely impregnable: mighty walls girded it, and there was an army of barbarians, some of whom stood in arms on the battlements, the rest, an innumerable crowd, poured from the gates and rushed at him, infantry and cavalry with their weapons. The sea, rising in stormy violence, threatened to swamp the ships. Although his affairs were in difficulties on every hand, he was not yet beyond hope. Escaping somewhat from the waves on the following day, he desired to join battle. Because matters did not / 139 / prosper for him (for some of the foe hurled down on him stones and timbers and anything handy in showers from the battlements, others from the ground darkened the air with arrows), he immediately brought about a withdrawal. He went outside arrow range and tried words on them. He informed them of the good things which he would immediately do if they offered the city without battle to the great emperor, and held out hopes of them for the future. When those in the city heard this, some rushed forth on horseback, others boarded skiffs, and invited him to approach the city, pointing to the opened gates. Fearing, as was the case, that the business was a trick, he first proceeded to a test. So he ordered one of the ships with him to approach the beach as if to anchor. But as soon as they saw it coming, the enemy, about five hundred, mounted to the battlements.

Observing this, Alexander [of Conversano], lest they go to arms, took coined gold in his bosom and swiftly boarded a ship. Showing it to those in the city, he cried out, "Whoever is desirous of wealth and liberty, let him come hither to enjoy them straightway." So he spoke, and a large crowd of them rushed forth from the city and immediately went over to the emperor. Once he had received them on oath, the general hastily led the army against the city. Thus nothing is more deceitful for men than golden bait. Knowing this, the other citizens, / 140 / who were displeased at what had happened, went at a rush to the citadel, and once coming within its walls, they fought for all [their possessions]. It was something really worthy of wonder, to see those lately united in race and purpose today sundered by gold as if by a wall, feeling hatred toward one another and already divided by deeds. So things went there.

There was another fortress above the city, in which was situated a church of Saint Nicholas; being minded to take it, the general acted somewhat as follows. Garbing armored men in black
clothing, he ordered them to rise at dawn and go to the church;
when they came inside they were to draw their swords and fight.
So they approached the fortress at dawn and knocked at the gate;
those within, supposing them to be monks, unbarred the gates and
admitted them. And thus it was taken by the Romans.

Although this had been occupied, those in the citadel were
still stubborn. So until the seventh day they thus continued opposing one another, but when Bassonville arrived there leading a very
large force, then they yielded it to the Romans. Indeed, out of
hatred directed toward Roger, because he had behaved inhumanly
to them, as is customary for tyrants, they demolished it to the
foundation and got rid of it, although the general was strongly opposed to this and asked to purchase it for much money.

/ 141 / 4. So matters went at Bari. When Palaiologos held
it, he sailed back to Trani; having won it over by treaty, he then
made subject Giovinazzo, a notable city. There was a certain Richard [of Andria], a cruel man. To slaughter like a sacrificial victim
a man who had quarreled with him even over trifles, or to slit his
guts and deprive him of hands or feet, was a punishment very
common with him. He was in command of the fortress of Andria,
and when he heard that the Romans laid claim to Giovinazzo, he
first bade them with threats to abstain from the enterprise; but as,
ignoring the threats, they possessed Giovinazzo by agreement and
planned to advance on other places, he joined with other counts
and with [Asclettin], William's chancellor, whom someone speaking Greek would call a logothete, and went with them to Trani to
recover the city without resistance. An army followed him, two
thousand knights and an extremely numerous crowd of armed infantry.

The Romans who had been left inside [Trani] with a small
and scanty force were in great dread for the city and all their af-

fairs. Therefore they speedily recalled Doukas, revealing in a letter the fate which impended over him. When he received the letter, he packed up and set out the same day on the road to Trani. As he reached a spot whose name is Ruvo,[9] the people there came forth, urging the Romans' army to take possession of their city without a battle. Doukas, however, / 142 / thought that to make a stay there was profitless, lest it allow Richard to shift the balance of the war without hindrance, and passed it by for the time being, as it was possible to lay hold of it later at the right time. He hastened against Richard at full speed.

There is a certain coastal town named Barletta, where the chancellor happened to be. As Doukas approached it, three hundred knights from his [Asclettin's] army together with a regiment of infantry who were making a sortie suddenly encountered him. In no wise astonished by the unexpected event, he quickly formed his men together in a solid mass and rushed upon them in a vigorous charge; after resisting briefly they were driven back. As to the other Romans there I am unable to say how each fared in valiant deeds, but charging with his lance Doukas allegedly hurled upwards of thirty to the ground, until, after they had lost many of their men, they got inside the [town's] gates. The Romans who had pursued them returned to camp, since it was already late in the day, having suffered no loss except one of the mercenary cavalry. So they camped there that night, but took the road at daybreak.

When Richard learned of this, he fled from there as swiftly as possible, lest the Romans encircle him and achieve something beyond remedy; once he reached Andria, he remained there. After he had rescued the army with Palaiologos, Doukas followed after Richard, although the force about him exceeded that of the Romans by a large amount. / 143 / For they were six hundred, no more, apart from the infantry, who themselves were inferior to the very numerous infantry force with Richard. A thousand eight hundred knights, and an innumerable army of infantry followed Richard.

When he heard that the Romans were approaching, Richard himself led forth his army. When they came near, the Romans, divided in three parts, were drawn up as follows. The Cumans and those bowmen who were on foot stood in front in a solid formation. Doukas, with half of the cavalry and especially a company of Cumans, himself held the rear, while Bassonville with some other counts and the rest of the cavalry occupied the middle ground. Richard, possessed by great anger and not capable of making any pretence of military science, charged with the cavalry around him, until, reaching the very center of the Roman army, he brought the battle there to a standstill, since the archer force on the front line did not withstand him even briefly. Then exerting pressure on Bassonville, he forcefully drove him back, and next attacked those about Doukas. There an obstinate battle developed, and many of those with Richard fell; but since they fell in the midst of a great press, no awareness of it reached the army. The pressure was immense, and a heavy din of spears breaking on shields arose; numerous arrows / 144 / flew and danger lurked everywhere, until, pressing heavily with a fierce charge, Richard constrained them to give back. Then Doukas himself, who had been overthrown with a lance, came near being captured.

But Providence conducts and directs all human affairs whithersoever It desires. Although the Romans had come to this pitch of fortune, in the end they won. For Doukas escaped in flight to one of the walls made of stone, without mortar or any other coating, which customarily stand outside [city] gates to mark off the meadows, and he was safe there. Then the Romans' infantry, coming to his aid, threw stones at those about Richard, so that many of those who had previously fled collected together there. Observing this, Richard rushed at them with thirty-six knights. One of the men from Trani who ranked among the priests, however, hurled a great mass of stone from higher ground, hit him on one knee, and brought him to earth. As he lay there rending himself in pain, the other hurled a second missile on his neck. Since he had already been defeated, and although he begged hard for mercy, he [the priest] laid him [Richard] on his back, and drove a dagger through his belly; spilling all his guts like food from a mouth, he [Richard] furnished an example of his own form of cruelty to a captive wretch. Thereafter Andria and the armed force around it went over to the Romans by treaty. / 145 / They, who had not expected to avoid danger, returned to Bari with trophies of victory. Chancing upon abundant supplies there, they took refreshment from their martial labors.

5. After a short time had passed, it seemed right to divide the army in half, one part to stay there with one of the generals, the other, with another leader, to go forth to raid the neighboring fortresses. The lot of fighting outside fell to Doukas. As there was a city which Castro, an outstanding man, commanded, he [Doukas] surrounded it and besieged it vigorously. But because, after he had often assaulted the wall, he recognized that he was attempting the impossible (for it proved hopeless to pry a stone out of it, although it was frequently smitten by siege engines), setting out from there about lamp-lighting time, he hastened to Monopoli, intending to attack it by surprise. At that time the people of Monopoli happened to be sending forth an army against the Romans, partly to discover what was going on, partly to oppose them wherever it would be possible. By chance the men of Monopoli encountered the vanguard of the Roman army and came to grips with it. When knowledge of this reached those in the rear, the knights almost all fled, and with much running and gasping reported to the other citizens that the Romans' army would immediately be at hand. Many of the infantry were captured. Disturbed by this, the city / 146 / decided to oppose the foe in their present circumstances. And so knights, over two hundred, together with more than a thousand infantry, went forth, while an innumerable crowd of slingers followed behind them, and stood before the city.

When it was day, Doukas halted and himself kept over half of the soldiers, but dispatched the rest to pillage the surrounding

areas. So he proceeded, after he had divided the army in half; he
did not indeed at once engage the men of Monopoli, but while
seemingly making a pretence of spying out the walls, he first advanced at a walk, apparently examining the city in detail. Then
without prior announcement, commanding thirty of his men to fall
upon the foe, he rushed into their midst. Stunned by surprise, they
turned to flight, but he did not leave off pursuing until he had followed the fugitives to the city's gates, and spearing one himself,
threw him to earth within the gates. Then after he had recovered
those who had been captured, he set out from there. Already the
other force had satisfactorily made a circuit and returned with
spoil, and it too returned with Doukas to Bari.

While these things occurred, envoys came to the Romans'
generals from the bishop of Rome, whom the Latins customarily
title pope.[10] The embassage desired of them that either both or one
of them go to Rome to discuss important affairs with the bishop.
For (they said) he had already assembled as many forces as possible and was preparing to fight alongside the Romans. To this the
Romans' generals responded with a letter, and sent a certain Basilakios / 147 / who ranked among the emperor's secretaries, but
who then accompanied them, with gold to hire knights from there.

They, however, prepared war on Monopoli. As the people
of Monopoli did not have the courage to oppose the Romans, they
asked that a specified time be granted to them, within which,
unless aid come to them from somewhere, they would hand over
the city without fighting. This was done, and an armistice for the
space of a month was accorded the people of Monopoli.

6. They were occupied in these matters. But, since Sicilian
forces were then attacking him, Bassonville summoned the Romans' generals by letter to come swiftly to his aid. Since they paid
no attention to what he asked, he sent again and inquired about the
same matters. The Romans first replied that they had not come
there from the emperor to fight in Bassonville's behalf (nor indeed
did the treaty between Bassonville and themselves mean this), but

specifically to take possession of Italy for the emperor, assisted in that by him. So they responded to Bassonville. He, however, urged the men no less, saying he was trapped in ultimate perils. So, considering, they went from Bari to the city of Bitetto, a route needing a day for an armed man. But since a rumor had previously been prevalent that Bassonville had planned to betray the Romans to Richard [of Andria] while he still lived, the Romans decided it was necessary to bind him by additional oaths; when this was done, / 148 / they treated him without further suspicion.

Meanwhile the emperor sent a fleet to Italy, filling it with Alans [11] and French knights and Romans. Ioannakios whom they surname Kritoples commanded the Alans; the French, Alexander [of Conversano], a Longibard [i.e., Apulian] by birth but who was extremely devoted to the Romans and the emperor's affairs. John, surnamed Angelus, had overall command.[12] When William's general learned this and also that the Romans' army was approaching him, besieging Andria and pillaging the lands there, he went with his whole army to the city of Molfetta, which was adequately secure.

The Romans intended to subdue Bosco, a fortress subject to the late Richard, stronger than any other and very difficult to approach. There, out of excessive ostentation, every sort of beast was reared in individual habitats, to afford him easy hunting whenever he wished. Leading a few of his followers, Doukas came to investigate it. When he approached, those inside took courage and went forth; falling upon his midst, they inflicted a loss of four men on him, but two of their men also fell. The engagement became hand-to-hand. But, drawing together, the Romans thrust the enemy back by their valor. In this conflict many of the Romans and two of the Alans performed nobly. So the fight was broken off there. When his other force came up, Doukas established a camp / 149 / and spent the night; getting his men in order at dawn, he advanced in formation. While the assault proceeded, the Romans galled those inside with arrows and missiles from war machines; the others defended themselves vigorously from the battlements.

There something rather remarkable happened. Two of Doukas' guardsmen, since they perceived that the fortress, while damaged by stones, was unyielding, covered their heads with shields, held torches in their other hands, and advanced to the gates to set them alight. But since the material was not combustible, they retreated unsuccessful, avoiding, contrary to expectation, the things flung down on them from the walls like hail. After the battle had been continued until sunset, since they had achieved nothing, the Romans returned to camp.

William's generals heard this and assembled in council; they considered whether they had to do battle with the Romans. Their opinion was to collect their force and advance to the Romans' camp; learning this, the Romans prepared to oppose them. Nine leaders were in charge of the Italians; the chancellor had overall command. Their army was completely armored, mounted on haughty steeds, and wielding long lances. At these things, panic seized the Romans' army, and wonder as to whether with a small army they could fight against so well-armed and innumerable a force. Yet they stood drawn up by companies while the general suggested to them many things which roused them to courage. / 150 / For a while neither side commenced battle. Then when the trumpets sounded from either hand and the signal was given, falling upon one another each commenced to fight hand-to-hand. You would have said that neither sunshine nor daylight was visible: a cloud overspread everything and dust rose on high; clattering resounded and a fierce din arose.

So until midday the battle was equally balanced. Thereafter, forcing their way by numbers, the Italians pressed those about Doukas. Swiftly recognizing the problem, he rushed into the midst of the enemy's formation. While he smote those on either hand, the Roman onslaught followed him with a shout. So the forces engaged anew, and the fighting waxed fierce, until by their valor the Romans drove back their foe. In their flight, up to three hundred of their knights fell, and a numberless crowd of infantry, but the rest escaped by fleeing. After they had succeeded in this, the Romans turned back against the fortress [Bosco]. After they had soon overcome it, they found abundant supplies in it; sated with diverse good things, they returned to Bari.

7. Not much later they became possessed of Montepeloso, a celebrated city, and took Gravina which Alexander [of Conversano] had previously ruled, and many other towns and fortresses. In addition, they held over fifty villages, and on every hand the emperor's affairs prospered greatly. But his forces continually slipped away from William, / 151 / and he was really in a difficult place. Running through the whole of Italy, rumor everywhere heralded the Romans' invincibility. Then the Italians observed the Romans, whose warfare they had not experienced for an immense period of time, driving away and carrying off absolutely all their property.

Hitherto the Romans' affairs had been moving with the current, but from then on fate began somewhat to begrudge their good fortune. A disease which fastened on Palaiologos inflamed the man with burning fever, nor did it cease consuming his natural moisture until it first constrained him to be tonsured,[13] then a little later bore him off from mankind. For just as he donned hair garments and seemed to be better, he directed Doukas to attack other cities which still were not in the Romans' possession. On the third day thereafter, he was in sore straits; learning this, Doukas returned to Bari. Finding him already dead, he committed the body to a coffin, after he had fulfilled what Christian customs allow in the way of ritual. After he had arranged matters well in Bari, he alone took up authority over affairs for the future.

8. So Palaiologos departed from life, a man who was generally shrewd and particularly very clever in dealing with martial affairs. Taking his army, Doukas made straight for Brindisi. He was then especially eager to unite to himself Bassonville, / 152 /

who had gone off for the following reason. Either, as I think, fur-
nishing himself pretexts for profit, or truly gripped by lack of
money, he asked Palaiologos, who was still alive, to lend him ten
thousand gold pieces. He at once proposed to offer him four
[thousand], as a gift from the emperor but not a loan, and absolutely refused the rest. Offended thereat, Bassonville departed
from the Roman army. But as soon as Palaiologos died and
Doukas was placed in charge of affairs, he [Bassonville] came into
his presence, obtained the money just as he had asked, and again
participated in the Romans' martial labors.

   Taking him, Doukas went toward Massafra with the whole
army. There was there a city named Polymilion,[14] where there was
one of William's followers, by name Flameng. But when he heard
that the Romans' army was approaching, he left there and went to
Taranto; taking Polymilion and pillaging the surrounding countryside, the Romans satiated the army with booty. Thence they
moved to the city of Mottola, which was situated high up, equally
strong and well-fortified on both sides: on one, rough and really
inaccessible ravines extended, on the other it was circled by navigable streams. But it seems nothing hinders those sailing with a
fair wind. Although Mottola seemed secure on all sides, yet it was
taken by Romans who had not toiled long at all, in a fashion about
to be related. Since they were / 153 / in high spirits from their
previous victories, when they observed those from the city, heart-
ened by the nature of the place, standing outside the gates, there
where it was rather open to attack, they charged up hill at a run.
Astounded at their boldness, the others rushed in flight to their
gates. When the Romans' army fell upon them, these had not yet
been barred, and so the city was taken by storm. After they had
achieved this, the Romans set out from there.

   Shortly, Flameng with a large army encountered them as
they advanced. Leaping out in front of their regiments, some of
the Romans clashed with the foe and displayed marvelous feats,
but being much inferior to the opponents' number, they retreated.

At this moment, Doukas with his whole force attacked Flameng, drove him back, and assaulted Massafra. Having carried it by assault, he discovered an immense quantity of supplies stored in the citadel; it held many arms and no less than two hundred horses. When they learned this, the men of Taranto gathered by guilds and neighborhoods and openly abused Flameng, imputing this charge to him, that he had made his own cowardice the cause of the Romans' courage. Unable to endure this, he again assembled troops and waited for the Romans' army. But just as it came within his view, smitten immediately by fear, he did not even recollect his courage. A few Romans attacked them as they fled and slew some.

/ 154 / When they came near Taranto, however, they perceived the city to be impregnable and left it, intending to approach Monopoli. Since they were deficient in siege engines, they summoned by letter the fleet at Bari to come as quickly as possible, so as to get plenty of such things from it. Meanwhile the Romans passed through a lush region, laden with manifold products, so that they were satiated with myriad good things. Allegedly a soldier would sell ten ordinary cattle for a gold piece, and a hundred thirty sheep. Then, too, they found some of the Romans who from a long time back had been committed to prison, and released the poor fellows from their fetters.

9. When they arrived at Monopoli on the fifth day, no one even came out against them (for rumor, which had struck terror into them, had already driven them within the walls), but they stood in full armor upon the towers, ready to defend themselves if any assault approached the wall. Pitching camp, they [the Byzantines] remained in a convenient place not far from the city. Since he [Doukas] had already brought to Monopoli the fleet which they had summoned from Bari, it furnished supplies sufficient for the siege; they then attacked the wall in full force. But, because they were hurling things down from above on their foe, the people of Monopoli beat back the advancing Romans and killed some. The

battle which had commenced in the morning lasted until night. Then, since it was getting dark, the Romans returned to their camp. / 155 / The people of Monopoli had guards appointed by turns on the towers, lest by night the Romans should covertly do some harm to the city. Myriad fires burned on every hand, and pipes and trumpets sounded.

Just as the sun, passing the eastern horizon, peeped down on the face of the earth, the Romans went out from their camp and returned to battle, while the men of Monopoli rushed to their battlements and stood to arms. Again a violent struggle was joined, with the Romans forcing an approach to the walls, but the oncoming foe being thrust back by the men of Monopoli. For some while they toiled in these circumstances; later the Romans' army hurled fire where the ships of the people of Monopoli lay at anchor, and caused a great blaze to arise.

Then one of the Romans' soldiers, Hikanatos by name, achieved feats worthy of telling and hearing. A double wall girded Monopoli: the inner rose very high and made no account at all of an enemy spear, while the other, which rose to a third the height of the foregoing one, ran around its base. Two of the men of Monopoli climbing onto this wall shot at the foe and urged others to it. Observing this, Hikanatos charged with his spear and hit one of the said men. He was immediately rolled on the ground, and a great shout was lifted up by the Romans' army; the noise became immense / 156 / and unendurable to hear. Astounded at this, those upon the towers, who thought that the city was already taken, left the fortifications and ran to the center of town. And save that, swiftly perceiving the situation, they again mounted the battlements, the city would have been taken at once by the Romans. In such circumstances the second onslaught on Monopoli ended.

Because the people of Monopoli knew that they were caught in sore straits, they sent a letter to Flameng and asked him to come as quickly as possible. He responded that after a short time he would join them with a large force, to drive the Romans away. Fear, however, kept him within, and he fell into limitless cowardice when he considered with whom he would fight and against whom the battle would be. When the seventh day thereafter passed and Flameng did not appear anywhere, then the people of Monopoli despaired of assistance from any direction and sent envoys to the Romans' army, to the effect that they would yield the city and themselves to the great emperor. Doukas told them that their pledge would not hold good in this agreement, unless they would accept a garrison placed over them by the emperor. When they agreed to this, a fixed time was given for the pact [to take effect].

Some of the citizen body of Monopoli (those who were displeased at what was being done), however, without the others' knowledge, revealed these things to Flameng. Aroused at the report, he selected no less than a hundred armored knights from his followers and dispatched them at once; he said he would come a little later / 157 / leading a substantial force. Those who had agreed to this deed waited for those soldiers on a night on which continuous rain poured down from above, admitted them to the city through a postern, and thereafter planned to take up arms again. As soon as this came to Doukas' knowledge, he deemed the embassage from the men of Monopoli a trick, and immediately led forth his army from camp. But as they [the people of Monopoli] reckoned that the hundred knights were scarcely sufficient for them, and since the Romans' army was in general fighting with more zeal than before, they sent and invited the general to the city again, ascribing the problem to others, who had rashly done the present deed without common consent. At first Doukas seemed to refuse: gripped by excessive conceit and arrogance, he declared that the matter had already been decided by battle. But when the citizens pressed him still more on this and begged forgiveness for their error, he at length relented and led his force into the city.

Just as the Romans took possession of the city, Flameng was reported to be about twenty stades [two-and-a-half miles] away. Learning this, Doukas chose knights from his followers on the basis of their excellence and dispatched them to intercept Flameng; he himself remained there to control the city. But when Flameng perceived from a distance the emperor's standards exposed on the walls, he turned back before coming to grips with the Romans' cavalry, who were already near at hand. Then the pursuing Romans slew many of them, / 158 / and took alive a hundred fully armed knights. The swiftness of his horse preserved Flameng from danger, as he came near to being captured. After they had thus been successful, the Romans returned to Monopoli.

10. Doukas, who daily observed fortune smiling on the Romans, was unable to trust it very much, but was reasonably cautious about its reversal, lest (he said), like some rascally fellow travelers, it should turn back, leaving them in mid-stream. So he wrote a letter and sent it to the emperor. It went thus: "If no conflict remained for us in Italy, most mighty emperor, there would be no need of another army or of anything else. Know that until this day everything has proceeded according to our intent, as we have overcome almost all the cities which exist in Italy [i.e., Apulia] and on the Ionian Gulf [Adriatic Sea], and have been victorious in great battles in a fashion worthy of your empire and of the Romans' race. Since a still greater struggle lies before us (for William, who pillages Sicily, very likely grieved at the destruction of his followers, is gathering troops from everywhere and has already launched a fleet of numerous ships on the sea, intending to attack us by land and sea), we must not treat lightly the preparations of the islander [William] nor conduct this war casually, lest our present renown should instead be terminated in infamy. For while it is agreed that successfully to pursue great ends with few men / 159 / is more gratifying than with many, yet failure imports manifold shame, because along with defeat it also implies ignorance of strategy in the defeated, as your majesty has often taught us. So that nothing of the sort should ever happen to us, we require a larger naval and land army here." The letter was in such terms.

Since all went well for him in Monopoli, he set out from there with his whole force; after he had acquired by treaty Ostuni, a city outstanding in strength, he hastened to another town, Brindisi, anciently named Temese. The long age which has since intervened has made anew most of the names by reversals, changing them to ones either absolutely dissimilar or somewhat different.[15] When the Romans reached it [14 April 1156], they remained quiet (for the Christians' Easter was the next day); those of the city, deeming this to be fear, frequently sallied forth and reached the camp, until the Romans rather unwillingly leapt forth at them, but when they thrust them back, returned to camp.

So the rest of the Romans returned to their previous occupations, offering reverence to the [holy] season; but one Thomas, an Antiochene by birth who had long since become an adherent to the emperor,[16] donned his arms and went forth from the camp on horseback into the plain. When he was near the town, / 160 / he summoned the noblest to descend for single combat with him. There was one there, Angelo by name, who was distinguished for bravery. When he observed Thomas demanding single combat, he armed and went out into the plain, going at a foot pace to face Thomas. Then wonder seized those from both sides who saw men so armed and so valiant prepared for combat in that place as if in a stadium. When they came near, spurring their horses, they collided with lances. Thomas' lance, passing through shield and breastplate, pierced up to the skin, but Angelo drove his lance through [Thomas'] shield, where he was raising it above his head, since the soldier was then lifting it up to protect the area around it [his head], and it pierced the helmet and scraped the flesh. Thus parting from one another, the one returned to the Romans' camp, the other to the city.

When the Romans had completed the celebration of their festival, they advanced in order against the city. As they decided that they were acting in vain in striking the walls with stones (for men of old, who invested much care in their public works, were probably more especially ambitious in construction of cities), they abstained from it; flinging stones like a discus to fly high, over the walls, they caused them to fall within the city. As soon as they let go the first one, an old woman strutting in the city received the shot on her crown, and it shattered her head / 161 / and broke every bone of her limbs. Lamentation arose, and the appearance of a captured city overtook those within, who even lacked courage to go see that unfortunate woman. As the Romans made a second cast and then many other shots, the frightened populace each individually imagined a stone above his head, but not in the fashion which legends relate concerning Tantalus.[17] Wherefore, as the soldiery who were on guard in the towers sensed that the citizens were planning to accord entry to the Romans, they went at a run to the citadel. Opened by the citizenry, the gates admitted the Romans' army.

So when Doukas held it [Brindisi, except the citadel], dividing his army in half, he kept one [part] in the city to combat those in the citadel, but sent the other to forage. So he acted there. But a populous and fertile region which they call Halitzion,[18] considering what had befallen Brindisi, went over to the emperor. A small force of the enemy (they were Normans)[19] which was lying in wait in a grove for those pasturing the Romans' cavalry, when they saw them settled for sleep, drove away the horses. Hearing of this, which was reported to them by those returning from foraging, the Romans swiftly pursued, recaptured all the horses, and took alive most of the foe. Then a particularly outstanding man among the Italians, by name Sycheren [Siger?], was captured. But since it did not become clear / 162 / who he was, he deceived his captor and released himself by a gift of gold.

11. A rumor prevailed among the Romans that a little later William would arrive leading large military and naval forces. So, having prepared as well as possible, they remained quiet. The fifth day thereafter had not come when one of the enemy's army who had deserted warned the Romans that William was so close at hand as to be taken in nets. When they heard this, the Romans' generals

laid out the battle. It seemed proper that Bassonville and John Angelus, who had the entire mercenary force and those from Italy who had gone over to the emperor, should undertake the struggle by land, and Doukas should contend against the [enemy] at sea: for so, they said, they would be able to assist one another. At dawn Doukas marched at a foot pace to the beach with the armored members of the cavalry which attended him, having the ships sailing on one side, while the rest, ready for battle by land, advanced in formation. The Sicilians' ships, as they were already near the city, were unable to enter the harbor in a body (for while sufficiently broad inside, it ends in somewhat of a strait); they entered in succession, divided in groups of ten.

Then allegedly Doukas, seeing that the Romans' fleet, because it was very small, was terrified at their number (for his ships were fourteen in all), / 163 / planned something as follows. He contrived to produce for them a letter as if just sent from the emperor. The letter specified that forces by land and sea would reach them about midday. When they had been elevated by hope, he said, "But I have vowed, fellow soldiers, that we shall first seize victory, lest we who have hitherto born the weight of toil shall have to share the blessings of victory with those who join late in the struggle." So saying, the general observed the enemy's ships arriving within the harbor, and then ordered battle to be joined. Once the battle commenced, the Sicilians, who were unable to endure the Romans' shots from land and sea, as they were subject to archery from both sides, retreated. The pursuing Romans slew many of them, and took with all their crews four [ships] which ran aground. For since their rowing was more hasty than necessary, they struck upon the beach, a ready prey for the land forces.

In this battle more than two thousand of the enemy fell; many another of the Romans did well, but especially a noble fellow, by name Skaramankas, one of those placed under Doukas' command. When the foe was thinking of fleeing, spurring his horse, he took hold of one by the stern as it was trying to depart and held it back by force, nobly performing the far-famed deed of old Kynegeiros.[20] / 164 / When blows from those within hindered him, he necessarily let go, yet, since he had cut short the time for its escape, he caused it to be captured by other Romans who then ran up.

Once they had succeeded in this, the Romans advanced on [the citadel of] Brindisi; after they had constructed a device which is customarily called a "tortoise," they brought it up to the citadel. When they observed this, those upon the walls laughed aloud, thinking that they intended thus to tear apart the wall-structure, something which was absolutely impossible. For the stones were so close to one another that the whole wall seemed to be a single stone. But when the Romans had brought the machine near the wall, entering it by night, they dug down close to the foundation and taking away the dirt carried it out the other end [of the machine], until they passed the final stones of the foundations and reached the earth underneath. Removing it, they created a hollow space, then thrusting in timbers they filled up the hollow. Thereby they supported the [part] of the wall which was suspended there, until, observing those within still steadfast, they set fire to the place. Swiftly devouring the material, it threw down the wall to the foundations. It cast down many of those on the battlements. But retiring to the inner wall, the barbarians resisted no less.

12. While the Romans were engaged in these matters, the emperor assembled a fleet of ships and sent it to Italy with a land army; / 165 / Alexius, son of the daughter of the emperor Alexius [I],[21] was in command of both these; he then bore the office of grand *doux* [high admiral]. He was commanded by the emperor to assemble another force and so make sail for Italy; but without doing this he went to Brindisi, partly because the generality were frightened at so fearsome a voyage, partly in suspicion of the perils which impended over them from the enemy.

Thereafter fortune more openly commenced to begrudge

[its favors] to the Romans. For Robert [of Bassonville], who had hitherto fought alongside them, hearing that William had come with large forces, and seeing that the Romans had not yet subdued the citadel of Brindisi, abandoned the alliance; he pretended that he was going away to collect forces which would assist him in battle there. Also, the knights from the March [of Ancona] demanded in the future to be furnished double their previous hire; when they did not succeed in their request, they departed. Learning this, William assembled his forces and marched straight for the Romans.

As the latter were planning how they had to manage the war, to some it seemed right to go to Bari and make themselves secure in the city by entrenchment, but others were displeased at this, declaring it was outright cowardice if they withdrew and let go what was in their hands. Because the latter seemed correct, not letting the interval pass in idleness, they again assailed the wall [of the citadel of Brindisi] and threw down a great part of it with war machines. Not that they were able to expel the barbarians: but at first taking courage, they [the garrison] sallied forth at them, then when the Romans pressed them hard, they ran back to the wall, / 166 / and if an intervening accident had not hindered the Romans, Brindisi would then have speedily been taken by storm. For they had already mounted the wall and were fighting those within from the towers, but a great many of them [the towers] which had previously been damaged by myriad stone-casts collapsed and fell to the ground, and pulled down many of them [the Romans], and so they withdrew unsuccessful.

Since William was not near, the Sicilians made a plan to yield the fortress to the Romans on terms. But fortune, as if it had promised to serve the Romans for a specified time, then sensing that that was measured out, departed from them out of the midst of the city. For while the Sicilians were planning this, it was reported to them that William was then at hand with a great army. Hearing this, they abandoned their intention, mounted the walls, raised a repeated clamor, and held a celebration as if they had already expelled the Romans.

13. This had been achieved there. William, who had set forth from Messina with his whole army, marched direct to Brindisi, while his fleet waited at anchor at an islet opposite Brindisi a few stades away. They planned to make an attack on the Romans simultaneously from both sides. But bad advice and, I think, the inevitability of defeat prevented the Romans from fighting at sea immediately, before William appeared against them. Carrying on battle against both, they brought ruin to the emperor's / 167 / affairs. As they then awaited for an army to come from Byzantion, they postponed an onslaught until its speedy arrival. But as William was reported near, then perforce they accepted battle with both.

Selecting two men tried in battle, Ioannakios Kritoples and Bairam,[22] a Turk by race, they sent them with Georgians and Alans to skirmish. When they encountered the enemy, who had pitched camp some forty-five stades [five-and-a-half miles] away, at [the moment of their] departure they attacked them from the rear, close at hand, slew many of those in the rear guard and drove off numerous horses from their baggage train; after they had taken a standard from them, they returned to Brindisi. But the Sicilians took no notice of this (because in their immense number, no information reached them), and encamping a little way from the Romans, so that foragers from both sides encountered each other, they planned their battle. Already their fleet, lying a little way off the harbor, awaited them. The Sicilians were thus occupied.

But by much previous desertion the Romans were inferior to the enemy's army, and then still more of their force slipped away. For very many others of their allies abandoned them, and in particular a not insignificant body of Normans who served the Romans for hire went secretly over to William. Observing this,

William realized he had to grasp the opportunity of the moment, lest after time elapsed / 168 / either Robert [of Bassonville] would come to assist them (for reportedly he had gathered troops and was returning) or else a military and naval reinforcement would reach them from the emperor. So he arrayed his army by regiments and advanced. Since Robert was late, either willfully or by accident, the Romans formed and arranging themselves as well as possible, stood face to the foe. Then it was astounding to see an insignificant body of Romans getting ready to fight with all the Sicilian forces [28 May 1156].[23]

For a while neither joined battle, then one of the hireling knights from the Romans' formation leapt into the space between the lines and stood inviting anyone who wished to single combat. Falling on each other in this fashion they commenced battle. The fight, starting at dawn, was equally balanced for a long time, while the Romans fought courageously; then the Sicilians, forcing their way by numbers, drove them back. Many of the fleeing fell and were taken captive, the rest with much shoving and violence burst into the city, among whom was the general Alexius [Comnenus]. Doukas, who had been left outside the walls, did not give over striking and being struck, until surrounded by the foe he became prisoner after many struggles. When the Sicilians took him, they then easily had those in the city netted as if in a trap.

To this end the folly of Comnenus and Doukas brought their earlier renown. So present-day men are: some survive entirely bereft of military science and bring affairs to ruin, / 169 / others perchance know a part of military science but are wrong about the more important part. For strategy is an art, and one who practices it must be supple and cunning and know how to make a timely alteration at every turn of it. For there is a time when it is not shameful to flee, if the occasion allows, and again to pursue relentlessly, each according to one's advantage; where success would seem more by cunning than by force, risking everything is

to be deprecated. Since many and various matters lead toward one
end, victory, it is a matter of indifference which one one uses to
reach it.

Since Alexius lacked the forces which the emperor had ordered him to bring, if the Romans had recognized that they were
not equal to the Sicilians, had embarked their army on ships, and
had engaged their fleet first, they would have forcefully overcome
it. They would have been consoled by victories at sea for their
withdrawal from the land and so when occasion warranted they
would have disembarked again on the mainland and won battles in
Italy with larger forces. But as they kept in mind the dishonor of
retreat, they fell into the disgrace of being destroyed with their
whole force.

14. So this happened there. Hearing of it, the emperor was
very likely angry, especially because / 170 / this had happened
after so many previous successes. For disaster occurring after
glory invites infamy, and in particular it usually brings grief, because it lacked little of succeeding entirely, then all was ruined.
Therefore he was grieved, yet he was not overcome by sorrow. He
dispatched Alexius [Axouchos], who then bore the office of protostrator, to Ancona to lay claim again to Italy, as if from a base.
For the men there had previously taken oaths to the emperor, that
while they would not willingly fight the Germans' king, they
would guard like themselves the emperor's money and those of the
Romans whom he would send. Why the emperor was persuaded to
this, I will forthwith relate. When he was campaigning previously
on Kerkyra, he recognized the Venetians' nation as malicious and
stubborn, and thought it very important to lay claim to Ancona.
Thereby he might to a large extent humble the Venetians' pride
and from there very easily wage wars in Italy. Therefore Alexius
went with much money to Ancona [1157]. Sending from there to
Italy [i.e., Apulia] Constantine Otto and Andreas, count of an Italian city [Rupe Canina], valiant in might and well-supplied with

bravery, he [Alexius Axouchos] assembled a large mercenary force and subdued numerous cities for the Romans.[24]

Then something as follows happened. As the bishop of Rome [Pope Hadrian IV] had previously agreed on an alliance with William, when he noted these two men [Constantine Otto and Andreas] going through the regions of Rome, he strongly forbade it. But / 171 / some of the nobles who had previously agreed on friendship to the Romans (for customarily emperor Manuel was allied to many of those there) roused the people against him, received on request the imperial standard very honorably, and freely allowed Kontostephanos to recruit whomever he wished. Angered thereat, the bishop subjected the people to a punishment [Interdict], the only thing he was able to do, saying that there was nothing in common between the newer Rome [Constantinople] and the elder, since they had anciently been broken apart. "We must rather fight in behalf of the Sicilians' lord: it were impious not to go to the aid of one who is a member of our own [body], nay more, someone who is faring badly in a struggle with one much stronger than himself." Fearful of this penalty, one of those who managed the emperor's affairs withdrew, reversed his opinion, and went over to bishop's side. But the Romans' leaders drew him forth with much violence; to pillory his breach of faith, in a barbarous fashion not far from tastelessness, they caused his full armor and horse to be raised on ropes hanging on a tree. Assembling openly against the bishop, they persuaded him involuntarily to release men from the penalties. Therefore the Romans' affairs again enjoyed great liberty.[25]

They overcame in war a city which has its name from Saint Germanus [San Germano, modern Cassino], and they placed upwards of three hundred others under the emperor; the name of each of these can be read by whosoever wishes from off the palace south [sic] of the city / 172 / built by this emperor in addition to the older palaces [i.e., Blachernai].[26] If there are inscribed there more

than these, it is excessive flattery and a servile fashion of those
who laid claim to the deeds, such as is usually the case with the
multitude, on which account I once heard the emperor himself
express his anger. Whether they were removed, I am unable to
state unreservedly.

15. Thus the whole land of the Italians lacked little of
coming again under the Romans. But Alexius Comnenus and
Doukas and whoever else of the Romans' generals had become
captive to the Sicilians' lord again ruined matters [1158]. For as
they had already pledged to the Sicilians many things not then
desired by the emperor, they robbed the Romans of very great and
noble achievements. What should one be capable of agreeing to,
when fetters hold him and underground dens imprison him? The
Sicilians did this so that the men there who expected the emperor
to make peace with William very likely deprived the Romans of
the cities too soon.

When the emperor heard this and understood what had
been done, dispatching letters to Sicily, he wrote as follows to the
Romans in prison. "It make me wonder, gentlemen, how you continually practice meanness in affairs. For previously you thus
ruined former excellent victories and invited on yourselves the fate
in which you presently are, and now, when others were eager with
God's aid to recoup by war what you had previously mismanaged,
you stand in the way. Or did it not occur / 173 / to you that the
Sicilians intended this to check our onward advance? For who of
the Italians will there be, who hears that the land which we now
hold will be restored to William by us, and will not straightway
revolt from us and without hesitation return to William's allegiance? There will not be one, save he were a fool and senseless
man, as many happen to be. I ask you, tell me, by God, when did
your fatherland seem nobler to you? When, after Italy and the
island of Sicily had all been brought under our authority, as outstanding men brilliantly rescued by your compatriots, you return to
Byzantion, noble champions of the Romans, regarded as a wel-

come sight to your peers? Or when, after we have yielded nothing and gained nothing, just as your oaths [to William] specify, we recall you hither?''

He wrote this to the Romans, but William he addressed as follows. ''Think not, noble sir, that we will not notice why this was contrived by you, since not even necessity excuses what has been done under constraint. So what was sworn by those bound and imprisoned men will not prove wholly satisfactory to you. The Romans will not abstain from warring in Italy until they shall place it and the whole island under our power, as it formerly was.''

When those around William received the letter, they responded as follows. ''If you wish to impose penalties on us for the errors previously committed in regard to your majesty, / 174 / most mighty emperor, you have already prosecuted Italy beyond what was necessary. You have overcome no less than three hundred cities in its midst, something which had been lacking in the Romans' realm for a long time back, and you have won renown which belonged to none other save your majesty since Justinian, the former emperor of the Romans. We ask that you compare our error (I mean when we overran your Corinth and Euboea) and the Romans' victories in Italy, which now for so long a time have driven away and carried off property there, filling the land with thrice as much blood, many times more often, and not merely pillaging as many cities, but also rendering them your subjects. Which seems greater to you?

''Nor should you desire to measure out these things against us, who are much inferior to your majesty, but turn back to the earlier emperors and observe with me the feats of the Romans in times past. Or did not someone even then trouble the Romans' realm? Was not your state many times vexed by Turkish and Hunnic [Petcheneg] peoples, and the late Robert [Guiscard] who crossed from Italy to Epidamnos [Durazzo, modern Durrës] and waged great battles with your grandfather [Alexius I]? Scarcely and with difficulty could he thrust Robert from the Romans' land, but you have overcome well nigh all of ours. If this was undertaken to avenge yourself on us, you have enough victories; you have punished us enough.

"For you who tread our soil / 175 / it is not ignoble to welcome terms of peace, nay, rather, exceedingly glorious. You will immediately obtain the Romans whom we have made captive, since fate has yielded us men thus eminent, regarding whom you are not justly angry at us. To a man waging war, it is no shame to take action against his enemies. So that it remains that you justly wage war on us on that one count, what we did wrong in regard to Euboea, for which you have as we said already exceeded [equitable] retribution. So if you have been eager to impose punishment on us for what we demonstrated in your land, we have done as much in defense against your majesty; but if you must continually wage war on our race, it is seasonable for you to consider whether or not the attempt is contrary to humanitarian laws. For it is humane to measure out wars by their pretexts, and someone else would say that to go further was bestial, but this is not to be said by us. We ask that you make a treaty and conclude this war."

After he had repeatedly perused this letter, the emperor agreed with what it said; when he had received the Roman captives and recovered whatever spoil of war there was, and in addition had obtained oaths from William that he would be his ally for matters in the west, he [Manuel] ended the war. A little later he honored him [William] as king, which he previously was not; he preserved so much good will toward him that, when William had measured out his life-span [1166], and his brother approached him [Manuel] and asked to be assisted to rule Sicily, he did not receive him at all.[27]

/ 176 / 16. So the business of the Romans' Italian wars reached a conclusion there. Since affairs in Asia had already been stirred up, while he still carried on conflicts in Italy, the emperor had much anxiety for matters there, but then he was wholly taken up by them. For the Turks' sultan [28] had overcome Pounoura and

Sibyla,[29] cities subject to the Romans, and the aforementioned
Ṭoros seized many of those in Cilicia, while Yaghi-Basan, who
was a chieftain of the Turks and ruler of the Cappadocians' land,
had overrun Oinaion [Ünye] and Pauraë [Bafra], both Pontic
cities.[30] Sending Alexius Giphardos [ca. 1158] against the sultan,
he recovered the said cities, while he constrained Yaghi-Basan to
abandon an expedition against the Romans' territory and become
his own devoted ally; he himself planned to campaign in Cilicia.

Meanwhile [1156–57] the following events happened in
Byzantion. There was one of the Levites whom we call deacons,
whose name was Basil. As he had been entrusted to unfold the
Holy Scriptures to the multitude at religious services anywhere, he
desired openly and covertly to abuse in these sermons some of
those who had lately quarreled with him, especially Michael [of
Thessalonica] and Nicephorus, by surname Basilakios [or Basila-
kes]. One of these, Michael, was at that time professor of rhetoric
and expounded the holy words of the Evangelists at the church of
Hagia Sophia; the other was generally esteemed by men of letters,
especially as an excellent author of speeches. Indeed, he was very
skillfully trained in many parts of rhetoric. / 177 / These men
labored at these things and took it ill if, being so far advanced in
scientific knowledge, they were sneered at by such a man,
whereby they became the causes of irremediable disasters to themselves and many others.

For when Basil was celebrating his usual liturgy at the
church of the apostle John the Theologian outside the city, they
went to listen, yet with treacherous attention, filled with malice.
For as he was going through a Gospel passage someplace, I think,
he declared the Son of God and the Spirit were one and the same
and received the Sacrifice [of the Eucharist] along with the Father;[31] they forthwith seized on the expression and going up and
down, mocked at it, saying that Basil thereby introduced two
hypostases [forms of Christ's being], if one was sacrificed, the
other received the sacrifice. Others of those esteemed for learning

agreed with this teaching, especially Soterichos, whose surname was Panteugenos, a man who excelled others at that period in knowledge and cleverness of speech, who had obtained the [patriarchal] throne of Antioch but had not yet been consecrated. Soterichos defended their doctrine not only by tongue and mouth, but also arraying a formidable amount of logic, which, in dialogue form, possessed an extraordinary similarity to Plato; in this composition he united many absurd things, on account of which he submitted to removal from the [patriarchal] throne, as well as whoever was associated with him, when the emperor made an arbitration on the points in question. Basil again obtained his rank, for he had previously lost it, / 178 / even though at a later time he again lost it, when he was allegedly detected as unorthodox in doctrine.[32]

17. That dogmatic dispute obtained this conclusion. The emperor set forth against Toros. For while he was as stated occupied with affairs in the west, the barbarian, who had awaited his opportunity, had taken possession of well-nigh all the cities in Cilicia. For he was clever as anyone at seizing the right moment and capable in contriving matters.

On this account the emperor went to Asia, and for [reasons] which I am about to narrate. When Raymond prince of Antioch passed from among those here, forthwith his wife Constance offered herself and the Antiochenes' property to the emperor, but when as aforesaid, the emperor sent the caesar [John] Roger to wed her, she changed her mind by common consent of the Antiochenes and joined in marriage [1153] with a certain Reginald [of Châtillon], since they [the Antiochenes] were anxious lest when the woman was wedded to Roger they should become subject to payment of tax to the Romans. Since the emperor did not accord him what he wanted, this Reginald tried to frighten him, brandishing many threats; asserting that he required money, he acted as follows [1156]. After he had constructed ships, he made sail for Cyprus, attacked those there in piratical fashion, and carried off an abundance of wealth. At first, however, the emperor's nephew John [Comnenus the protosebastos] who then governed the land, and Michael Branas and whoever else was stationed there for its defense, repelled and manhandled him. Then / 179 / when Branas was pursuing him more impetuously than was necessary at Leukosia [Nicosia], John went forth to join him, and so both were captured by Reginald. On these accounts, the emperor marched to Cilicia.[33]

When he reached Lesser Phrygia,[34] he encountered the Turks there, defeated them in battle, and made a great slaughter; he devastated the adjacent region belonging to the Turks, as he hastened toward Cilicia, pretending to wage war on the Turks. In this fashion he thought he could catch Toros unawares. To arrive still more unexpectedly, he acted as follows. He ordered Alexius Kasianos, who then governed the province of Seleukeia, to assemble the native force and be ready. Selecting the better-equipped part of his army, he hastened to Seleukeia. He ordered the rest of the Romans' army, which remained somewhere around Attaleia, to take care of its horses. For a disease, which specifically afflicts the equine species, had attacked their hooves and sorely injured them.

When he came forth on the plains at Seleukeia [1158], the forces were not at hand as he had ordered (for this had been neglected by Alexius), and he turned to something else, as he was eager to catch Toros with his full strength. He sent Alexius on ahead so that somehow he might be able to detain Toros, who encountered him there, while he [Manuel] marched behind him, leading no more than five hundred / 180 / armed men. The tyrant would have been swiftly taken and fallen into Roman hands, if fate had not unexpectedly rescued him. For one of the beggars [pilgrims], who in great numbers from the race of the Latins go to Palestine and as wanderers overrun mountains and forests, and leave nothing untrodden by their multitude, encountered the emperor; after he had been furnished a gold piece by him, he went to Toros as quickly as possible and warned him of the emperor's im-

minent arrival. Hearing this, he [Ṭoros] was very likely astounded,
and revealing the news to nobody at all except Thomas and
Korkes, his favorites, he hastily ran off to one place after another,
a fugitive.

Entering Cilicia the next day, the emperor could discover
him nowhere, but without a fight he captured the fortress at Lamos
[on the Lamos Çay], which was especially well-defended. Then he
took Kistramos and Anazarbos, a celebrated city. Advancing and
ravaging, he subdued Longinias with the whole countryside around
it. Passing on to Tarsus which is the capital of that nation, he easily took it, and sending troops to Tili [Toprakkale], a very strong
fortress, he placed it under the Romans.[35] How he won Tarsus,
which was not easily to be taken by many myriads, in a single
day, I will narrate. When he observed that it was well-nigh impregnable, he did not desire to make any delay there; so he
directed himself toward other cities, but he sent his brother-in-law
Theodore Batatzes / 181 / to besiege it. Theodore, however, had
not yet reached the city, when those upon the battlements, thinking
the emperor was approaching and frightened into an extraordinary
panic, flung themselves from the towers, wretches dying a painful
death; in this fashion the city was immediately taken.

18. So Tarsus was captured. Ṭoros and prince Reginald,
observing this, did not dare appear as envoys before the emperor,
because they were aware of their own great misdeeds, but sending
some from among the nobles [36] to him, they petitioned that the
emperor should be reconciled to them. As they failed in their purpose, Reginald, who was in difficulties on every hand, agreed to
turn over the citadel of Antioch to the emperor, if he were forgiven
his crimes. He was aware of the malice of the bishop of Antioch, a
compatriot whom they have established over themselves, forsooth
titling him patriarch, who nourished a quarrel with him from the
following cause.[37] Reginald, as we previously said, felt extreme
poverty and determined to ravage Cyprus; entertaining the bishop
privately, he [Reginald] asked him to give him money: he [Regin-

ald] knew he was very wealthy. Because he was unable to persuade him, he deprived the man of his garments and first thrashed his body with many strokes; since summer was at its height, anointing his wounds with honey, he left him to be burnt by the sun. So wasps, bees, flies, and other blood-drinking creatures / 182 / settled on his entirely naked body and sucked his blood. At this the man gave way, offering to yield all his wealth to Reginald. He, perhaps to propitiate him [the patriarch], after he [Reginald] had dressed him in his usual garb, led him on horseback through the midst of the city; he himself walked and held in his hand the cord which hung from the saddle. Although he did this, the other was no less enraged against Reginald and sought an opportunity to take vengeance on him. Repeatedly writing to the emperor, he offered to betray the man to him. When the emperor declined this (he desired to win by war rather than by treachery), he abandoned the attempt.

Knowing this, Reginald promised the aforesaid things to the emperor; when he [Manuel] did not allow it, he [Reginald] made the following supplication. He removed the covering from his head, bared his arms up to his elbows, and going unshod through the city with a multitude of monks, he appeared before the emperor. A rope bound his throat, a sword was borne in his other hand. A splendid dais was raised there; Reginald stood far off from the imperial tent, as if not daring to approach, while a crowd of monks who were not monks, unshod, with bared heads, approached the emperor; all bending the knee wept tears from their eyes and / 183 / held out their hands. At first the emperor refused, but later, being beseeched, he ordered the prince to advance. Moved by his coming in the said fashion, he forgave him his drunken offense, while he [Reginald] bound himself with oaths to many things, to wit that he would act according to the emperor's will, especially that according to old custom a bishop would be sent to Antioch from Byzantion.

Then indeed astonishment took possession of those who

were present, who had come as envoys from the nations in Asia, the Khorezmians and Susans and Ekbatanians, and all of Media and Babylon, whose ruler they call the Great Sultan,[38] and from Nūr-ad-Dīn the *atabeg* of Aleppo and Yaghi-Basan the Turks' chieftain, and from the Abasgai and Iberians [Georgians], even from the Palestinians [Crusading States] and the Armenians beyond Isauria [i.e., the former Armenian realm, north of Lake Van].

19. Thus he acted there. Baldwin [III] the king of Palestine sent to the emperor and asked to meet him to negotiate, as he said, concerning important matters. But the business was a pretext. Having his eye on the principality of Antioch, which was situated near him, he yet knew not how he might win it, since he had not yet learned the facts about Reginald; he [Baldwin] advised the emperor not to release him [Reginald] at all, so that either with him out of the way he [Baldwin] might treat the Antiochenes as subjects, inasmuch as they had been rescued by himself, or else he might no less impose order on those who were rejecting dominion from both parties [Reginald and Manuel].[39]

/ 184 / Once he had planned these things, he [Baldwin] arrived in Antioch, and addressing the Antiochenes he deceitfully reminded them how he had come there from Palestine to benefit them and that they were obligated to him for great favors. When they agreed, he again asked the emperor to meet him. Aware of the man's intent, he [Manuel] first refused, claiming that he [Baldwin] could not receive the appropriate [ceremonial] greeting and welcome, if he [Baldwin] negotiated with him while occupied in the midst of martial activities. But seeing him [Baldwin] still more pressing and making daily pleas about the same subjects, he [Manuel] agreed to the request and ordered him to come. The Antiochenes allegedly surrounded him as he went forth from the city and begged that if it were possible, he should reconcile the emperor to them.

In the meanwhile something as follows befell at the emperor's camp. There was one of his secretaries, Theodore by name, Stypeiotes by surname. This Theodore was especially close to the emperor and had been entrusted with the office of ἐπὶ τοῦ κανικλείου [keeper of the inkstand, a principal secretary]; but after he was detected and proven crooked and malicious toward him, the wretch was deprived of eyes and tongue. For he foretold to many, as if from a [prophet's] tripod, that the span of the emperor's life had already been measured out, and declared that the Romans' senate must bestow authority on someone not still a youth nor puffed with pride, but to a genuinely aged man, well beyond youth, so that when he, by way of argument, ruled he might rather direct the state's business as in a democracy. / 185 / So matters befell there in regard to Theodore. Then too, George, by surname Pyrrhogeorgios, chief of the imperial trumpeters, who is customarily called the *primikerios* of the court,[40] who had quarreled with the emperor over no small matters, again enjoyed his favor and suffered no other injury, but lost that office.

20. Learning that the king was approaching, the emperor sent some of the nobles one place, some another to meet him, with the more distinguished behind, up to his nephews-in-law, who greeted him and honored him appropriately, until he came into the emperor's presence. Then he [Manuel] honored and welcomed the man in a fashion worthy of the throne of David; but the other, either rendered proud by this or nourishing some inborn arrogance, when he arrived at the imperial tent, attended by the imperial staff-bearers and Romans of the aristocracy, dismounted from his horse there where the emperor customarily does so. Perceiving thereby his haughtiness, the emperor omitted many of those things which concerned his honor still more. Yet he paid attention to him and addressed him and furnished him a low seat to sit upon; he conversed often with him and entertained him at a banquet.

After Reginald had made these agreements, the force with which they were going to assist the emperor in war did not please the Antiochenes, because its ancient might had melted away from

the city, and also that a bishop / 186 / was to be sent to Antioch
from Byzantion [displeased them]; for these reasons they had come
to petition the emperor, and Baldwin interceded with the emperor
about this. Observing that it was not strongly refused, he made his
envoys throw themselves at his feet. Considering which of the two
[conditions] contributed more honor to the Romans, he [Manuel]
immediately allowed them to campaign with a lesser force (for
something demanded beyond one's strength has resulted in many
cases in subsequent transgression, and in general it suffices for a
demonstration of subjection that something very trivial be rendered
at some time); but he said a bishop was not to be received from
anywhere else than from Byzantion. Accepting this gladly, they
returned to the city.

21[A].[41] So Reginald's matters had their conclusion there;
the emperor intended to attack Toros next. The latter had at first
run off to desert places and the Tauros Mountains, and then when
Baldwin petitioned the emperor about him, he came to the Romans' camp as a pitiable suppliant. Welcoming him, the emperor
enrolled him among the Romans' subjects and so terminated the
war.

Since the emperor was about to enter the city [April 1159],
the Antiochenes probably feared lest the Romans' forces, once admitted inside, would attempt to drive them out; not knowing how
to divert the emperor's intention, they invented some false excuses
and presented them to him. These were that some rash fellows
from among their citizens had plotted that when the emperor entered the city entirely unarmed / 187 / (for it were not otherwise
fitting), they would practice some treachery against him. Comprehending the trick, however, the emperor declared that what was
pretended would not take place, and in reply to those about him he
specified how impossible this was: among other things not least
because the king was going to parade unarmed rather far from the
emperor's person, but Reginald and others [would be] around the
trappings of the [emperor's] horse and would be occupied with the

cords of the saddle, as they proceeded on foot and without any weapon. A large company of ax-bearing barbarians [Varangian guardsmen], as was customary, would escort the emperor himself.

Thus he refuted those pretenses, but when he was about to enter the city, he donned double breastplates, induced thereto by the inexhaustible strength of his body. Over these he put a garment decorated with precious stones, not inferior in weight to what was underneath, and a crown and other things customary for the emperor. I can wonder at this, that after he had celebrated a triumph in the way in which he usually did one at Byzantion, and had reached the church of the apostle Peter, he nimbly dismounted from his horse and, when he was going to remount, he leapt up with a bound, just as if he were entirely unarmed.

Then there met him the bishop of the city garbed in a priestly robe, with the whole order of priests. They held in their hands crosses, and bore the Holy Scriptures, so that the entire foreign and outland [populace] was astonished, observing in addition to these things Reginald and the nobles of Antioch running on foot around the imperial horse, / 188 / and Baldwin, a crowned man, parading a long way behind on horseback, but without insignia. After the triumph had been celebrated in this way, the emperor remained in the city for eight days, then departed. The Antiochenes exhibited so much servility to him that, while he dwelt at Reginald's palace, none of those who had disputes had the case judged by compatriots, but by Romans.

21[B]. After he had succeeded in these matters, the emperor prepared to attack Nūr-ad-Dīn. But since he [Nūr-ad-Dīn] knew of his advance, he released an Italian, the son [sic] of Saint-Gilles,[42] and the man in command of the knights in Palestine, whom the Latins call the Master of the Temple,[43] both distinguished men, and in addition many other well-born men. Also, of the common, ordinary sort, [Nūr-ad-Dīn released] upwards of six thousand, who had been taken captive by him out of the German and French army when they campaigned in Asia [the Second Cru-

sade]. Nūr-ad-Dīn did these things, but in addition he agreed to assist the emperor in his wars in Asia. Accepting him [as an ally] on
these terms, he [Manuel] gave up his purpose.

But a little later he [Manuel] proposed to break the agreement: yet he did not achieve his purpose, as will become clear
from what follows. For without Nūr-ad-Dīn's knowledge, a horde
of Saracens ambushed and wrought harm to some of the Romans
who were going foraging. Learning this, the emperor posted ambushes in a suitable spot there / 189 / and at dawn himself attacked
them, all unsuspecting.

When he had driven them back, desirous of sport, he went
out to hunt on the upper plains of Syria, something frightful to
hear of at these present times. Some men, no more than six, whose
task was to track down the beasts' lairs, went ahead of him. They
had not gone far, when four-and-twenty enemy warriors appeared
to them; they were engaged in trying to attract by trickery some of
the Romans toward their own army, which was in ambush behind
them. As soon as the huntsmen saw this, they threw themselves
into the current of a river in front of them, swam across, and came
to the emperor to report what had befallen them. The emperor was
not disturbed at this report; "Come," he said, "tell us where the
enemy are." Although the others were in great trepidation, he
allowed his horse full rein and charged at the enemy. An innumerable army of Saracens suddenly appeared watching over those
regions. Without delay, he fell upon the midst of so many armed
warriors with a great rush, and, driving them back, he did not
cease pursuing until the fleeing foe got inside the forts which had
been erected there, and the plain was filled with corpses. On this
account, after he returned to camp, he desired, as stated, to set
aside the agreement [with Nūr-ad-Dīn]. But some rumors brought
from the west, which / 190 / reported that matters were in an
uproar there, hindered him from the undertaking.

At this time Baldwin's arm was broken for the following
reason. He shared with the emperor in hunting and was a partici-

pant in the exercise. Astounded at the emperor in all other respects, he also desired to know whether he was esteemed in this activity. Being eager to equal the emperor's dashes, as he engaged in this activity in his marvelous way, he accidentally slipped along with his horse and, as stated, injured his arm; immediately binding it up, the emperor applied appropriate care, and a few days later he removed [the bandage].

In such matters he surpassed many who had been occupied in the physicians' art throughout their life. Indeed, during a shortage of trained men, I have seen him lancing veins and applying drugs to the sick. He also contributed much to the healers' science which had remained unknown to it for all time, what [drugs] are proper for anointing, what for drinking, as well as such things as can be gathered by whoever wishes from the public hospitals, which are customarily called *xenoneis* [guesthouses]. But so much for that.

The emperor then bethought himself of the road to Byzantion. To travel by the shortest route, he set out from Pamphylia and led his army through the midst of Lykaonia, albeit the sultan was strongly opposed to this. When he came near the city of Laranda [Karaman],[44] the frightened Turks departed in flight, thinking that the Romans were launching an immediate attack on Ikonion. But when nothing harmful befell them at the Romans' hands, they recovered courage, brought in quantities of supplies, / 191 / and furnished them to them. But it was impossible for the Turks entirely to restrain the hatred nurtured in them. So when the Romans reached Kotiaion [Kütahya], they attacked some of those separated from the rest of the army, and slew and captured them. The emperor then returned to Byzantion; after he had celebrated a great triumph and offered thanks to God for his victories, he returned to the palace.[45]

22. A little later [late 1159], being minded to take vengeance on the Turks for their drunken folly towards him, he assembled an army on the plains of Kypsella [Ipsala, in Thrace].

Meanwhile, writing to those who governed the Romans' provinces in Asia, he ordered them to attack Turkish territory at a specified time, one from one side, one from another. He did this so that the Turks should be incapable of coming to one another's aid: since this actually occurred, it wrought great harm to the Turks' land. When the season had reached the winter solstice, the emperor crossed the Hellespontine ferry to Asia and reached Dorylaion on its two rivers, one called Bathys [Muttalip Dere or Sarisu] by the natives, the other, Thybris [or Tembris, modern Porsuk Çay]; after he had overrun the whole surrounding country, he drove off a horde of men and a quantity of various beasts. Learning of their losses, the Turks commenced to appear in bands and companies. The emperor dispatched one force of Romans to pillage what lay before them, but he himself, ascending the heights of that region with a few of his followers, / 192 / ordered them to play loudly the imperial trumpets, contriving thereby to impart fear to the foe, who would imagine that the emperor commanded that battle.

As he had frequently inflicted great slaughter on those barbarians, whenever he appeared unexpectedly to them, he seemed veritably a thunderbolt to them, and thousands, they say, should it be so, even tens of thousands, armed and armored men, shamelessly fled. When they reached my ears, these things seemed unbelievable, just as even the deeds of [Nicephorus II] Phokas and [John I] Tzimiskes, who were not very ancient emperors, [are] not [credible], or if there are some others who had renown for valor comparable to them. For it is beyond belief that entire thousands should be defeated by one man and numerous fully armored men overcome by a single lance. Therefore, whenever I dwelt at the imperial court and heard such deeds of the emperor lauded, I turned from the assembly, dizzied. For my character is naturally unsuited to flattery, nor would I willingly allow the slightest expression to pass except truly and unfetteredly. Such things I used to leave to be spun out by those continually at home in the palace and those in high offices, until the facts of the matter came to my attention, as I was thus by chance encompassed amidst the foe and observed from close at hand that emperor resisting entire Turkish regiments. But the history will describe this at the right moment: / 193 / at present let us keep to what lies before us.

The emperor was on the heights of that region, while the Romans' army advanced to the interior and unexpectedly encountered Turkish forces. As the struggle then became hand-to-hand, and since the Roman force commenced to be worsted, the emperor learned of it and raced to them at full speed, without donning a breastplate or defending his body with anything else except a shield. Swiftly thrusting himself into the foe's midst, he displayed wondrous deeds of might, striking continuously with his sword at whoever came near; when they commenced to flee, without losing time he pursued them, once a lance had been furnished him. Not turning back, they fled afar, unable to perceive that so numerous an army was pursued by a single man. For fear which beset them absolutely darkened their eyes. When they recognized their situation, mocking at one another for cowardice, they suddenly turned about and stood facing him. Reining in their passions out of fear, they did not rashly pour themselves down upon him; while they emptied whole quivers at him, he turned his shield from one side to the other, thrust aside the shots, and preserved his body from the arrows.

Among the Turks there was one courageous and vigorous individual. When he observed that out of all those not one opposed the emperor in combat, boiling with rage, he seized a sword from the hands of one of his fellows and rushed to smite him. But grasping him by the hair, the emperor / 194 / took him captive along with three other nobles. At this, unable to oppose him, the rest departed in flight. With the said men [prisoners], the emperor returned to the army; since he perceived that winter was setting in very fiercely, he returned to Byzantion.[46]

23. Just at that time [early 1160] he was at the townlet in Bithynia where he had previously settled the captive Romans from

Philomilion (Pylai was its name),[47] and he dealt there with envoys who came from the sultan. When he recognized that they had nothing valid to declare, he dismissed them, threatening that, unless they acted in accordance with his will, the Romans' cavalry would shortly overrun their land and pillage everything even worse than now. Having passed some time at Augouste, then setting out from there (at this time a village called Rhitzion by the natives entertained him as he crossed to the farther side [of the Astakenos Gulf]), he went to the opposite shore. From there he advanced by the road through the coastal cities, and reached Philadelphia; thence, having made preparations, he attacked Turkish territory.[48]

The [Turkish] ambassadors, going through the plains of Dorylaion, were therefore wholly ignorant of the emperor's assault on them, and were confident that he was staying in Byzantion's environs. So when the Romans' invasion was everywhere bruited [winter 1160–61], the Turks at first deemed the matter absolutely incredible, but when they heard of it from many eyewitnesses, they set their army in motion / 195 / and hastened to meet it. For the barbarian suffers in no respect so much as in loss of money and goods. Deeming that the Turks still knew nothing of what he did, the emperor dispatched the rest of the Romans' army onwards to ravage, while he came behind with a few men. The Romans heard that the Turks were on the move in force, and they were very likely disturbed, especially since the emperor was not with them; but as he then rejoined them, since he had learned of the Turks' advance, they regained courage and marched more eagerly. As it was late in the day, they dismounted from their horses, gave the beasts their usual fodder, and rested for a while; then setting out when night had already commenced, they took the road by lamplight.

The business of cressets is as follows. On a cube [i.e., base plate] made of iron they fit uprights, separately, which gradually diminish from broad to pointed; on the center of the plate they fix another iron one [upright: a spike], not like the rest, but at first thick, then quickly becoming pointed. Having bound them [the uprights] around with some bands, they finish them like a lamp-stand and fasten them on spear points. Then, dividing some linen cloth lengthwise, they soak it in pork [49] fat, and, carefully twisting them, they put them each on the sharply pointed iron [spikes]; when they have been lighted, / 196 / they cause a great amount of light to descend from them, to simulate artificial daylight for the troops. Let this much be said about cressets.

Since driving snow was coming down and the roads had to-tally disappeared, the Romans' army, which had largely wandered out of the way on which it was directed, would likely have struck into perilous and dangerous regions, had not the emperor, sensing the mistake, seized a torch, roved hither and thither, recognized the route, and guided the army to the proper road. Reaching a village called by the natives Sarapata Mylonos,[50] it [the army] commenced to forage. He who controlled the emirate of that region (Suleimān was his name),[51] learning of the report which was everywhere current, still hesitated to trust what was said. So he dispatched his nephew Poupakes [52] who had often come in sight of the emperor, and ordered him to go as close as possible to the Romans' army, to spy out the emperor. Recognizing the em-peror at once, Poupakes dismounted from his horse and addressed him in servile fashion. Learning who he was and by whom he had been sent, he [Manuel] said, "Report this to Suleimān. 'You who desire to learn who is now pillaging the Turks' land, act as if, when fire sets alight your house, you make no account of how you might overcome it, but carefully investigate whence it had its ori-gin / 197 / and by whom it was started. Do not desire to conceal the vileness of your cowardice by pretended ignorance as if under a cloak. For, when it is illogical, the pretence of ignorance does not exonerate the user from blame. The science of generalship knows one excellent thing: that he who braves danger for his country sways matters in balance. Should one not grasp this, he loses everything. Otherwise your pretext has no place. Well, you have recognized, you have met him who whips the Turks: should you desire to oppose him, there is no excuse [not to do so].' ''

So saying, he sent him back. After he had pillaged and given over to destruction what lay before him, he took the road back, [but] something incredible happened first. For allegedly that army was no more than sixty fighting men, when the affairs of the Romans, which were in great peril, were unexpectedly rescued. Gathering in great numbers from that moment, the Turks held advantageous parts of the terrain, and when the Romans came there, a stiff fight broke out. Shooting from the heights, the Turks galled the Romans, who, being continually and forcibly squeezed together, were entirely unmindful of their valor, since the nature of the place was not at all suited to their passage. Then peril impended over the emperor himself, for some of those guarding him commenced to melt away. Although he was in such a strait, he did not abandon his accustomed / 198 / courage; he sent away his relative-in-law John,[53] often aforementioned, who approached and was eager to supply a shield to him (for he was then unarmed), saying it was impossible that one shield could adequately protect two bodies. The Romans passed through that region in thus great difficulty, and when they came to broader spaces, which allowed the horses' excellence and the men's strength to be tested, raising a war cry they headed straight for the enemy's spears. Driving them back, they slew many and returned bringing all the spoil which they had driven off. Then while many had acted bravely, the emperor excelled everyone. None engaged the foe before him, and none was author of so many valiant deeds. After this success, the emperor returned to Byzantion.

24. At what had befallen, the Turks were aggrieved and determined to injure the Romans in turn; biding their time, they seized Phileta,[54] an eastern city. Also, unexpectedly attacking Laodikeia in Lesser Phrygia, they seriously damaged it, carrying off at sword's point many of the inhabitants, from youth upwards, whom they had made captive, a great and innumerable multitude.

When he heard this, the emperor was vexed and grieved; were it possible, he wished to cross to Asia forthwith and commence a campaign on Ikonion. But since he knew this required a time / 199 / appropriate for such deeds and greater preparation for war than before, he deferred it.

Being minded to gather forces from every direction, he dispatched John Kontostephanos to Palestine [early 1160] to meet king Baldwin and lead back from there the men whom he had agreed by their alliance to furnish on request to the emperor, as well as a mercenary corps. He ordered Reginald prince of Antioch to start out as swiftly as possible with the troops around him, as well as the then leaders of the Armenians, Toros and Tigranes, and the Cilician Chrysaphios and those whom people call Kogh Vasilii,[55] who are commanders of martial forces, but who long since came over to the emperor as voluntary subjects. From the east he gathered thus great a band, and from the west he drew Ligurian [i.e., Lombard] knights and summoned the grand župan of Serbia with the troops under him, and he hired many Scyths from those tribes settled around Tauros [i.e., Tauroscyths or Russians]. Nor did he cease making preparation for war with these measures, but aware that the landfall for the Latin races bound for Palestine was at the island of Rhodes, he recruited a mercenary band of knights from there. For provision-supply and other service, he ordered an unutterable quantity of oxen with their carts to be driven from the villages in Thrace.[56]

So he had made these preparations, while in order to render the sultan hostile to his compatriots and relatives, he wrote to his brother Shāhan-Shāh, / 200 / who then governed Gangra and Galatian Ankyra [Ankara], and to his son-in-law Yaghi-Basan, who ruled both Kaisareia [Kayseri] and Amaseia [Amasya] and other outstanding cities which are situated in the Cappadocians' land. After he had rendered them suspect to the sultan, he was in a short time ready for war. The sultan learned of this, and since he was incapable of opposing either of those who had been roused against him by the emperor, he yielded his claim to many cities, especially ones recently acquired by him with great effort, in favor of those who lived near his own land. He wrote to the emperor and requested pardon. Should he succeed in this, he promised to restore the Roman captives, wherever they were concealed in his realm: the search would be his business.

While these things were under examination, something as follows befell. As he set out from Palestine [autumn 1161] with the knights, John [Kontostephanos] encountered a Turkish army which numbered upwards of twenty-two thousand fighting men. Stricken by surprise, he at first went with his followers quickly to a hill located nearby and took a stand; thereafter, cheered on by the whole army, he charged at them, and since the Romans engaged the foe with intense pressure, the Turks' retreat commenced. Many of them fell as they fled, many were taken by the Romans' soldiers, and the cavalry trampled many under foot. Then numerous other persons achieved deeds worthy of account and of their valor, but / 201 / in that conflict the demonstration of excellence rested with the general, John. After this success, John returned to the emperor with tokens of victory.

When the sultan heard this, pricked by goads of regret, he cursed himself for their untimely rashness, not so much disturbed by what had befallen, but that he had still further invited the emperor's advance against himself and thereby had behaved so that they [the Byzantines] threatened those who were not yet ready. Therefore he quickly supplemented his previous offers with other, greater ones. He promised to give the Romans annually an allied force on request, and agreed that no Turk would set foot on their land with his permission; should anyone from another [Turkish] principality trouble the Romans' territory, he would straightway wage war upon him, and he would in every way hinder any treachery from whatsoever source it arose. He would without hesitation do everything commanded by the emperor, and should one of the cities subject to the emperor have previously fallen under Turkish sway, he agreed to restore it to the Romans. Persuaded by these things, the emperor bound him with mighty oaths; ending hostility, he returned home.

Learning that the Cumans had crossed the Danube to ravage the Romans' land, he departed from the road which led to Byzantion, and marched to the crossing near the city of Abydos, where a small coastal town is situated in Thrace which, I think, takes its name from Kallias, general of the Athenians.[57] Crossing here, he hastened against the Cumans. / 202 / He had not yet attained the Danube, however, when they, hearing of the Romans' advance, quickly packed up and departed.

Book V

1. So things turned out there. Since there was nothing to be seen in any direction which threatened the Romans' realm, the emperor went to one of the villages near Byzantion for relaxation: its name was Longoi. While he was staying there, the last day of her life arrived for the empress [Bertha-]Irene, a woman who, as was previously stated by me, greatly exceeded others at that time in prudence, propriety, and mercy towards those in need.[1] She had been the mother of two daughters, the elder of whom [Maria Comnena, the Porphyrogenita] survived and dwelt with her father; the other, after she had completed the fourth year of age, reached the end of her life a little later.

   While, still struggling against her illness, the child yet lived, however, affairs in the west summoned him, and the emperor left behind matters of his own household and marched to deal with them. For at that time a rumor was current that Frederick, king of the Germans, was setting his whole nation in motion to attack the Romans' land. On this account, and because the Hungrarians' king Géza had ended his life,[2] he went to Sardika. He made a sufficient delay there, as he put a high value / 203 / on the overlordship of Hungary. For what was reported about the Germans was not yet genuine. Let us now state why the emperor desired to lay claim to Hungary. Géza had two brothers, László and Stephen [István]; having quarreled with him, I know not why, they became extremely hateful to him. After a lengthy exile, one one place, the other another, they both finally approached the emperor and came into his hands. Stephen married the emperor's niece, Maria, daughter of Isaac the sebastokrator, who as stated was extremely beautiful; the other remained unwed. Then when Géza died the rule of justice summoned one of the brothers to power (for it is law among the Hungarians that the crown passes always to the survivors of brothers), and the emperor was eager to restore them to their ancestral land. For, overlooking national custom, Géza had passed the royal office to his son. The Hungarians, partly in awe of this law, partly alarmed at the emperor's approach, deprived Géza's son Stephen [István III] of office and yielded it to László [II], one of the brothers. To Stephen, I mean the elder one, they gave the rank of *urum:* among the Hungarians, this name means he who will succeed to the royal authority.[3]

2. So regarding those two brothers, matters had a conclusion. The emperor proceeded to Philippopolis, a Macedonian city, / 204 / to settle matters in Serbia. For Primislav, who then ruled the country, as was elsewhere previously narrated by me, meditated revolt and possessed a spirit of independence; on this account, after he had come close to being dispossessed of power by the emperor, he found mercy again in his sight and remained in the same [office].[4] Then, making no account of agreement or oaths, he again engaged in rebellion. The emperor, who thereby fully comprehended the man, removed him from office and established his brother Beluš in it. Feeling pity for his fate, he exiled Primislav, lest he again work harm, but presented him with a region very fertile and good for the pasture of animals. While Beluš was for a short while resplendent in office, he laid aside the monarchical state, abandoned his fatherland, and went to Hungary. After he had lived there for a long time he departed from mankind. The emperor caused to be summoned the last of the brothers, who was called Desa and ruled the region of Dendra, a prosperous and populous one near Naissos.[5] After he [Manuel] had received pledges

from him that for the whole period of his life he [Desa] would preserve pure the condition of obedience to him, and in addition that he would entirely abandon to the Romans Dendra, which as stated was fruitful, he [Manuel] named him grand župan.

3. About this time [1162], also, the sultan Kilidj Arslan [II] [6] voluntarily came to Byzantion to petition the emperor regarding matters beneficial to him, / 205 / something tremendous and wonderfully extraordinary, such as I know never happened to the Romans before. Of the very magnificent [emperors], who is not outdone, that a man who rules so much land and lords it over so many tribes should appear at the emperor of the Romans' court in the guise of a servant? To describe the ceremonies for those who wish to hear, a splendid dais was reared, and a throne was placed on it, raised very high off the ground, a spectacle worthy of note. The whole was made of gold, but a great quantity of ruby and sapphire stones were applied on all parts of it, nor could one count the pearls. A sufficient number of them surrounded each of the jewels, which were fastened on at slight intervals: they were perfectly englobed, and gleamed whiter than snow. The throne abounded in such brilliances. The highest part, which extended above his head, excelled the splendor of the rest by as much as the head surpasses the [body's] other adjacent members. On it the emperor sat, filling the whole with the magnitude of his well-proportioned body. A purple robe, a wonderful thing, enveloped him. From top to bottom it was afire with rubies and illuminated with pearls, not indeed in disorder, but a marvelous artist's skill had embroidered it, since art depicted a genuine-looking meadow on the robe. From his neck to his chest there hung on golden cords a jewel outstanding in size and color, / 206 / ruddy as a rose, but in shape particularly like an apple. I deem it excessive to write about the adornment on his head. On each side of the throne, according to custom, stood the official body, since family and rank regulate the standing-place of each. The emperor's [official reception] was in this order.

When Kilidj Arslan reached their midst, he was full of astonishment. Although the emperor urged him to be seated, he at first very firmly declined, but because he saw the emperor still pressed him, he sat down on a low stool, very humble alongside the lofty throne. After he had said and heard what was appropriate, he departed to the residence appointed for him in the palace.

Glorying in the magnitude of his successes, the emperor made preparation for a triumphal procession from the citadel itself to the famed church of Hagia Sophia, so as to march in procession with him; yet he did not accomplish what he had intended. For [the patriarch] Loukas [7] who was then in charge of ecclesiastical matters was opposed to the action, saying that impious men must not pass by consecrated furnishings and priestly adornments. Then something else occurred to prevent the matter. When it was late at night, an immense upheaval suddenly shook the earth. The Byzantines, deeming that Loukas' counsels had been transgressed, declared that the undertaking was contrary to God's will. For men naturally pay attention to matters close at hand, without inquiring about anything more remote. / 207 / The conclusion of the affair, however, clearly produced an explanation of what had happened. For when, after many years had passed, Kilidj Arslan became careless of his engagements toward the emperor, he caused the Romans to attack the Turks in full force. By some chance the army fell into difficult terrain, lost many of the aristocracy, and came near a great disaster, save that in warfare the emperor was there seen to surpass the bounds of human excellence. [8] But, as I have already said, these things will be related later by me.

Conducting him to the palace south [sic] of the city, the emperor received him with magnificent banquets and entertained him in entire amity. [9] Then he charmed him with horseraces, and according to custom set alight some boats and skiffs with liquid fire, and absolutely gorged the man with spectacles in the hippodrome, whereby the grandeur of cities is particularly likely to appear. After he had passed sufficient time in Byzantion and had confirmed his prior agreements with additional oaths, he returned to his own land. The terms of the agreement went thus: throughout his life to be hostile to those who cherished enmity against the emperor, but to be friendly to those who, on the contrary, were settled in his favor. Of the cities which he had won, he would give the greater and more notable to the emperor. It was not allowed for him to make peace with any of the enemy unless the emperor directed. He would fight as ally with the Romans on request, and come with his entire force whether the conflict was an eastern or a western one. Nor would he allow those who lay beneath his authority, but / 208 / who are clever at living by thefts and customarily are called Turkomans, to do any harm whatsoever to the Romans' land, unpunished. He agreed to these things, and those of the grandees who attended him [pledged] that, should he be unmindful of them, with all their strength they would hinder the attempt.

This was achieved in Byzantion, but a rumor [thereof] had previously crossed from Europe to Asia. The tribal leaders there, deeming that it would not be to their advantage if the emperor dealt with the sultan, sent envoys and begged to be reconciled with the sultan. He [Manuel] heard them with friendship, but seemingly entrusting everything to the sultan's choice, he sent them to him, who, as was stated, was staying in the palace. As soon as they came before him for discussion, they prevailed on him to abandon his hostility to them and persuaded him to be suitor on their behalf to the emperor. Accepting the petitioner, he [Manuel] brought them too into the party of his friends, and from then on peace was settled on the Romans' realm.

4. Since the empress [Bertha-]Irene had departed this life, while the emperor was not yet the father of a male child, he then considered a second marriage. There was a certain girl in Tripoli in Phoenicia [Lebanon], a Latin by birth but outstanding in beauty. So, to seek her, he sent [1160] the sebastos John Kontostephanos and an Italian, Theophylact, whom men title Exoubitos.[10] / 209 /

The men saw the girl and admired her beauty; since nothing whatsoever appeared to impede them, without delay they embarked on
the trireme. Just as they were about to set forth, however, severe
illnesses beset the girl, and she was in serious danger. Therefore,
continually postponing their departure until the morrow, they
passed their time in idleness. Should she get free of the pains a
little and expect to depart, yet as if by some providence the suffering would commence to return; when she lay down, her body
shuddered and shook extremely, fevers seized upon her, and mor-
tification and consumption ensued. The radiance of her appearance, which previously gleamed beautifully, was shortly altered
and darkened. Seeing her, one was filled with tears at such a
meadow withered untimely. Thus the maiden was in a bad state
while staying at home; should she ever embark on the ship and
depart a little from Tripoli, a double flood assailed her there. So
Tripoli again entertained the ship, but there she caught still greater
diseases which did not at all abandon her. As this happened repeatedly, it led Kontostephanos to endless reconsiderations. So in all
likelihood grieving and turning over ideas one after the other, he
finally entered one of the churches there and inquired whether it
was proper for the girl to be betrothed to the emperor. The holy or-
acle answered him, "The wedding is ready, but those invited were
not / 210 / worthy" [11] to enter. When he heard this and comprehended the meaning, since a rumor had already crushed them that
the girl was not born of lawful wedlock, something especially
capable [of causing] shame, he gave over the enterprise and set out
for Byzantion.[12]

Raymond prince of Antioch had daughters who were at that
time outstanding in beauty. To view them, the emperor sent Basil,
by surname Kamateros, who was then *akolouthos* [commander of
the Varangians]. When he swiftly reached Antioch, he saw that
both were beautiful, but Marie appeared to him the more beautiful.
That envoy's inquiry proved correct. Our era, the Byzantines used
to say, has never yet been acquainted with such beauty. But this

[comes] later. Since the decision favored Marie, the emperor learned of it and sent members of the aristocracy to Antioch to betroth the girl to him, to wit, Alexius [Comnenus], daughter's son of the emperor Alexius [I], who was then grand *doux*, and Nicephorus Bryennios, who was the emperor's relative-in-law through his niece, and had become a sebastos. Among them also was Andronicus Kamateros, who then held the office of eparch,[13] and who, being also a relative of the emperor, had been deemed worthy of being a sebastos. They saw and wondered at her, embarked her on a trireme, and magnificently escorted her to Byzantion.

On the twenty-fifth of the month Apellaios, which / 211 / people who speak Latin call December [1161], after she had been splendidly conducted into the renowned church of Hagia Sophia, he wedded her there, with Loukas who then held the church of Constantinople, Sophronios of Alexandria, and Athanasios of Theoupolis [Antioch] laying hands on them, as is customary for Christians; then, proclaiming her Augusta, he returned to the palace. He feasted those in high office with magnificent banquets, and set dinners for the people in all the byways of the city. On the next day he had the patriarchs to dine with him, and after he had welcomed each one with immense amounts of gold, he sent them away; indeed, before everything else he had presented the church with a hundred-weight of gold. A little later he entertained the people with horse races, and desired to neglect nothing which conduced to mirth.[14]

5. This was done in Byzantion. But after László [of Hungary] died [14 January 1162], Stephen [his brother] became possessed of power [as István IV], and seemed grievous and was excessively oppressive to the principal personages. Therefore the Hungarians reviled him greatly and were evidently on the verge of pulling him down from his authority. Troubled at this, Stephen again besought the emperor. Then setting forth, when the season

was at the equinox [spring 1162], he [Manuel] hastened to Philippopolis, and himself remained there with the greatest part of the
Romans' army; but entrusting a division of the army to his nephew,
Alexius Kontostephanos, he sent it to Hungary. At this time, however, Stephen / 212 / thought that he was reconciled with the Hungarians and did not require it, so the Romans' army then set out
for home. But in the meanwhile the Hungarians again rose up
against Stephen; they accused him of many things, and in particular asserted that under him the Hungarians' state had been utterly
ruined. Therefore the emperor again collected an army, but Stephen who had from the outset taken heed of the peril came as a
fugitive to one of the cities near the Danube which were from a
long time back subject to the emperor; proceeding on to Sardika,
he met the emperor there. Strongly moved at what had happened
and pitying the man for his fate, he [Manuel] presented him with
money and with sufficient forces conducted him back to his ancestral office. The aforementioned Alexius Kontostephanos commanded these troops, and the emperor marched a little behind.

When he reached Naissos, a plan came to him as he
camped there, to settle in passing affairs in Serbia. For that place
is on the road to both Hungary and Serbia, and one must enter either one from there. Desa, who then ruled Serbia by the emperor's
gift, once he was in charge of the land, forgot the agreement and
again laid claim to the region of Dendra. Rebelling against the
Romans' authority, he wrote to the Germans, intending to unite to
himself a bride from there, and did everything which was in every
way contrary to the Romans' desire. Then when the emperor summoned him to join him in the campaign against the Hungarians,
/ 213 / he appeared wayward, stubborn, and buoyed up by very
great hopes; he continually promised his arrival for the future. So,
when he reached Naissos, where, of two roads, one leads to Serbia, the other to the Danube and Hungary, the emperor pitched
camp midway between them; perceiving the peril which hung over

him, Desa gathered his attendant troops and arrived in the Romans' camp. The emperor treated him favorably and honored him
suitably.

No vice, however, seems more shameful than an unbridled
tongue. For once Desa perceived that no harm resulted from his
previous folly, he elevated his purpose and resolved to do greater
harm to the Romans than before; yet he kept the plot secret. Thus
in the vilest of men the supposition of goodness usually becomes
the working material of very great crimes. For a little later, envoys
came to the emperor from the Hungarians' nation; but by some
chance he [Desa] met them, and on being asked by them as usual
how his affairs were, he answered unreservedly that they went
well and were deserving of favor toward himself from their king,
whom he openly called "lord." Learning this, the emperor decided not to hesitate, and summoned him to trial; when he was
convicted, since his accusers and accomplices stood face to face
and displayed the man's faithlessness, he [Manuel] then kept him
securely, without dishonor. Circumscribing his tent with a ditch,
/ 214 / he held him by regulation within palings, so that from him
the place is named "Desa's Camp" (for thus the multitude
vulgarly call the trench); dispatching him to Byzantion a little
later, he made him prisoner in the palace.[15]

This happened there. The emperor, dealing with the envoys
who had arrived from the Hungarians, saw that they promised
nothing genuine, and ordered them to depart at once from the
Roman camp and journey back the way they had come. So they
left; but when he reached the city of Belgrade, he camped there.
[It is] one which, as stated, the Romans' army had constructed
after they had torn down Zeugminon, while they had many of the
Hungarians as participants in their labors. It was indeed a plaything of fortune, which mocks continually at human affairs; one
might laugh at those who formerly demolished the buildings,
seeing colonists again. From such things I think the name of fortune is very commonly used among men. As they are unable to

comprehend the reasons for acts of Providence, on account of what seems to them to be correct, they attribute catastrophes to fortune. Let each think and speak as he pleases about this, but let the narrative cleave to its earlier matter.

When the emperor came there [Belgrade] and realized that it was then impossible for Stephen [István IV] to rule the Hungarians' land (for already they had hastily installed Stephen son of Géza [István III] again), he turned to something else. As stated, he desired with all his might to lay claim to Hungary, which is situated in the midst of the western nations. He therefore / 215 / intended to unite in marriage Béla, who was Géza's son after Stephen, to his own daughter Maria. He sent to Hungary George, a Palaiologos by birth, who then commanded the imperial foreign guard and who had risen to the rank of the sebastoi, and ordered him to investigate regarding the marriage tie; he himself took the road to Byzantion again. After they had discussed matters with Palaiologos, the Hungarians quickly handed over Béla to him and gladly assigned him [Béla] the territory which his father, while still alive, had apportioned to him. Taking him along, together with the said agreement, Palaiologos arrived in Byzantion. The emperor viewed favorably matters relating to the marriage connection, and the youth was then renamed Alexius and hailed as "despotes" [i.e., "master"].[16]

6. So Béla's arrival in Byzantion had this commencement. Supposing everything was going well in the west, the emperor next paid attention to Asia; after he had been stirred up by what happened to it, he was distracted from it by western affairs. For Nūr-ad-Dīn, who ruled Aleppo and Damascus, both outstanding cities in Syria, since fortune had smiled favorably on him, and governed many other cities which drink the waters of Euphrates, also acquired many regions not to be despised. He came to grips with numerous princes there: some he held captive, among whom was Joscelin the ruler of Edessa,[17] others he had slain in battle, to wit Raymond of Poitou, of whom we have given an adequate account

in the foregoing / 216 / narrative, a man like unto those legendary Herakleis in strength and might, and Baldwin who had then ruled Marash. Continuing onward, he opposed in battle the *doux* of Cilicia, Constantine whom they surname Kalamanos the Younger,[18] noble in visage and active in martial affairs. But at first he was severely defeated by the youth and fell into irremediable disasters, then by chance he captured him and Reginald prince of Antioch, and among them also was the ruler of Tripoli in Phoenicia. Constantine, when he was winning the battle, was not to be restrained, but borne along by foolish rashness and unskillfully engaging in pursuit, he himself was taken and the affairs of the Romans collapsed [August 1164].[19] Nūr-ad-Dīn had also defeated Ṭoros in battle and was buoyed up by hopes of seizing Antioch immediately. Therefore the emperor was at first grieved at what had occurred and intended to cross to Asia; seizing the moment he was then about to hasten thither with all his force. But affairs of the west again prevented him.

For the new king of the Hungarians [István III] again usurped Béla's heritage and then openly broke the treaty; also, Stephen [István IV], whom the Hungarians had previously expelled from office, crept back to Hungary through Anchialos and intended to reclaim power [1163]. He undertook the affair secretly, rashly rather than cautiously. As he was going around he won over some of the Hungarians; / 217 / when he learned this, Stephen [III] rushed at him with his whole army. Therefore the emperor dispatched to Cilicia an army sufficient to defend it; he himself marched back to the Danube, crossed the Sava, and stationed his army opposite Titelion [Titel, on the Tisa],[20] intending to recover his ancestral heritage for Béla and to rescue Stephen [IV] from difficulties before him. Already his forces were slipping away and he was really in a tight spot, since at every opportunity the Hungarians with him were going over to the king [István III]. Sending Andronicus son of Kontostephanos, who a little later was entitled grand *doux*, with an army, he rescued Stephen from peril.

Setting out from Titelion with his whole force, he advanced further. For the Stephen [III] who had usurped power, since he was unable to engage the emperor with equal force, at first marched with his attendant troops to someplace in the remotest part of Hungary; then, after he had assembled allied forces, he hastened to oppose the Romans. Reaching a certain place called Petrikon [Petrovaradin?], the emperor encamped there; this place is the outermost limit of the approach to inner Hungary. After he reached there, he wrote thus to Stephen [III]: "We have come, my boy, not to wage war on the Hungarians but to recover his land for Béla, your brother, not something which we have torn away by our might, but which you and your father long before granted. Also to rescue from peril your uncle Stephen, who is related by marriage to our majesty. / 218 / If it is according to your will that Béla should be our son-in-law, something which was previously agreed by you, why do you quickly abandon our friendship by failing to render him the land? If you oppose the marriage, and something else seems right to you in regard to it, know that we abstain from constraining you further."

7. The emperor wrote this. The other, as stated, assembled an allied force of Germans and of Scyths settled at Tauros [Tauroscyths or Russians], and he had associated the Czechs' nation with himself since their ruler had come to him with his whole army. He it was who had campaigned along with Conrad, formerly king of the Germans, when as was narrated by me he set out for Asia, and on this account he had become king under him.

Yet both were deceived, the one who granted the title, the other who gave thanks. For the title of empire disappeared in Rome a long time back, since the attributes of power passed, after Augustus whom, alluding to the youthful age at which he assumed office, they call Augustulus, to Odovakar and then to Theodoric ruler of the Goths, who were both tyrants [i.e., usurpers]. For as long as he lived Theodoric called himself king and not emperor, as Procopius narrates. From the time of Theodoric and a little earlier,

until now, Rome existed in a state of revolt, although repeatedly
recovered for the Romans by Belisarius and Narses, generals of the
Romans in the period of Justinian; / 219 / it was again rendered no
less subservient to barbarian tyrants, who were entitled kings in
emulation of Theodoric the first king and tyrant. As they have no
claim on the lofty status of the empire, whence do they propose for
themselves such offices [kingship], which as I have already said
descend from the empire's majesty like distinctions? [21]

This alone is not enough for them, but, although it is not
fitting, they usurp the highest peak of authority and confer the imperial dignity on themselves. This piece of drunken folly requires
explanation. Now they rashly declare that the empire in Byzantion
is different from that in Rome. As I consider this, it has repeatedly
caused me to weep. The rule of Rome has, like a piece of property, been sold to barbarians and really servile men. Therefore it
has no right to a bishop nor, much more, to a ruler. For the one
who ascends to the greatness of empire runs on foot in a fashion
unworthy of himself alongside the mounted bishop and is like his
groom.[22] But the other titles him *imperator,* considering him on
the same plane with the emperor [the Byzantine *basileus*].

[To the Pope:] How, noble sir, and whence did it occur to
you to treat the Romans' emperors as grooms? But you know not
wherefrom, and you abuse the [title of] bishop, while he [the western emperor] falsifies [that of] emperor. For if you do not agree
that the throne of the empire in Byzantion is the throne of Rome,
whence did you become possessed of the rank of pope? / 220 /
There is [only] one Constantine, the first Christian among the emperors, to whom this [grant of title] seemed proper. How could
you welcome part of it favorably, the [papal] throne, I mean, and
the excess of dignity, but reject the rest [acceptance of imperial
supremacy]? Either acquiesce in both or reject the other also.

But, he says, I can designate emperors. Yes, as regards
laying on of hands, as regards consecrating: these are spiritual
matters. But no, as regards granting empires and innovating in

such things. Since if it was in your power to transfer empires, why did you yourself not change the one in Rome? But when someone else enacted something, he who then possessed the church amongst you unwillingly used to respect his decrees.[23] You, however, are caught in your own snare and somehow are covertly doing contrary things. Those whom, not long ago, while you were behaving properly toward the emperor, you did not receive when they requested it, since it was impossible, but enrolled among [your] grooms, now, I know not how, you are accepting as emperors; you deem that he by whom and through whom and from whom you claim the [papal] throne is not possibly identical with the barbarian, the tyrant, the slave. But, he says, I am compelled, I am under constraint. Your excuse has no validity: previously and not long ago you conceded these things to emperor Manuel. Should you deny it, the documents which received your signature at the bottom proclaim it. But really the matter is a joke, a shabby and servile trick, and in the fashion of a timeserver you adapt to changes of fortune.[24] But we have protracted this more than is suited to historical narratives; let the tale return to its former matter.

/ 221 / 8. After he had thus made preparation, Stephen [III] hastened against the Romans [1164]. As the emperor was in the Hungarians' territory, the men there came forth in a crowd to welcome him, both those enrolled among the priests, who were wrapped in woolen mantles and held the Holy Scriptures in their hands, and those who were of the common, ordinary people. They sang most tunefully a hymn elegantly composed by some among us. It went thus: "O Lord, Who aided humble David," and so forth. Passing by those regions, he hastened to cross the Danube, and going by the island there [25] he intended to march to the interior.

Then, while the Roman [force] was crossing, allegedly one of the boats, filled to the brim with cargo and arms and as many men as possible, which was not far from the bank, canted to one

side, so that water poured into it. The rest of the Romans' army,
those who had embarked on ships and were borne on the surface of
the river and those who still stood on dry land, some gripped by
fear of danger, others by negligence, ignored the affair. The ship
lacked little of going to the bottom with all its men, save that the
emperor leaped into the water and advanced as far as possible on
foot. While the current swirled down with great violence and had
formed some mud there which was difficult to get out of, he put
his shoulders under the boat and forestalled the moment of danger,
/ 222 / giving an opportunity for others to come to its aid.
Ashamed at his zeal, they went to assist those in peril and deliv-
ered them from danger. Thereby the emperor had a great reputa-
tion for humanity.

Then, after he had crossed the Danube somewhat higher
up, he hastened to a city, Pagatzion [Bács or Bač] by name—this
city is the metropolis of the people in Sirmion, and there the
bishop of the people makes his dwelling—an innumerable crowd
of inhabitants came out to serve as his guard there.[26] So he
camped there, but learning on the next day that Stephen [III] was
then approaching, he immediately prepared for battle. Summoning
one of the Romans who knew the Czechs' language, he ordered
him to disguise himself and creep into the enemy's camp; when he
came in sight of the Czechs' king, he should address him as follows: "Whither do you journey? What expedition do you make
with the army under you? Or do you not know that you are daring
to lift your hands against the great emperor? It is perilous for one
to oppose him in battle for valid reasons, not to mention one who
risks being despised by these Hungarians, who gave and then took
away Béla's heritage, because they treat their own oaths as jokes.
One who deals with a private individual and, should it happen
thus, scorns his agreement does not go unpunished by the law;
shall the Hungarians, who have acted against their treaties with
such an emperor, remain inviolable? Far from it. Then / 223 / does
the emperor wage war justly? The result of battle goes always ac-

cording to justice. Consider this. You have come as a slave eager to fight against a master, and as a slave who bears the yoke without compulsion (otherwise it would have some reason: naturally such a thing is hateful to masters), indeed as a voluntary subject (your allegiance [*lizion*] signifies this),[27] if what you formerly did in Byzantion, when you set out for Asia with Conrad, has not escaped your memory. As the issue of the affair depends on your decision, choose what will be beneficial to yourself and all the Czechs. Regret, coming too late, usually benefits very little someone who practices it."

He spoke thus; Vladislav [II] (this name was applied to him) [28] answered thus. "We do not come here to wage war on the great emperor, noble sir (we would not be thus unmindful of our agreements toward him), but to defend this Stephen who has been unjustly injured by his paternal uncle, who first drove him from his ancestral land and heritage, then when right had restored him, the other again attacked him and intended to regain by force the office which he had lost by ruling badly. For these reasons I have come to beseech the emperor and to petition that he rather protect an orphan boy. But if anything has been done to injure that same empire by this younger Stephen (for I learn that none of the land belonging to Béla himself / 224 / has been seized), with ourselves as mediators he would immediately yield the land and will in every way render satisfaction for the mistake." So saying, he sent the man back.

Returning to the Romans' camp, he communicated the reply to the emperor. He [Manuel] heard the words without displeasure, yet he was unable to believe them entirely. He felt anxious lest they were not spoken according to Vladislav's [real] intention, but that some treachery lay hid in them. Sending some of his attendants to him, he [Manuel] ordered the agreement to be confirmed by oath, and the other unhesitatingly did this at once. Not only that, but also he reiterated with additional oaths what, as aforesaid, he had previously pledged.

A little later Stephen sent envoys to the emperor, rendered
the land, and added a petition that he [Manuel] never allow his
uncle Stephen [IV] to campaign against Hungary.[29] Accepting
these terms, the emperor concluded the war in order to cross to the
Romans' land, and he advised Stephen [IV] to depart from
Hungary, because he had learned by experience his compatriots'
disaffection toward him. But being unable to persuade the man, he
said to him, "Now I am leaving: since I have recovered the land
for Béla, there remains no excuse for conflict save an unjust one.
Know that soon you will be betrayed to your enemies. But if you
wish, I will prove the fact even to your face. Here is your nephew
Stephen, so similar to you in appearance that / 225 / it is difficult
for those who look at you superficially to distinguish one from the
other. After you have dressed him in your armor, order him to take
your army and march against the foe. Keep yourself concealed
someplace here, and you will at once know how the Hungarians
treat you."

So, entering a boat, he [Stephen IV] lay at anchor unno-
ticed somewhere about the Danube's banks, while his nephew
Stephen hastened with the Hungarians around him to engage king
Stephen. But the armies had not even met each other, when the
Hungarians with Stephen laid hands on him and hastily presented
him to the king as the elder Stephen. The Hungarians' error ended
at that point, but the emperor learned of it and sent advice to
Stephen [IV], saying, "Enough, fellow. As it is dangerous to
withdraw needlessly, so it is stupid to be unseasonably bold. See,
you have twice been able to learn how many evils each occasion
offered you. Do not abide a third attempt, noble sir. It will not be
possible swiftly to make amends according to your wish." So the
emperor said, but the other replied, "Instead, the Hungarians are
now ashamed, as they have been apprehended in treachery." Thus
a spirit once gripped by lust alters and constrains every argument
in its direction.

After he had refused [aid] for these reasons, the emperor

left there Nicephorus / 226 / Chalouphes with an army, to accompany Stephen and take charge of whatever might befall. He himself returned to the Romans' land. Not much later [1164], the Hungarians' king, learning that Stephen still remained in Hungary, assembled still more forces and hastened to decide everything by battle. Meanwhile, many of those with Stephen [IV] passed over to the king and caused the other to be left bare on every side. When he learned this, Chalouphes offered a plan that he abandon Hungary and come to Sirmion. Since that region lay under the emperor's sway, he said it would be possible for him without hindrance to undertake whatever he wished. As the other firmly refused, he [Chalouphes] schemed as follows. Pretending that a letter had come from the emperor, he marched to the Danube, in order to meet with those who bore it, who out of fear of the Hungarians were staying someplace alongside the Danube. When he reached there, he crossed and went to Sirmion. A little later Stephen, who had come near to being captured by the enemy, reached him as a fugitive. When he heard of this, the emperor sent a notable army to Sirmion, partly to defend the region (for he treated the Hungarians with great suspicion, lest they should revolt again), partly on the pretence of security for his adherents and to contrive Stephen's safety. Michael, by surname Gabras,[30] commanded this force; as he had married a niece of the emperor, he, along with Chalouphes, had been entitled sebastos.

/ 227 / Conveying the arm of the martyr Procopius which he took from Sirmion, the emperor restored it to the rest of the body in the church in Naissos; it had been broken off a long time back for the following reason. The nation of the Hungarians has repeatedly overrun the Romans' land, but a little before the reign of Alexius Comnenus they took Sirmion and after they had enslaved many Danuban cities, they reached Naissos. There, finding the martyr's holy coffin, they judged it inhumane, I think, to carry off the entire body, yet after they had cut off the arm they departed. Reaching Sirmion, they deposited it there in the church of the martyr Demetrius, which in former times he who governed the province of Illyricum had constructed. When he discovered it there, the emperor took it away and, as stated, quickly restored it to the rest of the body.

9. In that year these things had been accomplished by the emperor against the Hungarians. He also dispatched Alexius, son of the domestikos [Axouchos], who as has often been stated controlled the office of the protonotarios, to Cilicia with a noteworthy expedition; he named him commander-in-chief of that conflict [1165].[31] For Nūr-ad-Dīn, the *atabeg* of Aleppo, exalted by his previous victories, was impelled by hopes of soon overcoming Antioch. Also, Ṭoros who tyrannized over the Armenians had then seized by treachery many Isaurian cities out of those subject to the emperor, since he was hostile to Andronicus Euphorbenos, / 228 / the emperor's cousin, who then governed Cilicia. For he [Ṭoros] accused him of many things, and in particular blamed him for the murder [1162] of his brother Stephen [Sdefanē]. So this happened there.

The power of Frederick, king of the Germans, moment by moment advanced and waxed great. For he contrived many and various things for the stability of the state and especially laid claim to money, something not previously customary. He took Milan, a famous city [1162], and put to flight the nation of Ligurians or Lombards; proceeding further, he marched to the innermost parts of the west. He who had previously been unable to conquer in battle those nearest at hand, then overcame those furthest off. He subdued Rome itself in battle.[32] Therefore the emperor Manuel himself became concerned as to how he could check his advance, lest his unexpected success should turn him against the Romans' land, at which from a long time back he had cast a greedy eye. So, dispatching secretly some undistinguished persons to the nations there and those situated within the Ionian Gulf [Adriatic Sea], he ordered them to remind them of Frederick's insatiable greed and to arouse them to resistance. To the Venetians' nation he sent Nicephorus Chalouphes with money, to make trial of that people's good will toward himself and to direct affairs there for the Romans' benefit.

After he had subdued Rome, Frederick made many alterations; especially, removing from the throne Alexander [III] who was then bishop there, / 229 / he substituted Ottaviano,[33] thereby I think deeming that he would assimilate to himself the rank of emperor of the Romans. For no one except the emperor of the Romans is allowed to nominate a bishop for Rome. Since the time when this custom was extinguished by the negligence of the emperors in Byzantion, no one has established any bishop in Rome, but this has been done by episcopal synods and the high-priestly order [i.e., cardinals] at Rome. Frederick, however, had earlier eyed the office of emperor, and as he laid hands on this, he seemed to possess an important token of it. He won over many bishops, and seemingly validated his innovation by a synod. To the other kings, however, this did not seem praiseworthy, but no one was able to oppose Frederick, who had advanced to a high degree of strength, except that the emperor hindered him with money and other devices for this purpose, and reestablished Alexander on his throne. But this was later.

When he reached Epidamnos, Chalouphes left there most of the money entrusted to him and went on to Venice by ship, meeting with favorable winds [ca. 1166]. When he came to speech with the doge of the region [Vitale Michiele II] and others esteemed among that nation, he spoke as follows: "Let no one of you, gentlemen, imagine that I have come here from the emperor in fear lest good will toward the Romans' empire should ever desert your shrewdness, [and so] to strengthen your possible weakening of determination. You are not thus / 230 / ignoble and unworthy of your own race, and the emperor has not erred in his former opinion about you. But since out of the rest who exist under his sway, he is particularly confident of your good will, he decided to extend his principal solicitude to you. It is shameful to utilize subjects who are prospering, but refuse the rescue of those who are in difficulties. Because you along with others who do not share in the emperor's benevolence have been wronged by Frederick, who out of lust for power has striven to undo effortlessly what has been long established by time and custom, he sent me to you, as you see, to supply everything which you might wish to obtain from him. With the emperor's assistance, you took on yourself the conflict against this Frederick at Milan, and you know how you prevailed over him. Therefore he bears hatred for the emperor, and trusting in his unexpected success he requires something unsuitable, to be titled emperor of the Romans. He does not know that fortune's unexpected results usually slip quickly away, because they are not fixed in a firm seat. These are the reasons I have come to you. You should take care to carry out in deeds what you lately agreed to when you sent to the emperor's court. You said that the neighboring cities of the Ligurians [i.e., Lombards] would support us if someone came from Byzantion to take part in the enterprise with you. This, as you see, has happened.'' Nicephorus spoke thus, / 231 / and the Venetians, who welcomed his words, undertook to fulfill everything. Indeed Cremona and Padua and many other of the most outstanding cities in Liguria went over to the emperor. The emperor accomplished this in Italy, but not yet openly; he still desired to conceal his hatred toward Frederick.

10. The Hungarians' king [István III] again took Sirmion from the Romans and held it, and laid claim to Zeugminon itself [1165]. When he learned this, the emperor wrote to him as follows: ''You do not act justly, noble sir, dishonoring oaths which you previously swore to our majesty regarding Sirmion and other places. Know then (for proof of what you have done precludes lengthy speech) that unless you swiftly withdraw from what does not belong to you, you will not achieve so much in taking Sirmion as you will forthwith suffer, when the Romans again overrun your whole territory with arms. Or have you forgotten how many myriads Hungary was bereft of by your father, when he long ago

quarreled with the Romans' state? Repentance for what has been done has been your salvation: look you lest there be no profit even from your former penance. The sword of justice which has previously been sharpened through many years has indeed turned to dullness during equally many. One could not, I think, avoid its edge before all others.'' The emperor's expressions were in such terms, but Stephen neglected the words and returned to the same courses. Therefore in every / 232 / way the emperor prepared for war on him, and even desired to reestablish on the throne his paternal uncle Stephen [IV], something he had not previously intended.

Indeed a certain Manuel, who traced his lineage to the Comneni, reached the Russians' nation [ca. 1165] to remind the ruler of the agreement which he had previously made on oath with the emperor, and in addition to reproach him for his friendship to Iaroslav [Osmomysl] the ruler of Galicia. For Iaroslav had broken faith with the Romans in various matters, and in particular he had received and honored with friendship Andronicus, of whom we shall forthwith make much account, who came to him as a fugitive from prison in the palace, where he had I think been confined for nine years. What the facts of Andronicus' flight were, I shall now relate.

11. At another time, previously, in a wonderful fashion, he had escaped from prison, but fate I think still required punishment for what he had done and effortlessly placed the wretch in the hands of his pursuers. When he then reached the Sangarios [Sakarya] River, they say, driven by necessity from the cold, he entered a miserable hut and was immediately recognized from his appearance by the men there. For he was by nature continuously agitated and looked somewhat fierce and terrible, as if his inner emotions had I think emerged and were on the outside. The peasants, who surrounded him as he strongly denied it and asserted that he was not Andronicus, / 233 / bound him and went to Byzantion, taking him along; again fetters and a cell restrained him.

Finally imprinting the keys on wax, he sent [the impres-
sion] to his wife and son [1164]. Using other conspirators for this,
they made some [keys] of iron and sent them to him. When he
received them, since they say the sun had just gone down, at
which time this had been agreed upon, after waiting for an absence
of guards, he went out. There is a certain courtyard which has a
wall, in which he was imprisoned. There, because the place was
seldom trodden, some weeds which spontaneously grew there had
shot up to very great height. Running there he concealed himself
like a rabbit, drawing his body into the smallest possible compass.
Since it was already night, his usual night guards had to surround
the prison; he who had been entrusted by the emperor with his
wardship approached, posted the guards, and shaking the bars, as
was his daily custom on going to bed, tested whether he could find
any damage. As he found them entirely uninjured, he left and went
to sleep. For Andronicus, fearing lest Kladon (this was the man's
name) finding the door open would speedily set forth in quest of
him, had closed it again and departed in security.

When midnight came, he went to the farthest part of the
courtyard, where the wall overlooked it as it came to an end. It
[the wall] was not very high but / 234 / projected enough above
the water that, when roused by the wind, it [the sea] often beat
against it with watery violence. There he fastened a small cord and
holding it descended to the shore. There fortune for a short time
greeted him with grim visage, then smiled and released him by its
favor, being somewhat coy and evidently jesting. For one of the
guards at the palace, who customarily live quartered in the towers
and keep watchful by shouting to one another in turn and uttering
the agreed word, when he saw him, approached and required that
he declare who he was. The prisoner said that he was one of those
held in the palace by the *papias* [34] for fiscal reasons, and said, "If
you let me go, this will be yours as a favor from me," and so saying he pulled out and displayed the amulet from his bosom. The

other (since he was one of the peasantry and continually struggled with the facts of poverty), when the gold flashed in his eyes, took the thing and let Andronicus go. Meanwhile he approached the skiff lying not far off which was to carry him; taking him up, they conveyed him home. Removing the shackles which bound his feet, he again boarded a ship, set sail, and went outside the walls. Finding there the horses which were prepared for him, he mounted and departed in flight. After he had thus fled from prison, Andronicus went to Russia. But our narrative must return to its previous subject.

/ 235 / 12. On account of the said reasons, Manuel came to Primislav's court and requested from him an allied force for the Romans. For he had been dispatched to him and to Rostislav who himself was a ruler in Russia to discuss an alliance.[35] Indeed, he succeeded in his purpose. Being extremely delighted because the emperor utilized such an envoy to them, they promised to fulfill everything the emperor required. Nor did the emperor on this account overlook Iaroslav [of Galicia], but he roused him to war against Stephen by various devices, writing to him as follows: "We shall not imitate your lack of affection, which you have unnecessarily displayed toward us, neglecting the terms and treaties previously sworn by you. But I place before your eyes the facts of his injury, since you are risking being abused in the highest degree. Consider that you are marrying your daughter to the Hungarians' king, who is an ill character and really unsteady in purpose: he pays no respect at all to justice or truth. I think anything can easily be done by a man dissolute by nature and generally carried beyond laws. Therefore Stephen will neither marry your daughter nor do anything else lawful for her. Even if he weds her, he will treat her like a streetwalker. For as he thus injures our majesty and shamelessly reckons null the oaths recently sworn by him, on the pretext of a joke, consider what he might not inhumanely do to you." Primislav [36] hearing these words / 236 / with a certain barbaric simplicity was immediately captivated, regarded his son-in-law as an enemy, and agreed in every way to assist the Romans who were fighting against him.

In Russia there is a city, Kiev by name, which excels the other cities which are located there, and which is like an [ecclesiastical] capital to the nation. To it a bishop comes from Byzantion, and it has a claim on the rest because they ascribe to it special honor in seniority. The ruler of this territory, who likewise agreed to wage war on Stephen, confirmed his treaty with oaths.[37]

While this took place, Frederick king of the Germans learned that the emperor strongly opposed him in affairs in the west, resolved their differences, made peace with the Romans, and himself agreed with the emperor to wage war on Stephen. Nor did Henry, who as has often been said [sic] had married Theodora the emperor's niece, intend to be absent from this conflict;[38] there was also a numerous army of Cumans and Serbs subject to the Romans, and according to his agreement the sultan dispatched his allied troops: a powerful force was gathered from every hand.

At the same time Vladislav, one of the principal persons in Russia, came as a refugee to the Romans with his children and his wife and all his forces, and a property along the Danube was granted to him. Previously the emperor had given it to the refugee Vasilika the son of George, who had the principal place among the chieftains in Russia.[39]

/ 237 / The Venetians too then agreed to aid the Romans with a fleet of a hundred triremes for conflicts by sea, renewing their previous treaties again. And in addition they gave pledges to maintain opposition throughout his life to Frederick king of the Germans and all the others in the western region if they should wage war on the Romans.

13. So matters went in regard to the west. Baldwin [III] king of Palestine who had wedded the emperor's niece[40] perished from among mankind [1163]. Because he had ended his life childless, the sovereignty of that land passed to his brother [Amalric I];

as soon as he assumed it, he sent to the emperor and asked to have a bride from among the Romans, and at the same time he wished to test his opinion regarding the situation in Antioch. The Antiochenes, because they were naturally oath-breakers, had resorted to Baldwin in Palestine and by their own will were managing the governance of the city and of themselves.[41] Knowing, however, that the city was subject to the emperor, he thought he had to inquire of him first, as stated. He [Manuel] answered him as follows: "The request concerning a marriage relationship, since you wish to obtain our favor, will shortly be fulfilled; but since the city of Antioch was anciently tributary to the Romans and now is subject to our majesty, so long as we live it will be impossible for you or anyone else to exercise authority over it. When they forthwith receive from our majesty punishment for infidelity to the Romans, the people of Antioch / 238 / shall know with whom they have dared to quarrel." His letter was in such terms. The other [Amalric], since he was disappointed in his hopes for Antioch, pressed on in asking the emperor about a marriage tie. After he had married one of the daughters of [John Comnenus] the protosebastos, he too took an oath [to the Byzantine emperor], as his brother Baldwin had previously done.

Since he had not yet completed preparations for the conflict before him, the emperor feared very much for the city of Zeugme which was already besieged by Stephen [III]. Prior to the outbreak of war in all areas, he sent a notable army to aid it, under the generals Michael Gabras and Joseph Bryennios, under whom others of the most distinguished of the Romans were placed, John whom they surname Angelus, a man of military experience, and John Ises ['Īsā],[42] a Turk by birth who had participated in Roman upbringing and way of life. Desiring still further to succor the city, he filled numerous ships with soldiers and supplies and ordered them to sail by way of the Danube, to furnish the people inside with necessities, until he himself reached Hungary with the whole army.

The Hungarians had wasted much time around the wall [of
Zeugminon] and after they tested it repeatedly had recognized they
were undertaking something impossible (for the Roman ships
which were anchored at the nearest bank of the river Danube contributed greatly to the Romans within, and in addition took away
men who had experienced injuries in battle and furnished others
sound in body). / 239 / They themselves collected boats, as the
force with Gabras and Bryennios had not yet reached Hungary,
and rushed across the river against the Roman ones in order to sink
them and easily prevail in battle, even if they were proven inferior
by this attempt. Their ships, because they were not constructed
very skillfully and spread out to immoderate width, were inferior
in speed to the Roman ones. As they went across the river, the
Romans, who had formed a type of battle array, intercepted them
at mid-stream and fired upon them frequently with arrows; hindered by these, they backed water. The rest of their ships, drawing
nigh the river's other bank, avoided danger, but one of them, full
of men who held commands among them, became prey to the
Romans as they hit it with artificial fire.

Since they were unfortunate in this attempt, the Hungarians
turned to something else. Corrupting with money some of the
Hungarians who served Stephen [IV], they induced them to mingle
something deadly for the man. Thereby the city was taken and the
whole of Sirmion again became subject to the Hungarians [April
1165]. The Romans and Hungarians inside, who had sided with
Stephen [IV], were unharmed, because they yielded the city on
condition of such an agreement. Triumphing over Stephen's
corpse, the Hungarians at first neither offered it holy rites nor
deemed it worthy of anything else lawful for the dead, but they
caused it to be cast out before the city's / 240 / gates and condemned it to remain unburied. Later, stirred by natural inclination,
they conveyed it to the church of Stephen the Protomartyr and
there committed it to a tomb.[43]

14. When the emperor heard of this, albeit the empress

was then oppressed by a grievous sickness, he himself, spurred as usual by marvelous zeal, set out for the war. Reaching Sardika the capital of the Illyrians, he assembled his army there. He set out when June was waning [1165], and went to the Danube. As he was going to cross, he acted as follows. He stationed the part of his army which was outstanding in weaponry and ready for battle opposite Chramon,[44] a Hungarian city, offering the expectation that he would forthwith cross from there. So when he observed the Hungarian force established on the farther side, he set out for Belgrade and at dawn sailed across from there.[45] Thereby he divided in several parts the enemy who planned to oppose him.

The Romans, however, were seized by great trepidation at the crossing; observing this, the emperor himself, as he had often previously dared, entered a skiff before all the rest and hastened to the opposite shore. Thereafter, the Romans' army, shamed at the emperor's rashness, proceeded to the boats. When the Hungarians saw that the emperor had crossed, they abandoned their formation and withdrew. Then in the disembarkation on enemy soil the emperor jumped further than was proper / 241 / (for the shallows did not allow the ship to ground on dry land), missed his mark, and severely twisted one of his legs. He did not wish to abate his zeal, but hastened to a backwater of the river; while he passed the day in this pain, the injured part of his leg increased in swelling.[46]

Numerous barbarians garrisoning Zeugme ran forth from the walls and took a stand to oppose [the Romans]. But as soon as they saw the emperor, each hastened to outrun the other; in confusion and tumult they rushed back into the city and dared not come out. Then the Romans prepared for a siege. On the third day thereafter they joined battle. The barbarians who defended the battlements filled the air with their cries and indistinct shouts, and continuously shot and were shot at. In these activities, however, that day and the next were wasted, and neither the Romans nor the Hungarians were successful. I am capable of astonishment at many things done at this siege, but I would scarcely believe those who reported the emperor's daring if I had not been present as a witness of what happened. For when the Romans had constructed a wooden tower, they intended to move it up to the city so as to combat the barbarians on the battlements hand-to-hand. He demanded to mount before all the rest, saying, "Romans, you will earn my favor more than any others [will] if you do not hinder my ascent." Yet / 242 / he did not accomplish his wish. The principal commanders who accompanied him forcefully prevented it.

Making a circuit of the wall, he sought out the place where it was particularly subject to attack; in the absence of stones, he ordered the ditches which girdled the city, and which were rather deep and wide, to be filled with fagots and firewood, so that the war machines could cross. But nothing yet was accomplished toward the capture of the city. For, although they were severely pressed by the Romans' soldiers, the Hungarians shouted more than before, and were borne up by hopes that the Hungarians' other army was rapidly approaching them.

15. While matters were still in suspense in this fashion, the Romans' scouts came up and brought word of the approach of a large army. Dust was to be seen rising in the greatest part of the air. One of the Hungarians of outstanding position who had gone over to the Romans, Vasas by name,[47] asserted that the Hungarians' king was not far off, leading men beyond count, especially a joint Cuman and Russian army; in addition to these, he said that the Czechs' lord had returned with him in full strength. When the emperor heard this, he called a council of outstanding men, to consider how they must manage the present situation. "Fellow Romans," he said, "the natural order of affairs is not familiar with one thing only, that one should only be bold, but that one should not rashly attack insurmountable problems; I in particular think it is of great importance for someone who is little by little learning self-control. / 243 / Then, since that nation was successful some time ago by an unexpected turn of fortune and has become difficult for the Romans' state to face, we must not therefore think it

enough for us if we only campaign on their soil. But we must allocate what is proper to each occasion and apply the requisite action to the present situation. Identical policies are not suited, I think, to the successful and the unsucessful. As for the Romans' realm, even if it no longer enjoys its old good fortune, but (to speak with God's help) will appear in a much greater [fortune] under ourselves as its champions, it will redound to its glory absolutely to avoid the Hungarians' king, who as they say is approaching with a large native army, with still more levied by way of a mercenary force. In order thereby to preserve both renown which he had already transformed to something better, and strength which would thus escape intact, we must take counsel as well as possible." The emperor spoke thus.

To some Romans of the council it seemed proper to depart and camp at the Sava, as from there they might oppose the enemy with impunity; others were not pleased thereat, and thought it proper to set out from the siege and resist the approaching foe with all their might. The emperor, however, did not approve either; he forthwith stigmatized the one as cowardice, the other as folly. / 244 / "It is possible," he said, "that when we abandon the siege, a far greater force than at present, and supplies in sufficiency, would be conveyed to the Hungarians who form the garrison in the city." It seemed proper to him that the less serviceable part of the army and whatever household force was armed should remain there at the city under some rather insignificant generals, while all the rest should go with himself to fight the other Hungarians. As this [view] prevailed, they prepared to set out on the ensuing day.

But when nothing definite was reported to them, they armed themselves at dawn and conducted a third attempt upon the city. Again battle was joined, and the Hungarians on the battlements defended themselves from the Romans' army with stones and arrows and anything handy, but the latter more than before undermined the [walls'] foundations and smashed [them] with casts of stones from engines. Frequent cheers and exhortations were heard on both sides, and there was shouting and outcries, and an indistinct din arose. When the Hungarians observed some of the Romans prying with crowbars at the foundations, they acted as follows. There was a stone of great size lying within the walls; girdling it with wooden beams, they fastened their ropes to the timber and drew it up to a wooden turret which they had constructed projecting over the walls, to drop it on the Romans from there. But just as the stone reached the turret, unable to endure the weight (for it [the boulder] was exceedingly large), it [the turret] suddenly broke and crashed to earth with many of the Hungarians, / 245 / and none of them avoided the danger. Again a din was raised and the fight raged still more. Then allegedly the emperor observed one of the Romans shooting very accurately; he ran over and, holding out his shield, kept the man safe from arrows.

16. Since they recognized that their affairs were really in difficulty, the Hungarians sent and begged the emperor that they might yield the city to him and depart uninjured. At first he said he would not do this until Gregory and the rest of their župans fastened ropes to their necks and came with their feet bared and heads uncovered. On such terms he sent them back, but the Romans pressed more furiously and took the city. When it was already taken, Gregory and his fellow generals of the Hungarians approached the emperor in disgrace in the stated fashion of guise as petitioners, and made lamentation. For some time he [Manuel] declined to look upon them; later, however, when Béla requested it, he prohibited their execution, but dispatched them to prison.

With great fury the Romans rushed into the city and slaughtered the people there like sheep. Then it caused me to weep, in contemplating human life, with how many voluntary evils this sorry race binds itself. Their valuables and clothing and silverware were carried off, and all their goods pillaged. / 246 / Even of the naked and unarmed warriors, each girded himself with the enemy's weapons. Then a wretched old woman was found, who had an arrow driven through her fundament. Why this happened, I will at once relate. While the city was still uncaptured, she, standing atop the walls, threw down filth; indecently pulling up her garments and turning around, she displayed her rear to the Romans' army; while singing some endless babble, she thought to bind the Romans with a diabolical spell. But one of the soldiers loosed an arrow at her and hit the wretch, just where nature placed the channel which conveys excrement.

Likewise, one of the Romans was found a suffering prisoner, confined in an irregular and lightless cell for the following reason. When the Hungarians had taken him prisoner, because he was known for excellent archery, they constrained him to shoot at the Romans from the wall. This was contrary to his will, yet he shrewdly allowed it, but acted so as to miss everyone. When the Hungarians observed this, they repeatedly beat the man's back and kept him securely shut up.

Thus Zeugme was again taken. Then many others did deeds of note and valor, but Andronicus Doukas [48] not least. For when he saw the Romans scrambling up the wall on a ladder, he approached the emperor's cousin Andronicus, under whose command he happened to be placed and who had then returned from Russia and been graciously received by the emperor, / 247 / and asked to be allowed by him to attempt the ascent; when the other permitted it, he went thither with great speed. When some of the Latins who were coming up from behind strove to go past him, he opposed them firmly and did not desire to forgo glory. While this was happening, the ladder suddenly broke and fell to earth. But Andronicus [Doukas] clung to his accustomed courage. When he saw some men mounting another which had been brought, he ran and ascended it. So matters went there.

King Stephen [III] had trusted in the security of the city (for in addition to other things, a channel from the Danube's currents watered it, one which had first lain open to the air as it reached the city, then had been placed underground by the emperor when he was allied with the late Stephen [IV]); he [the king] was unable to believe that it had been captured so easily by the Romans. But the emperor passed on from there and renovated another fort, in which he hastily settled many of the Hungarians in Sirmion, who are customarily called by them Chalisioi (and as stated they are heterodox, agreeing in doctrine with the Turks).[49] Once he [Stephen] learned accurately what had befallen at the city of Zeugme, he sent envoys to the emperor, men of the aristocracy and one who enjoyed the office of bishop, and agreed to render Sirmion again to the Romans, and in addition the whole of Dalmatia.

When they came in sight of the emperor, they uttered what had been commanded to them and / 248 / petitioned the emperor to abandon his wrath. At first he refused, saying, "It would indeed be estimable, envoys, if someone thought it proper to restore those things which he had previously stolen. We hold Sirmion, we have regained Zeugme, we are already masters of the Dalmatians, we are lords of all those together, of which you the givers have been deprived. So then is there among you another Sirmion? Is there another Zeugme and Dalmatia which you now come giving us? If so, show us them, so we may immediately receive them in the hollow of our hands, knowing that we shall not possess them securely in regard to your power (for you care nothing about breaking the law), yet, to speak with God's favor, holding them by our own strength, just like these. If then these things lie now in our power, and nothing remains of what you mentioned to give, on what terms will the agreement be? Or what will there be to exchange with us?" So he at first answered them, then changing his mind, he said, "But then, so that you may know that we wish to make peace as a gift to you, who are Christians, come, take the oaths." The emperor spoke thus, and after they had sworn to everything, they departed; the emperor then returned to Byzantion.[50]

17. Already John Doukas, who had subdued Dalmatia, had turned it over to Nicephorus Chalouphes, as he had been directed

by the emperor. He [Manuel] had previously sent him [Doukas] there with troops to take it either by force or by agreement, / 249 / since the Hungarians had designated it by treaty as Béla's heritage. Passing by the country of the Serbs he thrust into it, and in a short while entire authority [over it] was completely placed in the emperor's hands. Then Trogir and Sibenik came under the Romans, and in addition Split and the nation of Katzikioi and Diokleia, a famous city which Diocletian the emperor of the Romans built, and Skradin and Ostrovica and Solin, and whatever other [cities] are situated in Dalmatia, fifty-seven in all. So matters turned out in Dalmatia.

The emperor, as we said, returning to Byzantion, conducted a triumphal procession from the citadel to the great church of Hagia Sophia. Celebrating liturgies of gratitude there and having presented the priests with gold which reached the Romans as tribute from Sirmion, he relaxed in the palace. But it almost escaped me: for that triumph a chariot of pure gold was made, on which the emperor was to be mounted. He did not ride, however, partly rendered circumspect at the ostentation, partly because when the horses which pulled the car were first harnessed, they were extremely restive, so that it almost risked being overturned.

No long time passed, and when he [Manuel] learned that the Serbs and the nation of Hungarians again were striving [for revolt], he hastened to anticipate the attack. But as soon as they heard of his [Manuel's] coming, they broke off the incursion and preserved the treaties intact.

Book VI

1. The emperor honored Andronicus, who as stated had returned from Russia, with every kindness, presented the man with quantities of gold, and sent him to Cilicia to settle matters there [1166]. In order that he might be able to engage in lavish expenditure, he granted him the taxes of Cyprus. Remaining in his appointed place for very little time, however, he first made the empress' sister Philippa [of Antioch] his betrothed wife, something which was not permitted him at all by our law; then, abandoning her without any reason, he passed over to Palestine [early 1167], taking with him much of the emperor's money which he had levied in taxation from Cilicia and the Cypriots' land.

He met there [Theodora] the daughter of the sebastokrator Isaac who, as stated, had married king Baldwin [III]; when he died and the attributes of power passed to his brother, she lived as a widow at Acre. Because she was a relative, he frequently visited her and held private conversations with the woman. As he went on, he became extraordinarily besotted with her, in an unlawful and unholy love, until after he had had intercourse with her he carried her off and went with her to the land of the Saracens. On her he later begot children. / 251 / After he had passed through extensive foreign countries, he then entered the eastern land of the Iberians [Georgians]. Not much later he again went to the Turks with the woman; from there the wretch made frequent raids against the Romans' territory and took captive many men. He rendered the spoils of war to the Turks, and therefore was subjected to anathema by the church.[1]

2. About this time [1160–66] an inquiry occurred in Byzantion regarding Christ's teaching, for the following reason. There was a certain Demetrius, a Roman by descent, sprung from the Asian village of Lampe [near Atramyttion],[2] who had I think studied a little general education and secular learning, but who generally spent his time on holy doctrines and constantly talked endless nonsense about them. As he had frequently been sent as ambassador to the west and the Italian peoples, he returned from there full of drivel and indulged in many strange things and in particular he could not leave off meddling about the nature of God, a subject allowed to no one except the professors and the principal priests, but equally to the emperors on account of their rank.

As he had returned at that time from the land of the Germans, he asserted that the peoples there evidently had a wrong opinion, and once conversing with the emperor he discoursed of some such matters. When the emperor inquired what this was, in reply he set forth his entire doctrine; it went thus: "They dare to say that the same Person [Christ] is inferior and equal to the God who engendered Him." / 252 / When the emperor said, "But why? Do we not call Him God and Man?" he said, "Yes." "Then," said the emperor, "we agree that He is inferior as regards His Manhood, but equal as regards His Divinity. We hear the Saviour saying this same thing, for He says someplace, 'My Father is greater than I.'[3] And if we must not apply this to the one [divine] nature (for it would be most unsuitable), then necessarily we must apply the statement to the other [human] one. That it was said of neither is unthinkable. Therefore mankind's doctrine is sound, as our majesty has long known." The other, however, again said, "Yet they openly speak impiety." In such terms they concluded the discussion, but a little later Demetrius enshrined his teachings in a book and offered it to the emperor. He [Manuel]

said, "If it is possible to conceal this underground, bury it forthwith, lest by it you should be the agent of ruin for many people.
For in regard to this [present] view I happen to stand firm, and I do
not think one would easily be able to move me from it."

The other, however, became still more bold, and proposed
it privately and in assemblies. Then he communicated it to many
of the bishops and those from the class of Levites, whom we call
deacons. When he found that many agreed with him, he breathed
and spoke still more openly against those who were somehow less
minded towards it. He elevated the developing controversy to great
size, and there was nobody anywhere who did not then talk and
inquire about it, of whatsoever faction he happened to be. When
/ 253 / the emperor learned this, he hesitated and declined to put it
up for a synodal investigation, treating the matter with precaution.
Observing that almost all were inclined toward the opinion of
Demetrius, he received them one by one, then in pairs and in
larger groups; he examined what they said, and thus he converted
many of them to the other [true] doctrine, as they were unable to
argue against it.

Although he had not experienced training in logic, by the
acuteness of his mind and the breadth of his intellect he surpassed
everyone who lived in our times. There was no one who denied
this, not only of those who dwelt much in the emperor's presence
(or one would suspect flattery), but even of those who were unknown to him. Should he desire to explain something, he set it
forth with extraordinary wisdom and clarity and simplicity of expression. And it did not matter which type of philosophy the problem under investigation depended on, natural or theological or any
of the rest. He plunged himself in divine and profane learning, and
esteemed both Ares [War] and Hermes [patron of learning], although he could spare almost no time from martial activities. Thus
by the keenness of his natural ability, as we said, he won over to
his own opinion many of those whom he met.

At first there was no one who was not of the faction opposing him except Loukas who was then in charge of ecclesiastical matters, who himself did not dare to speak freely, and no more than six of the deacons. / 254 / All the rest, as they observed many abandoning their [theological] position by private discussion with the emperor, anticipating that by the excellence of his mind and his tongue's cleverness he would attract many of them to himself in private meetings, established a rule among themselves that no one of them would ever meet the emperor individually and privily. "For not now, but later, after his death, he shall be absolutely subjected to anathema." They spoke thus while they were holding meetings at each others' houses, especially those of prominent persons.

Still unaware of these matters, the emperor privately invited Euthymius the then bishop [metropolitan] of Neai Patrai [Hypati, near Lamia]; [4] he inquired what had been said and wished to study doctrine with him. Closing his lips he stood in silence. When the emperor asked the reason for his silence, in reply he set forth the entire story. Enraged thereat, although it was not previously customary for him (whatever he did he used to do quietly and without passion), he threatened to thrust him over a cliff, if they who were perverting sound doctrine concerning God charged him with this. Changing his mind, he said, "So that you will first perceive who you are and how you think about God, you who cast jibes at me (but although insulted I am restraining myself, lest by willful action I should impugn orthodoxy; for there are sufficient similarities of good books to bad to render synonymous the propositions from which / 255 / both sides are proceeding), arm yourself so that you will be able to combat me, who alone of all the rest will oppose you, not by force of arms, but by action of words. For it is hateful to me to overcome an inferior, and this action is witness. While I have clearly been insulted, as you see, I am holding back my vengeance; yet you must not ridicule these matters in corners. For who constrains you? Or who removes your freedom of speech? When have you been expelled by me as you spoke before the pulpit? What will I profit, should I defend an absurd doctrine? Then lest I disgrace my doctrine in words, something which happened to many among you (indeed I have never professed such things), it absolutely remains that I should not betray doctrine regarding God. Yet if someone speaking in accordance with the Holy Scriptures were able to alter my opinion, it would be no shame at all for me to change to them: let this one thing only be guarded against, that God be not impugned. For this [purpose] I myself have many times endured being affronted.''

These things went forward there, but a few days later he supplied numerous books which spoke clearly in regard to this, and put the matter up for synodal investigation [1166]. Many of the opposing faction then slipped away from moment to moment, until all were of the same mind with the other patriarchs and agreed that the emperor had gathered the purport of the Scriptures. Yet they were openly bitter at Loukas and lavished abuse on him, whereby they cried out to remove the man from his throne, / 256 / since they knew that he very unlearnedly attended to matters. Confessing that they had been defeated by Loukas' opinion, because it had come long before the emperor's, and being defeated by them [emperor and patriarch] in religion, they indicted him on other charges. At this, I think, the emperor observed them attacking Loukas with diseased reasoning, and said, ''Let this be kept secret for a while; when the conclusion of the present matter comes, this will be examined, and we shall apply to it an appropriate termination.''

He repelled them on these terms, and the doctrines were declared valid. The emperor subscribed them. Then, after having inscribed the text in stone, they speedily placed it in Hagia Sophia on the left as one enters. So the investigation obtained its conclusion.[5]

I have always thought this about these things, that it is not without reproach for a living man to meddle in the nature of God. Yet I am capable of astonishment at what is reported to me regarding this emperor. For once as he was investigating this affair (for the matter under debate was in contention for six years), one of those who served in the imperial household came and quietly reported to him that the empress had suffered a miscarriage, and that it had been male. Not even displaying his suffering in appearance, he remained attentive to what was being said. But when that part of the inquest reached its conclusion, having stood upright, he threw himself at the priests' feet, and said, ''Just now, holy fathers, word has come from the women's quarters, saying that a male child, my greatest hope, has been born untimely. I ask of your holiness, / 257 / make supplication to God, do so, I beg. Should I have wrongly undertaken combat in this holy conflict, may my seed never again be brought to fruition for either sort of offspring, nor may I enjoy my hopes; but if my opinion is pleasing to God, may this hope be granted to me in no long time.'' So saying, he rose from the ground, but the others each knelt and tearfully besought God. On such terms they departed. No long time passed, and the emperor begot a son, a figure of the Graces, a flower of nature. But at the proper moment my narrative will describe what sort of person he is to behold.[6]

On such terms those controversies ended. Loukas, since nothing worthy of note was imputed to him by his accusers, still remained upon his throne. But John, who possessed the see of Kerkyra, and one of the monks, whom they entitled Eirenikos, who remained true to their earlier doctrine, were subjected to anathema, and one after another others were expelled from ecclesiastical orders.[7]

3. Setting in motion again affairs which had been settled, the Hungarians' king dispatched Dionysius,[8] one of the aristocrats of his court who was experienced in many wars, to lay claim to Sirmion with a large army [1166]. When they learned of this, the Romans' generals laid their plans about it. The schemes of the council did not succeed, since the councilors looked not to what would profit the Romans, but how one might deceive the other,

especially both / 258 / the Michaels, one who was surnamed
Gabras and ranked as *doux* of that region, and Branas who separately commanded the soldiery; both were extremely warlike, but
Branas was rather the superior. As it seemed right to the councilors to attack Dionysius by night, they set out and advanced with
their whole force. Coming where Dionysius was encamped, since
they found the camp totally deserted of men, they commenced to
feel afraid. For in enemy country, if a place is deserted and its
wonted employment lacking, this is sufficient to shake a soldier's
spirit.

Yet scouting out their tracks, they advanced, and would
speedily have accomplished something if they had attacked the
Hungarians sooner. Since daylight was already distinctly visible,
the Hungarians perceived them and commenced to launch their
cavalry against the [Roman] camp (for they were setting it up for
pasturing); they formed into ranks and attacked those who customarily stood in front of the tents. Observing the Romans rushing
about in great disorder (being attacked by the Hungarians who
rode in the cavalry, the greater part had been scattered), they [the
Hungarians] charged them, and after they had turned them back,
they were able to drive them into some of the Roman regiment
who were coming up from the rear. Confused thereby, they turned
to retreat. So the Romans fled full speed, deeming that they were
attacked by a force much larger than the army visible to them. For
in such circumstances one can discover understanding and compre-
hension of reality in very few men.

Since they were all speedily exhausted, / 259 / both the
generals stood for a while with the standards and a few of their followers, thinking that some of the Romans would assemble again;
but because no one joined them from any direction, they too then
turned their backs. But Branas in the meanwhile wheeled about
and struck one of the foe with a lance, while the other [general]
fled. Then there became clearly evident the matter of their previous disagreement in the council. For when Branas rejoined the

fleeing Gabras, he mocked him and said triflingly, "Then do you agree with me, sebastos, as to how I have hitherto resisted the foe: I have attacked them with a spear?" And when the other assented, he said, "But, by the emperor's head, I have not observed you save in retreat." Thus the present-day Romans individually do not work for the common profit, but so that one might seem admirable, he undertakes every task.

The pursuing Hungarians did not slay very many of the Romans, nor take many. For they [the Romans] were possessed by great fear. One might infer it from this: an individual from the infantry regiments went as a fugitive all the way to Zeugme, checked by none of the Romans. So slowly did they travel. Then Dionysius, intending to elevate in importance what he had done, gathered together the few bodies of the fallen and reared a very large mound over them, considering that the slaughter would be equated to the size of the mound.[9]

These matters turned out thus, but the emperor / 260 / was aroused thereat and desired to attack Hungary himself. Wishing rather that a display of the Romans' might be made to them, he planned as follows. He sent to the Danube Alexius [i.e., Béla, brother of king Stephen of Hungary], to whom he had bethrothed his daughter, with numerous forces, which Alexius [Axouchos] who was protostrator commanded, to give the Hungarians the expectation that he would again attack them by way of the customary regions. But he ordered Leo by surname Batatzes, who led a force from abroad, among many other sorts a large group of Vlachs, who are said to be formerly colonists from the people of Italy, to fall upon Hungary by way of the regions near the so-called Euxine [Black] Sea, whence no one had ever assailed them. So Alexius [Béla] and the other army of Romans reached the Danube and imparted fear to the Hungarians that they were going to cross over from there, while Batatzes striking from the aforesaid place pillaged everything mercilessly and trod down whatever he encountered. Then he caused a great slaughter of men and made a not in-

ferior number of captives. In addition he returned to the emperor
driving herds of cattle and horses and every other sort of beast.

Wishing to inflict a second blow upon them, he [Manuel]
again sent an army against them, ordering it to attack from someplace higher up the Hungarians who live near Russia. Commanders of this force were Andronicus Lampardas and Nicephorus
Petraliphas and a sufficient number of others; yet the oft-mentioned John Doukas was placed in charge of all. Soon, / 261 / after
they had passed through some wearisome and rugged regions and
had gone through a land entirely bereft of men, they burst into
Hungary; encountering many extremely populous villages, they
collected a great quantity of booty and slew many men, but took
captive many more. When they were about to set out from there,
they erected a cross made of copper and inscribed it thus:

> Here terrible Ares and an Italic band
>   Slew countless tribes of Pannonian race,
> When noble Manuel ruled renowned Rome,
>   The pride of the wise Comnenian kings.[10]

4. While this happened, Henry duke of Austria, together
with his wife the emperor's niece Theodora, came to Sardika to
reconcile the Germans' king Frederick to the emperor and to
request an armistice in the war with the Hungarians [1166]. For, as
has been narrated by me in the preceding account, since the emperor was taking action against him, Frederick came close to being
deprived of the rule of Rome, when the bishop in Rome agreed to
return to the ancient usage.[11] He [Frederick] also promised many
other things against his will, since the peoples there had been
roused to war against him by pressures from the emperor. Therefore, a little before, when he was in sore straits, desiring to win
over the emperor, he wrote and negotiated with him in friendly
fashion, / 262 / and as stated agreed to cooperate with him against
the Hungarians.

When, however, [Manuel's] agreement with the pope about

the rule of Rome was rendered null, because, while the emperor asserted that the throne of Rome would remain at Byzantion, the pope would not accept this but demanded that he rule in Rome, Frederick therefore regained his bravado and again displayed his malice. As he intended to invade the Romans' land, with barbaric folly he commenced to divide it among his followers. Since, because of the emperor's opposition, he was unsuccessful in other schemes, he resorted to the embassy of this Henry and [Otto of] Wittelsbach. He planned by an appearance of friendship to persuade the emperor to desist from what was being undertaken against him; thus he could easily prepare for war against the Romans. Appreciating this, the emperor treated Henry favorably and agreed to his request for an armistice in the war with the Hungarians, but reached no final conclusion in regard to Frederick. As Henry was returning home, when he reached Hungary, he persuaded Stephen, who had rejected the Russian girl, to marry his own daughter. This indeed happened.

Not much later the Hungarians planned to rob [us] of Dalmatia again. Various forces went thither, as well as he who has the rank of bán [12] among them (this means someone who has authority after the king in the nation), / 263 / but, as they were unable to overcome the men there in battle, they withdrew, after having brought Chalouphes [the *doux*] into their power. How this happened to Nicephorus [Chalouphes] will forthwith be related by me. Learning that a Hungarian force was attacking the region, he gathered a few from his own army and went out from Split. But as he advanced, most of his followers melted away little by little and caused the man to be easily captured by the enemy. Surrounding him, after he had wrought deeds of mighty valor, they held him captive.

5. When the emperor heard of this, he returned to Byzantion, intending to come upon them in spring with another larger expedition. Indeed, he was unable to go there in the campaigning season, since a piece of bad luck hindered him; what this was the

narrative will reveal. Winter [1166–67] had passed, and when the mist had been swept away, he devoted himself to a certain temperate exercise which has from a long time back been customary for emperors and sons of emperors. It is as follows. Some youths who divide themselves equally cast a ball made of leather, comparable in size to an apple, into some level space which seems right to them when they measure it out. As it lies in the middle like a prize, they charge [their horses] at full speed toward it, against one another. Each holds in his right hand a stick sufficiently lengthy, but which abruptly terminates in a broad loop which / 264 / is divided in the middle with cords of gut, dried by time, intertwined with one another in the fashion of a net. Each side makes great haste to sweep it up and get it first to the other end, which from the outset has been assigned to them. Whenever the ball, driven by the sticks, comes to either end, this constitutes victory for that side. Such is this sport, very perilous and dangerous. It is constantly necessary that one participating in it turn backwards and swing his hips, spin the horse in a circle and engage in every sort of race and be carried along in as many types of movement as the ball happens to make.

Such is this sport. The emperor was astonishingly devoted to it; but his horse fell to earth on him with its whole weight. Borne down underneath, he labored and exerted himself greatly to rise from his fall, but was unable to thrust away the horse which had come down on him, as stated, with its full weight; he badly injured a thigh, as well as an arm by the twisting of his cloak. He endured it gallantly, so that although suffering very severely, he quickly stood up, when many had surrounded him, and sprang on his horse again and made some circuits sufficiently slowly, until feeling the pains very violent he went to bed. In consequence he was so overcome by pain that, on account of the faintness which overwhelmed him, he had no memory on the morrow of what had then been said and done.

Such was the matter then, but / 265 / two days later, becoming better, he went to Apameia.[13] Probably because of exertion occasioned by the journey, the swelling mounted again and frequent pains stabbed him. Having passed the Easter [9 April 1167] season at Selymbria [Silivri], since he felt himself getting better, he went to Philippopolis. He negotiated there with envoys who had come from the Hungarians. Since he perceived that they had nothing valid to offer, but were only striving in every way to obtain an armistice and suspension of the war, he sent them back unsuccessful. But along with them he sent one of the Romans, to ask for Chalouphes and to threaten that, if he [István III] did not straightway respect the treaty, the emperor and the Romans' army would again be seen. Reaching Sardika, he assembled his forces there.

6. While he was making a stay there, something as follows befell. Alexius [Axouchos] who held the office of protostrator, as has often been stated, had from a long time back meditated revolt; being detected at that time, he was shorn of his locks [tonsured]. After he had been installed among the monks, he was led off to one of the mountain monasteries, which are situated in great numbers on Mount Papikion on the river Strymon [Struma]. When he had stayed there for some time, he died.

But why and from what cause the fellow came to this turn of fortune, let us now declare. When he had previously journeyed to Cilicia, after he had been declared commander-in-chief of that war by the emperor, going on purpose to the sultan in Ikonion / 266 / he secretly won him to friendship and discussed with him many things which tended toward usurpation, and receiving and answering letters from him in which was written their agreement, he then went to Cilicia. Returning some time later to Byzantion, when he wished to adorn one of his suburban dwellings with murals, he did not emblazon on them ancient Greek feats, nor did he set forth the emperor's deeds, things which he has achieved in wars and beast hunts, such as is more often customary for those who hold governmental offices.

For he [Manuel] had combated so many and fought with
such naturally great beasts as we have heard concerning no one
else who has ever lived. And lest I be somewhat carried away
from historians' rules, let me set forth just something of that sort
from them [Manuel's feats]. It was around the winter solstice, and
so much snow was piled on the ground that not only were all the
ravines and clefts in the mountains concealed, but bodies were almost frozen by the excess of cold. Indeed, all the beasts which
lacked someplace to lie hidden came forth from the thickets and
rushed over the snow in crowds; flocks of birds which were unable
to use their wings (for ice clogged and held them like a fetter, as it
is possible to see in the case of bird hunting) went on foot instead
of wings, and lay a ready prey for beasts and men. The emperor
went to hunt in one of the eastern regions, whose name is Dama-
trys.[14] As he was occupied in this activity, / 267 / a great mountain of a beast encountered him, yet not a lion, nor is it possible to
call it a leopard, but the size and similarity to a lion prevent this. It
had a double nature, taking something from both, a leopard in a
lion and a lion in a leopard, a monstrous mixture of qualities, terrible in valor, courageous in frightfulness, and all the properties
belonging to both in each other. Such was this beast; most of those
who attended the emperor fled when they saw it. For it was unendurable for many people to see. But when it came close, there was
not one who then opposed it. But while they fled, the emperor
drew the sword with which he was equipped, and rushed to strike
the beast; bringing the blow down on its forehead, he drove it up
to the chest. Such was the emperor in hunting.

Neglecting these [subjects], Alexius (for I return to where I
made the excursus from my narrative) commemorated the sultan's
martial deeds, foolishly making public in painting in his residence
what should have been concealed in darkness. Learning of this, the
emperor often received him in private discussions and proferred
him advice, as he was eager to lead him away from what he meditated. But the other clung fast to his scheme; he frequently invited

into his presence a man, a Latin by birth but a magician and out-standing in wizardry, unfeignedly conversed with him, and com-municated monstrous plots. These were as to how the emperor might always be unfortunate in lack of an heir; he used to receive many drugs / 268 / from the wizard for the said purposes, and the wretch did not leave off doing such things. Therefore the emperor again reproached him and exposed his madness. Seeming to be regretful, the other was the same again. For having let a little time pass, he again resorted to that wizard and discussed the same mat-ter.

Then, meeting Constantine Doukas, who himself had mar-ried a niece of the emperor,[15] he said, "Noble sir, if it should be according to your will that we share a single purpose, know (he said) that no one would be able to overcome us." This, however, was said not very clearly, but something else was much more dis-tinct than it. Kasianos once approached Alexius, since he observed him unnecessarily falling back when he campaigned in Hungary with Béla, and undertook to spur him on in regard to this. But the other [Alexius Axouchos] receiving the man privately, said, "Would you know why I restrain myself very much from the wars? Because I have in me great pity for the human race." When the other blamed this statement, he said, "Because, unwarily, whatever might chance, the emperor desires to destroy the Roman [force], he orders me to thrust it forward strongly in battles. But, if you will keep safe this statement of mine, you will be our friend." He said so much, but Kasianos advised the emperor of this.

This, however, was previously; what he finally was busied at was something as follows. A force of Cumans who had come in mercenary service to the Romans at first made difficulties about their pay, / 269 / then were satisfied. But meeting them privately, the protostrator persuaded them with money to pretend to return to their ancestral home, and when it was midnight, to assail the em-peror's tent in crowds and engage in strife. This was indeed deter-mined and planned. But a little boy from among those who served

in his tent, when he observed the plot, went hastily to the eunuch
Thomas, who then was high in the emperor's favor, and warned
him of the plan. Taking the whole account to the emperor, he then
produced the boy for him. Still the emperor was loath to believe
what they said, until about dawn the Cumans commenced to withdraw for no reason. Fawning upon them with promises, he was
able to restrain them, but he sent some to Alexius to seize him at
once, and speedily the wretch was a prisoner. Soon afterwards,
when the emperor ordered, men from the aristocracy came to him,
John Doukas and Michael, who at that time was logothete [of the
bureaus?], and in addition the eunuch Thomas and Nicephorus, by
surname Kaspax, who was one of the judges of the velum. They
furnished him [Alexius Axouchos] three accusations, and ordered
him to respond to whichever of them he was able to make a
defense. But when he heard them, he admitted his guilt of all; he
begged them that, after he had first been tonsured and had participated in the holy sacrament, they should then inflict on him whatever seemed correct in justice. Moved to pity thereat, the emperor
had him tonsured as a monk.[16]

/ 270 / 7. In regard to Alexius, the turns of fortune ended
there. Since Hungarian forces were crossing toward Sirmion, the
emperor sent troops there, which various of the Romans' generals
commanded, and in particular the emperor's nephew Andronicus,
to whom was applied the surname Kontostephanos, was named
commander-in-chief of that war by the emperor. He was directed
how he had to array the men and where the battle would be located, as if painted in a picture. So after he had crossed the Sava,
when he came near the Hungarians' camp, Andronicus acted as
follows. He understood that to send forward spies and scouts, as
usual, to the enemy's army was not at all useful. But he ordered
some of the Romans who went ahead of the army to try to take
alive and bring back one of the enemy. According to command,
they returned conveying one of the foe, and he [Kontostephanos]
inquired of him how well supplied with forces were the Hungar-

ians who had come to Sirmion, and what were their plans. The other truly set forth everything. "Thirty-seven of the generals among us," he said, "command this force, but Dionysius has overall authority. In total, the army numbers upwards of fifteen thousand men, armored knights, bowmen, and light infantry. They excel so in courage that they believe the Romans will not resist their first onset."

When Andronicus heard this, / 271 / he let him go to report to Dionysius that the emperor, who was unable to endure the injuries which had been inflicted by them on the Romans, was (behold!) at hand to apply the requisite punishment. He led the Romans' army, fully equipped, out of camp. It was drawn up as follows. He ordered the Cumans and most of the Turkish force, together with a few knights who fought with lances, to lead the way, then on either hand followed regiments of Romans, which Kogh Vasil and Philokales commanded, and in addition Tatikios whom they entitle Aspietes. Behind them marched infantry mingled with bowmen and an armored regiment of Turks. Thereafter, on either hand marched Joseph Bryennios and George Branas and Demetrius his brother, and Constantine Aspietes the sebastos; then both Andronicus by surname Lampardas, who was the emperor's chartoularios, and . . .[17] together with picked Romans and Germans, and also Turks. Andronicus [Kontostephanos] the general marched behind with many other men worthy of note, who usually were arrayed under the emperor when he went to war, and Italians from the mercenary force, as well as Serbs, who followed behind him, holding spears and broad shields. Thus arrayed, the Romans took the road. When they came to the place where Dionysius had reared the mound, they dismounted from their horses, lamented fervently, and gave pledges to one another / 272 / that each would die for his fellow countryman and relation.

When Dionysius learned that the Romans were approaching, he was filled with courage and very ironically ordered the Hungarians to raise their cups and drink the health of the Romans.

Rising, they drank hastily, went to their arms, and were arrayed in their usual fashion. For their custom is always that the picked men among them fill the foremost regiment; long since aware of this, the emperor directed Andronicus that his array should be in reverse. So when they came near one another, Andronicus ordered the leading regiments to shoot arrows at the Hungarians. When they saw them [the Hungarians] charging at them, they were to flee, not straight toward the Romans' army, but rather to the sides, so that as they divided on either hand, the Hungarians would be left in the empty space in the midst of the battle array. But at their assault, the others [the Roman van] turned their backs and fled at full speed until they reached the Sava. Finally two of the Romans' regiments on the left, which Kogh Vasil and Tatikios commanded, held out, but the rest were swept aside. Demetrius Branas, who was left with eighty men when his followers were scattered, engaged the enemy, and fell there, struggling valiantly, after he had been struck a deadly wound on the face; after he had been made captive, he was carried off to the Hungarians' camp. His brother George, however, alarmed at their superiority of number, lacked courage for the conflict.

The left-hand / 273 / wing of the Romans thus turned to flight, but the right-hand one attacked the Hungarians' left and clearly drove them back. When Dionysius observed this, he was minded to attack those about the general Andronicus. Many of his followers, however, commenced to be afraid, wherefore they reined in their cavalry. Noticing this, Dionysius reproached their cowardice, but yet begged them to remain there, lest they make their fear evident to the Romans. Comprehending what was happening, Andronicus Lampardas feared lest the multitude with Dionysius, when he went elsewhere, would then fall upon Andronicus the general; he decided that he had to engage Dionysius first. As they clashed with each other, a din arose, and a clatter occurred everywhere as spears were broken against shields and fell to the ground. Although those arrayed under the other Branas, George, came to aid them, the Romans were exhausted.

When the general Andronicus observed this, lest, after those with Lampardas were seriously defeated, the whole conflict should devolve on him, he burst forth upon the foe and made a mighty onset, so that at the first encounter eighty of the Romans fell, but many more of the barbarians. By their valor, however, the Romans, who sustained the struggle with unutterable might, finally drove them back. Such a slaughter of barbarians occurred there that the plains were almost covered with carcasses. For when their spears / 274 / were broken and their swords shattered, they smote the wretches' heads with maces. Then the standard was taken, which, being very large, was carried by these barbarians in a cart, and also Dionysius' horse with his complete armor, while he himself fled danger with difficulty in a fashion I am unable to relate. Those of the barbarians who succeeded in running away and reaching the river were taken by the Romans' fleet. Five of their generals, whom they call župans, were taken alive, and about eight hundred of the soldiers. Among them were many of the well-born and generally distinguished men. In this conflict many thousands fell. There was not a Roman who was not the hero of many noble deeds, but most particularly John Kontostephanos and Andronicus Lampardas.

After they had been successful in this, since it was midnight, the Romans' army returned to camp, leading some of the Hungarians captive and [bringing] upwards of two thousand breastplates, nor could one count the helmets and shields and swords. In this situation they camped that night, but putting on their arms when day broke, they went to the Hungarians' camp. Since they found it barren of men, they pillaged it and returned. The war on the Hungarians concluded there.[18]

8. The emperor paid attention to the walls of Constantinople, which in many parts had been ruined by time, and when a lack of water / 275 / beset it [the capital], he carefully cleansed the channels. Since he noted that the old arcades which conveyed water to Byzantion were long since collapsed, and that it would be a difficult task to reconstruct them, one requiring much time, after

he had considered a place not far distant from Byzantion, which was named Petra,[19] he constructed an underground reservoir. Being situated in a hollow amidst hills on either hand, it was capacious, with many intakes to it, and, gaping, received water which descended to it through clefts and hollows as if from myriad channels. It communicated this [water] to the city through the usual underground ways.

This emperor uprooted from the Romans' commonwealth a custom, one of the most monstrous, which had lacked little of ending in law. What this was let us now relate. Man's inexorable necessity of remaining alive has caused manifold innovations in his way of life and in particular has constrained many to alienate their liberty for hire. So even some of the wellborn, should it chance thus, not to mention common, ordinary people, serve for hire those in superior positions and ranks. What evil does human greed do? Receiving these wretches, those who purchase their service treat them like persons bought with silver, and the day's wage paid down as hire was equally the purchase price of free men, and so a sign of misfortune. Indeed, if those burdened by toil from this servitude ever wished to reject it, the others [employers] / 276 / treated them like runaway slaves and imposed punishments for their daring. Then it was like Aesop's fable, in which the lion lay sick in his cave and the beasts went to him: many were the tracks of free men going in, but of those coming out by the same way, not a one. So terrible was the custom, but the emperor, desiring to extract it by the roots from amidst the state, decreed by letter freedom for those who were naturally free. For he wished to rule free Romans, not captive ones.[20]

In the fifteenth year of his reign, he decreed that no molestation should be inflicted on the holy monasteries at Byzantion in regard to the properties which they held anywhere [March 1158]. He confirmed the gift by a document which, because it is sealed with gold, is commonly termed a "chrysobull" [gold-sealed document]. Therefore none of the monks can now be seen pounding on the courtroom's door, because there is nothing possible for which someone from the government would go to law with them. Such is this.[21]

Since the law set aside very many from the total number of days, to wit those on which one of the Lord's sacraments is celebrated by Christians or else the memory of one of the great men [i.e., saints] is brought up, legal cases in the state reached to infinity without conclusion. Therefore I observed men growing old in legal actions, and indeed dying in them. But by new legislation [March 1166] he banished this abuse from the Romans' state. For the emperor's / 277 / decree said that festivals should not entirely pre-empt days, nor should they allow cases to be dragged on day after day by these delays, but those days were to be entirely debarred from legal disputation on which God procured something beneficial for mankind, and of the rest some were left completely available for legal action, on others the morning was prohibited to legal suits, but they [courts] were to be open for the entire afternoon and allow whoever wished to enter.[22]

Also, he very splendidly conducted to Byzantion the holy stone which had from a long time back been in Ephesos, and committed it to the other holy [relics] there [1169]. What the stone was and whence it reached the Ephesians' land, the narrative will next relate. At the end, there was the Saviour's sacrifice upon the Cross, and His Mother receiving Him, laid Him prone, as was customary, on this stone; falling down, she lamented deeply, as was reasonable, and the tears from her weeping reached the stone and still remain there, unexpunged, something rather miraculous. Then Mary Magdalene, they say, took the stone and set sail straight for Rome so that, coming in the presence of the caesar Tiberius, she might accuse Pilate and the Jews as Jesus' unjust murderers. When by some chance she put into the harbor of Ephesos, she left it there, but she departed and went to Rome. From then until now the stone remained there. When it had been brought to the region of Damalis across [from Constantinople], a splendid procession from Byzantion received it. The whole senate of the Romans composed it, and whoever / 278 / was among the priests and monks, while Loukas, who then directed the church, and the emperor went ahead of their respective portions of the official body. The emperor indeed lifted the stone with his shoulder, being unnecessarily modest in such things and desiring very humbly to render them service.[23]

9. About these times Egypt, which was in danger of being captured by the Romans, proved able to survive in a way which is going to be related. Not very recently it formed a part of the Romans' realm, and furnished it annually a great amount of revenue; when Asia was severely afflicted and the Arabic people prevailed for the moment, it too was taken and fell under the sway of the Easterners. But emperor Manuel, who had already recovered many of the regions in the east for the Romans, longed very intensely to reclaim this one too. So, dispatching envoys there, he ordered them to remind the land of its previous custom and of the tribute which, weighing many talents, used to come to us; but when it refused, to promise that in no long time war would be waged on them. In such terms was the content of the embassy. Since the Egyptians vigorously rejected this, the emperor constructed a fleet of vessels, horse transports, and very numerous warships, embarked an army on them, and sent them to Egypt [1169]. The oft-mentioned Andronicus Kontostephanos commanded it; as stated, he had previously become grand *doux* [grand admiral]. Sailing swiftly he reached Egypt, and sending to Palestine / 279 / he summoned the king there [Amalric I] to join the Romans in this conflict, according to the treaty.

While the king was delaying, Andronicus, lest his time be spent there in vain, decided that the army had to effect a landing. So they effortlessly took the city of Tenesion [24] and, frequently sallying forth, overran the region. When the king was reported then approaching, they transferred the war to Damietta [Dimyāt], a city filled with inhabitants and exceedingly rich. There many fearsome battles were waged by the Romans, but nothing succeeded for a reason I am going to relate. It was agreed by the emperor and the Palestinians who joined in the war on Egypt that the Romans would receive a half portion of the conquered region, and they would have the rest. So at the outset the king, when the Romans reached Egypt first, treacherously decided to come late for the war, so that while the Romans ran all the risks he might effortlessly take possession of the country; because he was late, he continually deferred battle and advised the like to the Romans, while they, paying little heed to his words, daily sustained heroic struggles. Whether, as I said, they [the Palestinians] did this desiring the Romans to run the risks, so that they might enjoy effortless victory, or were utterly envious of the emperor's lordship over Egypt, I am unable to state. Allegedly, however, those inside [Damietta] corrupted the king with money and induced him to this.

/ 280 / Since the Romans recognized that they were insufficient for the war, they withdrew and returned to Byzantion; but when a storm overtook them, many of the ships were lost. The Romans' expedition to Egypt had this conclusion. The people of Egypt, lest a second expedition of Romans be made against them, sent envoys to the emperor and agreed annually to furnish the Romans a specified amount of gold from there. Rejecting the embassy, he [Manuel] sent them back unsuccessful, as he intended to overrun their whole land again.[25]

10. In the meantime the king of Palestine came to Byzantion to petition the emperor for what he required [1171]. Obtaining what he sought, he agreed to many things, including his subjection to the emperor upon those terms.[26]

At this time [Manuel] committed the Venetians who lived in Byzantion and anywhere else in the Romans' land to public prisons and caused their property to be registered in the state treasury, for a reason which I am about to narrate. The Venetians' land is situated at the farthest part of the Ionian Gulf [Adriatic Sea], and projects rather far from the shore, sea-girt, like a sandbank. Frequently the sea advancing during the day makes it available for shipping at that time, but, retreating again, makes the strait entirely impassible for ships and men. The nation is corrupt in character, jesting and rude more than any other, because it is filled with sailors' vulgarity.[27] As they formerly offered an allied force to emperor Alexius [I] when / 281 / that [renowned] Robert [Guiscard] crossed from Italy to Dyrrachion [Durazzo, modern Durrës] and besieged the place [1081], they received various recompense, and in particular a confined space in Byzantion was assigned to them, which the commonality call the "Embolon" ["Quarter"].[28] Also on this account they alone of all the rest [other Italian and Byzantine merchants] pay tithes on commerce to none of the Romans from it [the Embolon]. Their immoderate enrichment from that source quickly elevated them to boastfulness. They used to treat the citizen like a slave, not merely one of the general commonality, but even one who took pride in the rank of sebastos and who had advanced to some greater position among the Romans' grand offices [was scorned].

Angered thereat, emperor John expelled them from the Romans' state [1122]. They were therefore eager to take vengeance on the Romans. Having readied a fleet of their ships, they assailed the land; they took Chios and ravaged the celebrated islands of Rhodes and Lesbos. Landing in the Palestinians' territory, they besieged and took Tyre along with them; the wretches pursued a course of piracy by sea and had no mercy on mankind [1122–25]. Therefore the emperor admitted them on the previous terms, and raised them to still more bragging and pride [1126].[29]

Willfulness which appears to be successful is capable of being swept on to folly. Therefore they inflicted blows on many of the wellborn who were related to the emperor by blood, and generally insulted them savagely. Even in the time of emperor Manuel, they no less continued the same practices, taking for themselves Roman wives and dwelling like other Romans in their houses / 282 / outside the residential area granted them by the emperor.

Unable to endure these things, he commenced to impose on them punishments for their misdeeds. Separating those who lived in Byzantion from the Venetians who came by way of trade, he called [the former] in the Latins' tongue "Bourgesioi," after they had prudently given him pledges that they would maintain obedience to the Romans so long as they lived. For the name ["burgesses" or "citizens"] is to be interpreted thus.

Not much later the Venetians who were angry at the Lombards [i.e., Genoese] because they had broken away from their wishes, rose up against them, pulled their houses down to their foundations, and did them great damage [1170]. Summoning them to the bar of justice, the emperor condemned them to rebuild the Lombards' houses and immediately restore what had been taken from them. But the Venetians did not wish to do any of these things and threatened to work harm on the Romans, reminding him of what they had done while emperor John was still alive. When he comprehended this, the emperor decided not to delay. So, because he intended to take them on the same day in a net, he dispatched letters throughout the Romans' land, whereby he specified to those who governed the provinces the moment at which they had to lay hands on the Venetians. Thus at the same time those in Byzantion were seized along with those in the farthest corners of the Romans' land, and prisons and holy monasteries received them [12 March 1171].

When some time had elapsed, since the prisons were crowded by so great a multitude, / 283 / the Venetians (for it seems that nothing is harder to defeat than desperate men) dared something as follows. As each one offered himself as security to the emperor for the other, they were able to go free from the prisons. One among them was outstanding by birth and distinguished by wealth; he had sold to the treasury for much money a ship of immense size, such as had never before put into port in Byzantion. Therefore, having been entrusted with its care by the emperor, he plotted with the Venetians that, when they had boarded it, they would set sail by night for their homeland. Seizing the suggestion, when a favorable wind came, they jumped in and departed in flight. When they learned this, the Romans pursued, and getting close to them when they were someplace near the strait of Abydos [the Dardanelles], they intended to burn them with Median [i.e., Greek] fire. But the others, because they were familiar with Roman ways, boldly made preparations, dipping some cloth in vinegar and wrapping the whole ship in it. Since the Romans were unable to succeed (for the fire was either hurled at the vessel farther than necessary, or did not reach it, or, even reaching it, was repelled by the cloth and quenched in the water when it fell), they returned unsuccessful.

When in no long time they reached their own land, the Venetians constructed a fleet and made an attack on the Romans [1171–72]. First they assailed Euripos [i.e., Euboea], but when they were repelled, since the emperor had installed garrisons of soldiers which were adequate for the cities there, they hastened to the island of Chios. After they had hauled their ships up there, / 284 / they went forth to ravage the place. They encountered there, however, forces which had crossed to the island by the emperor's foresight, and when they came to grips, they fought, lost many of their own men, turned back, and retreated to their ships. The emperor was minded to take them by force and planned to dispatch a military and naval force against them. But there was one, Aaron by name, who then possessed the office of *akolouthos* [commander of the Varangian Guard], a really presumptuous and bragging fellow. But as he was always hostile to the emperor's affairs, he was repeatedly caught in misrepresentation and convicted of devoting himself to diabolical works. But this was later, when righteous justice overtook the criminal. At that time, because he revealed the plan to the Venetians' nation, he caused the emperor's undertaking to fail.

The Romans' fleet set sail to reach Malea (this is a promontory [of the Peloponnesus] separated by many days' journey from the island of Chios), to lie in wait for the Venetians there. Already they were expected to be driven out by the Romans' infantry, which as stated lay in ambush for them on the island and engaged them from superior positions. But partly because they were overcome in battle by the Romans on the island, so that they suffered damage to the greatest part of their army, and partly because they had learned that the [Byzantine] fleet was under way, they set out late in the day and departed from the island. At dawn the Romans' fleet reached Lesbos, and when they heard what had happened, they pursued them. But it [the Byzantine fleet] was unable to decide matters in a pitched battle, / 285 / since the foe continually fled headlong. Overhauling many of their triremes, they took and sank them with all their crews, but the rest reached their own country in flight. Thus being short of men they fled peril, so that when those from Epidamnos [Durazzo] came to grips with them, not one of theirs was forcibly taken by them.[30]

The Venetians found such profit from their boastfulness. Desiring to mock their rashness, the emperor wrote them as follows. "From a long time back your nation has displayed great ignorance regarding what ought to be done. For when you formerly poured into the Romans' state as wanderers really gripped by poverty, you showed extreme disdain towards them. You had a great ambition to betray them to their enemies; it is superfluous to enumerate in detail what your present circumstances are. Detected thereby, you were justly expelled from their land. Out of vainglory you decided that a conflict with them would be on equal terms, [you] a nation not even anciently worthy of the name, but at length now well-known on account of the Romans, yet not comparable [to them] in strength: imagining this, you have incurred much laughter from every hand. How can that be? With them [the Byzantines] not even the pick of nations, anywhere whatsoever, could wage war unpunished." So much the emperor wrote. As

they were still unable to make war on the Romans with a large
fleet, / 286 / from then on they lay in wait and acted as pirates,
until they experienced a second blow.[31]

11. So these matters went thus. The affairs of Cilicia,
however, commenced to be in a bad state. For after Toros had
measured out his life [1168], his brother Mleh who took possession of the country began to behave no less ill toward the Romans.
Michael Branas had first been chosen governor of the Cilicians
[ca. 1160–61], then Andronicus by surname Euphorbenos, who as
stated was cousin to the emperor [1162]. But since he achieved
nothing worthy of note there, the Isaurians' affairs were in a state
of collapse; thereafter, many succeeded one another in the governorship, among whom Constantine, whom they surname Kalamanos, was distinguished, yet he achieved nothing [1163–64, and
again ca. 1173]. Kalamanos indeed, who had distressed the Armenian in many ways, was injured in greater ones.[32]

About those times, [Henry the Lion] the duke of the Saxons, a numerous and prosperous people, came to Byzantion with a
very great suite in order to reconcile the king of the Germans [with
Manuel] (for they practiced great suspicion toward one another).
After he had achieved what he came for, he departed [1172].[33]

At this time the Serbs, since the Venetians pressed them to
it, looked toward revolt; [34] also, since Stephen [István III] who
ruled Hungary departed this life [1172], matters there became full
of turmoil. Aroused thereat, the emperor went to Sardika. While
he made a stay there, the Hungarians sent and asked that Béla
/ 287 / be dispatched to them as king. For, when Stephen died, the
principle of justice looked toward him. Béla had previously been
set apart for son-in-law to the emperor, as was stated in the foregoing account, but since the law of consanguinity hindered it, he
wedded the empress' sister. Therefore, after he had been proclaimed caesar, he excelled in rank the greatest then in Byzantion.
So when he had proclaimed him king, he [Manuel] sent him to
Hungary with his wife, after he had promised on oath to observe

for the whole course of his life whatever would be beneficial to the emperor and the Romans. There accompanied him on behalf of the emperor those restoring him to office, John [Comnenus] the proto-sebastos and others of the aristocracy.[35]

When he had established Béla in power, the emperor turned to the nation of the Serbs, eager to take vengeance on their rashness. But, something which I myself am capable of astonishment at, the whole army had not yet been assembled, yet the emperor invaded the land with a few thousands through steep and precipitous regions and pressed forward to engage the grand župan. Although the latter had gathered to himself a numerous allied force from every hand, he at once fled, because terror beset his spirit. Sending envoys to the emperor, he asked to enjoy forgiveness for his evil deeds. Being unable to persuade him of this, he asked that he might gain an audience with him without personal risk. So when the emperor assented, he came and approached the tribunal, with head uncovered and arms bare to the elbow, his feet unshod; a rope haltered his neck, and a sword was in his hand. He offered himself to the emperor for whatever treatment he desired. / 288 / Having mercy on him for this, he [Manuel] dismissed the accusation. After he had thus been successful, the emperor departed from Serbia, while the grand župan accompanied him.[36] At this time Aaron, whom I mentioned a little before, was seized for the reasons mentioned and blinded.

12. In the west matters went thus, but Asia suffered difficulties again. For Nūr-ad-Dīn the *atabeg* of Aleppo, and the sultan who ruled Lykaonia [i.e., Kilidj Arslan II of Ikonion], and Mleh lord of the Armenians, and the ruler of Ankyra and the rest of Galatia agreed on the same thing, to launch an attack on the Romans [1173].[37] Therefore the emperor hastily marched from the west and camped somewhere around Philadelphia.

While he was busied at this, the Germans and Venetians came to besiege Ancona, some by sea, the rest with a land army [1173]. One of the men among them [Christian of Mainz], who adorned an episcopal throne, commanded the Germans. After some time had passed in the siege, necessities failed the people of Ancona, and the city was expected to be taken shortly. There was, however, a woman, an Italian by race [Aldruda Frangipane, countess of Bertinoro], but more generous than anyone else, and in particular masculine; since she had been bereft of her husband long before, she had maintained a chaste life from then on. When she learned the facts regarding Ancona and that it was in its ultimate straits, inflamed by ardor (for she maintained friendship for the Romans), she hastened to assist the city by outlays from her own household. Since this was wholly insufficient for the necessities of war, she / 289 / pledged her children [i.e., their property], and thus furnished a great quantity of gold; writing to the city, she declared that they should be of good courage and not betray themselves to the enemy. When the people of Ancona learned this, they felt encouraged and planned to attack the enemy. The latter, once they noticed this, forthwith shifted their ground. Meanwhile she, who was established as general over the city, united the men of Ancona with her own army. When an assault was made, the Germans, not enduring the onset, fled from a woman's host and lost many of their men. Their general, the priest, was almost taken, save that he snatched safety by flight. She, however, turned on the Venetians, who as stated beset the city by sea; after she had overcome them in battle, she returned to the city, hailing the great emperor with acclamations of praise.[38]

The emperor, who was as stated camped at Philadelphia, planned how he might easily alienate the said barbarians from one another. Indeed, writing to the sultan of Lykaonia, he reproached him for his faithlessness and inquired the cause for which he so suddenly waged war on the Romans. The other alleged many and various [excuses] and said that their caliph,[39] the high priest among them, was angry at him for having agreed to such an extent on friendship with the Romans. So saying, he sent the envoys back empty-handed. When the emperor heard this, he responded to him with a second embassy, writing to him / 290 / thus: "If it has from some time back seemed right to you, combined with others of your fellows, to attack the Romans, abandon your rashness. Place a guard on your land, since the Romans' army will reach it within fifteen days." When the sultan received this letter, he was terrified at heart and, abandoning his plans, discussed terms of peace for the future. And those parts of the [Turks'] plot which had not yet been finally confirmed were again broken apart, because a very large portion among them went over from the sultan to the emperor.[40] Glorified by this bloodless triumph, the emperor set out for Constantinople.

Learning of this and filled with courage thereby, the king of Palestine together with the prince of Antioch moved against the barbarians of Aleppo and did great damage to them.[41]

13. At this time the emperor composed for himself the speech in council, not, as was customary, with the *a secretis* [42] dictating it as if from the emperor. Its purport was deep in thought and proceeded from an extremely noble spirit; it was sufficiently furnished with ideas and provided with numerous logical arguments. The diction was pure and the style simple, and in short unadorned yet natural and clearly revealing its author. As has often been said by me, he was comparable to no one in natural attainments. I myself, / 291 / who frequently discussed the works of Aristotle with him, observed many of the deeply debated problems naturally resolved, something I think had never been possible for anyone else. With marvelous simplicity he clarified many of the points in the Scriptures which had hitherto remained inexplicable or else had not been rightly interpreted. But for these to be written here seems to me contrary to historical rules.

Book VII

1. Such were what had hitherto been achieved by emperor Manuel on either continent. Hereafter there will be recorded by me what befell him as he campaigned in Asia. For Kilidj Arslan, of whom we have made much account in the foregoing, who had been furnished much money by the emperor, as I said [sic], had risen to a very great height of power and had been able to deprive various rulers there of their principalities. Especially he applied constraint to Shāhan-Shāh, who was his brother born of the same seed, and who ruled Gangra and Ankyra, Galatian cities; he placed them under his authority, and, since he was unable to put him to death, necessitated him to wander among all the nations of mankind as a stranger and foreigner. Neither / 292 / did he render to the emperor any of the cities of which he had become possessed, nor did he desire to fulfill any of the other things to which he had previously agreed. He treated all men haughtily, and was unrestrained in passion. Considering this, the emperor was at first angered and indignant at the matter; but as he was drawn away from these things by western affairs, he did not at all wish to stir up those of Asia. When no other war from anywhere in the west appeared in the future, since he had been successful in everything, he assembled a sufficient army and determined to cross over.[1]

    Once Kilidj Arslan heard this, he sent envoys to the emperor, agreed to carry out various matters according to his will, and asked that forces of Romans forthwith be dispatched to Asia to garrison the cities which the emperor should choose. He himself would join them in the struggle for this purpose. When the emperor received this [letter], he sent Alexius Petraliphas with an army numbering upwards of six thousand, and entrusted him with money which he thought would be sufficient for that war. On these conditions, Alexius set out for Asia. When Kilidj Arslan heard that the Romans' army was approaching, he notified the cities which still remained unconquered by him and proferred them the fearful anticipation of the emperor's army. Being unable to resist both armies, they involuntarily yielded to him. Once he gained authority over them, he did not wish to yield any to the Romans.

/ 293 / The emperor was thereby displeased, and intended to set forth for war immediately. But since his affairs did not permit him (for spring [1175], which is the season especially suited to martial affairs, had passed, one in which he had planned to arrange various things beneficial to the Romans and in particular to erect cities wherever he pleased; in addition, Amaseia, an eastern city, was then trying to come over to him, and, since war had not yet openly broken out, it was likely that the Romans would easily acquire it), on this account he acted as follows. He dispatched to Paphlagonia Michael whose surname was Gabras, a man who as has often been said by me had risen to the sebastoi's rank and who was quite experienced in military activities. Part of an army he took with him, the rest he was to assemble from the villages which are situated there around Trebizond [Trabzon] and Oinaion, Pontic cities, and after he had collected them he [Manuel] ordered him to proceed to Amaseia.

In the meanwhile, something as follows befell. John Kantakouzenos, whom we have often mentioned in the foregoing account, had a son, Manuel, handsome to look upon, who was inferior in strength of body to none of his fellows.[2] As he was allegedly usually engaging in forbidden [i.e., treasonable] activities, the emperor first offered him advice, attempting to restrain him from such things. When he held fast to his rashness, without restraining himself, the emperor committed him to prison. But [something happened] which is usual with those in office (for in many cases they do what would draw to themselves the emperor's favor): / 294 / when he arrived in prison, they deprived the youth of his eyes, contrary to the emperor's will. When the emperor heard of it, he was angry and swore that this had been done to him without his knowing; yet he endured the pain, for he knew not how he could justly punish those who had done it.

2. But as we said, he sent Michael [Gabras] to Amaseia. He himelf crossed the strait of Damalis [the Bosporos] and went straight to Melangeia [1175]. After he had assembled an adequate force from the villages of Bithynia and the Rhyndakos, he went to the plains of Dorylaion, to fill the Romans' forts there with supplies while the peace still lasted and to encourage still more those who were hostile to the sultan, and in addition to reconstruct Dorylaion.

This Dorylaion was once as great a city as any in Asia and worthy of much note. A gentle breeze blows over the land, and plains extend around it, extremely smooth and exhibiting an extraordinary beauty, so rich and fertile that they yield abundant grass and produce splendid grain. A river, fair to see and sweet to taste, sends its course through the midst. Such a multitude of fish swims in it that, while fished in abundance by the people there, there is no lack. Splendid dwellings had been erected there by a former caesar of the Melissenoi, and there were populous villages and natural warm springs and porticoes and baths; whatever / 295 / brings pleasure to men, the place used to offer in abundance. But the Turks, when their assault against the Romans reached its peak, threw down the city to its foundations and rendered it entirely bereft of inhabitants; everything there vanished, even to the barest trace of its former splendor. Such was this city.[3]

At that time about two thousand Turks, wanderers, were as usual encamped around it. After he had repelled them from there, the emperor set up a palisade not far from the city and made preparations for wall building. It [the city] was speedily erected, contracted far inside the earlier plan, with the wall circling around it at a uniform distance on every side, a little way off from a mound which previously been built there for a citadel. Going out each day with a few men, in ambushes by surprise and in encounters face to face, the emperor killed many of the Turks, even those outstanding among them. For many [Turks] did not fail to come rushing in from the interior regions, thus to hinder construction. Then, too, the emperor dispatched Shāhan-Shāh, whom I have already mentioned, and who in former times had come as a refugee to him, to lands beyond Ikonion, after he had furnished him with money. An army also accompanied him as he took the road to Paphlagonia. But it had not gone far, when a force of Turks which was lying in wait killed many of the Romans with him and sated themselves on sufficient spoil. Escaping with difficulty, Shāhan-Shāh returned to the emperor in terror. Thus the man's affairs always ended in ill fortune. / 296 / This was what was done at Dorylaion.

With his army Michael Gabras reached Amaseia, and was invited by those who held the city to enter it forthwith; [4] since a force which had come for the same purpose from Kilidj Arslan was also encamped not far from the city, he lacked courage to enter. For he exercised great suspicion toward those inside, lest perchance they intended treachery against him. On this account they sent hostages to him and freely granted the citadel to the Romans. But some fear which suddenly overcame the man caused him to withdraw on one pretext or another, until those in the city became anxious lest, when the town was taken by Kilidj Arslan on account of the Romans' long delays, they should become forever hateful to their future master; without their ruler's knowing, they betrayed it to the said [Turks]. Setting out from there, Michael returned to the Romans' land, making no account of the Romans, who were as stated in the citadel, or of the others.

In this way the business of Amaseia ended. When the em-

peror, who was still occupied around Dorylaion, learned of it, he
dispatched the eunuch Thomas to Kilidj Arslan. He pressed him,
demanding back Amaseia, and charged him with neglect of his
oaths. He threatened that, if he did not cease thus injuring the
Romans, in no long time he would experience avenging justice.
Who this Thomas was I shall forthwith reveal. He was sprung
from the island of Lesbos, but came from an ignoble family;
/ 297 / since he had no profession worthy of account, he went to
Byzantion, became practiced in cutting men's veins [bloodletting],
and thereby earned his living. But it seems there is nothing at all
which cannot serve when fortune is favorable. Although Thomas
had reached the lowest of trades, by this skill he became as great
as any other man in the imperial court. After he had gained a large
amount of money in a short while, he some years later departed in
flight to Palestine with it. Since matters there did not fall out according to his intent, he returned again to the emperor. After he
had found him favorable, he was later proven disaffected; after he
had been committed to the prison in the palace which is customarily called Elephantine [i.e., "Ivory"], he there passed the
remnant of his life. But this was later. Going then to the sultan, as
we said, since he did not desire to fulfill any of the things for
which he had come, he returned empty-handed to the emperor. At
that time, too, the Turks who were lying in wait on the road came
close to killing him.[5]

3. Within forty days the emperor had erected the city,
and when he encircled it with a trench, settled a great many
Romans there, and left a sufficient garrison, he departed and
camped in the regions around the Rhyndakos. Having made a short
delay, he led forth his army. When he observed that very few attended him (for the greater part of the regiments had left for home,
without his being aware of it, although reportedly he had previously given firm orders that none of the army was meanwhile to
depart), / 298 / he sent a certain Michael, a barbarian by birth (indeed, his name was previously Ishāq),[6] one of those who had at

first served in his household, to punish some of the soldiers bodily for desertion. He himself, with a few men, passed through the plains toward Lampe [in Phrygia],[7] and reconstructed a certain fort (Soublaion was its name)[8] situated someplace around the origins of the Maeander, which had collapsed with age. From there the emperor commenced to engage the foe, not in the way in which he was accustomed, but he raged and dashed irresistably like fire or water.

The emperor was engaged in these activities, but the above-mentioned Michael, as if he had been enraged against the Romans from a long time back, made the emperor's anger his excuse: without first inquiring he stretched each of those whom he met prone on the ground, plunged the iron in his eyes, and left him there wretched, not even comprehending why he suffered. Sometimes it was not even a member of the army, but a peasant or someone dealing in trade or some other sort of men. He, however, went on to other places and maimed numerous men's bodies, until when the emperor learned of what was being done (for already having successfully completed the business of the fort, he had returned to Byzantion), he stopped him from his rage. He allegedly came close to being awarded similar punishments. But considering that he would not again dare inflict the same things on Romans, the emperor / 299 / relieved him of the accusation. In no long time, however, justice overtook him and removed him from mankind; it beset his descendants with misfortunes.

The emperor then summoned [Michael] Gabras to trial; when he had convicted him (for it was decreed that he might treat him with punishments according to his will), he fettered his legs with irons and committed him for some time to one of the prisons in the palace, but afterwards he recalled him and honored him again with his previous rank.

When Kilidj Arslan learned of the emperor's attack (for what had befallen around Dorylaion severely affected his spirit), he dispatched to Byzantion one of those who were especially power-

ful in his court, Gabras by name,[9] and begged of the emperor that
he [Manuel] should take whichever forts of his seemed right to
him and desist from anger against him [the sultan]. Refusing his
letter, however, the emperor sent him [Gabras] back; he summoned numerous troops from the Serbs and Hungarians and very
carefully prepared for war. Lest horses and men lacked necessities
of life, an immense number of oxen were driven from the villages
in Thrace, and over three thousand wagons.

When spring [1176] appeared, he crossed to Asia and as
usual assembled his troops at the Rhyndakos. The allies, Hungarians and Serbs, who were subject to the Romans, did not arrive at
the right moment, and caused him to campaign in the summer
season, on which particular account his affairs were ruined: in
martial activities, more than anything else, timing is most essen-
tial. Thus the emperor journeyed through Laodikeia and the
regions adjoining the Maeander, having in mind / 300 / to settle
down with his whole force for the siege of Ikonion. Since Nea
Kaisareia was trying to come over to him, he sent his nephew
Andronicus Batatzes to go to it with an army through the Paph-
lagonian regions. Before he [Manuel] set out from Byzantion, he
dispatched a fleet of a hundred fifty ships to Egypt, while he was
going with his whole force to the war on Kilidj Arslan.[10] Therefore, lacking troops sufficient for the [expedition] against
Egypt. . . .

[Here the text breaks off. During this march
toward Ikonion, on 17 September 1176, Manuel
was severely defeated and his army largely destroyed at the battle of Myriokephalon. He died in
1180.]

Appendix I

GENEALOGY OF THE HUNGARIAN KINGS (House of Arpad)

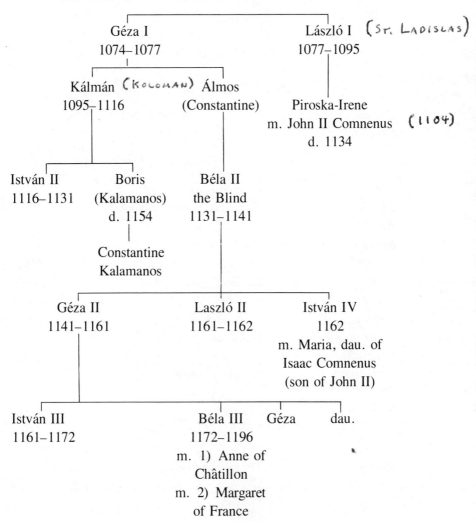

Géza I
1074–1077

László I (St. Ladislas)
1077–1095

Kálmán (Koloman)
1095–1116

Álmos
(Constantine)

Piroska-Irene
m. John II Comnenus (1104)
d. 1134

István II
1116–1131

Boris
(Kalamanos)
d. 1154

Béla II
the Blind
1131–1141

Constantine
Kalamanos

Géza II
1141–1161

Laszló II
1161–1162

István IV
1162
m. Maria, dau. of
Isaac Comnenus
(son of John II)

István III
1161–1172

Béla III
1172–1196
m. 1) Anne of
Châtillon
m. 2) Margaret
of France

Géza   dau.

Appendix II

Names Used in the Translation	Names Used by Kinnamos
Alans	Μασάγεται
Arabic people	Ἰσμαηλιτικὸν φῦλον
Austrians	Ὀστρίχιοι
Bretons	Βρετανοί
British	Βρίττιοι
Cumans	Σκύθαι
Czechs	Τζέχοι
French	Γερμανοί
Gauls	Γαλατοί
Germans	Ἀλαμανοί
Hungarians	Οὕννοι, Παίονες
Iberians	Ἴβηρες
Normans	Κελτοί
Petchenegs	Σκύθαι, Πετζινάκοι
Poles	Λέχοι
Russia	Ταυροσκυθική
Russians	οἱ πρὸς τῷ Ταύρῳ ἱδρύμενοι Σκύθαι
Saxons	Σαξόνοι
Serbs	Σέρβιοι, Δαλμάται
Turks	Πέρσαι

Notes

INTRODUCTION

1. Anna Comnena, *Alexiade: Règne de l'empereur Alexis I Comnène* (*1081–1118*), ed. and trans. Bernard Leib, Collection byzantine publiée sous le patronage de l'Association Guillaume Budé, 3 vols. (Paris, 1937–45). The English translations are: Elizabeth A. S. Dawes, trans., *The Alexiad of the Princess Anna Comnena* (London, 1928); E. R. A. Sewter, trans., *The Alexiad of Anna Comnena* (Harmondsworth and Baltimore, 1969). Ioannes Kinnamos, *Epitome rerum ab Ioanne et Alexio* [*sic*] *Comnenis gestarum,* ed. Augustus Meineke, Corpus scriptorum historiae byzantinae (Bonn, 1836; repr., Athens, n.d.); there is an unannotated Russian translation, *Kratkoe obozrienie tsarstvovaniia Ioanna i Manuila Komninov,* (*1118–1180*). *Trud Ioanna Kinnama,* trans. V. N. Karpov, Vizantiĭskie istoriki, perebedennye s grecheskago pri S. Peterburgshoĭ dukhovnoĭ akademii (St. Petersburg, 1859), and a Serbian translation, thoroughly annotated, of the sections relevant to Serbia and Hungary in *Vizantiski izvori za istoriju naroda Jugoslavije,* IV, trans. J. Kalić and N. Radošević-Maksimović, Vizanto-loški institut Srpske akademije nauka i umetnosti, Posebna izdanja, Knj. 12 (Belgrade, 1971), 1–105. Nicetas Choniates, *Historia,* ed. Immanuel Bekker, Corpus scriptorum historiae byzantinae (Bonn, 1835; repr., Athens, n.d.); the German translation is by Franz Grabler, in the series Byzantinische Ge-schichtsschreiber, VII–IX (Graz, Vienna, Cologne, 1958). There were other By-zantine historians in the 12th century, but they either wrote on short periods (Eus-tathius of Thessalonica, on the Norman capture of Thessalonica) or on world history (John Zonaras, Michael Glykas).

2. Kinnamos, 4–5; all citations to Kinnamos are to pages of the Bonn text (cited in n. 1 above), represented by numbers inserted between virgules in the transla-tion which follows.

3. See the Typikon of St. Neophytos, in Ioannes P. Tsiknopoullos, ed., Κυ-πριακὰ Τυπικά, Κέντρον ἐπιστημονικῶν ἐρευνῶν, Πηγαὶ καὶ μελέται τῆς κυπριακῆς ἱστορίας, No. II (Leukosia [i.e., Nikosia], 1969), 78. In 1195 a Manuel Kinnamos was one of the clerks of the Bureau of the Sea: F. Miklosich and J. Müller, *Acta et diplomata graeca Medii Aevi,* VI (Vienna, 1890), 129.

4. Györgi Bánhegyi, ed. and trans., *Kinnamos Ethopoiiája: Cinnami Ethopoeia,* Magyar-görök Tanalmánok: Οὑγγροελληνιχαὶ μελέται, 23 (Budapest, 1943), which has not been available to me. See brief accounts of its contents by F. D[ölger] in *Byzantinische Zeitschrift,* 43 (1950), 59, and Gyula Moravcsik, *Byzantinoturcica,* 2nd ed., Berliner byzantinische Arbeiten, 10–11 (Berlin, 1958), I, 324.

5. Kinnamos, 3.

6. Kinnamos, 69, 146–147.

7. Kinnamos, 5; it was possible to be enrolled "since childhood" among the imperial secretaries (19).

8. This has been the conventional view: see Carl Neumann, *Griechische Geschichtschreiber and Geschichtsquellen im zwölften Jahrhundert: Studien zu Anna Comnena, Theod. Prodromus, Joh. Cinnamus* (Leipzig, 1888), 93–95, 98–99; Moravcsik, *Byzantinoturcica,* I, 324. One must, however, bear in mind that the ancient historians who formed his model concentrated on warfare, and his Byzantine predecessors (Attaleiates, Anna Comnena, and Bryennios, to name but a few) found only the emperor's person and especially his martial deeds worthy of attention. Convention thus dictated his concentration on military history.

9. Kinnamos, 134–69. The description of Mottola, for instance, seems accurate: 152; his account of the siege of Bari, 139–40, seems to be that of a witness. If he was present, to whom was he attached? Possibly Michael Palaiologos, for whom he has outstanding praise, 70, 151. For John Doukas, the other leader of the expedition, he has very high regard and lavish praise (indeed, he claims to be able to state his thoughts, 158), but condemns his conduct after his capture by the Normans: 168–69, 172–73. He did not participate in every part of the campaign, since at one point he says that "allegedly" booty sold at specified prices (154). Nor does he seem to have shared the captivity of the leaders, so he may have returned to Constantinople at a late stage in the struggle. If he did not participate in this expedition, he had available an unusually complete and reliable source, whether a written memoir or living persons.

10. Kinnamos, 170–71, 290–91.

11. Ibid., 241.

12. Ibid., 192–93.

13. Ibid., 207. These quotations were noticed by Neumann, *Griechische Geschichtschreiber,* 93.

14. Kinnamos, 4, 257.

15. Kinnamos, 82–83; for the French version of these events, see Odo of Deuil, *De profectione Ludovici VII in Orientem: The Journey of Louis VII to the East,* ed. and trans. Virginia G. Berry, Records of Civilization, Sources and Studies (New York, 1948).

16. Kinnamos, 119, 120–21.

17. Kinnamos, 123–25, 129–31, 232–34 (his escape from prison), 250–51. The orations of Michael Choniates, before and after 1185, show what could be said both in eulogy and excoriation of Andronicus I: Michael Choniates, Τὰ σω-ζόμενα: Τὰ πλεῖστα ἐκδιδόμενα νῦν τὸ πρῶτον κατὰ τοὺς ἐν Φλωρεντίᾳ Ὀξωνίῳ, Παρισίοις καὶ Βιέννῃ κώδικας, ed. Spyridon P. Lampros, ι (Athens, 1879).

18. On the regency period, see my Byzantium Confronts the West (1180–1204) (Cambridge, Mass., 1968), 30–40. Several other details point to the regency period as the date of composition: Pope Alexander III (1159–81) is subjected to a violent invective (Kinnamos, 219–20), as if he were still alive, and the Kontostephanoi family, who were important supporters of the regency, receive consistently favorable treatment (96–98, and many other places). The date of composition of Kinnamos' history has aroused debate: Neumann, Griechische Geschichtschreiber, 99–100, believed most of the work was compiled during Manuel's reign, only the introduction being later; this ignores Kinnamos' reference, p. 4, to his present special opportunity for writing history (see below). Karl Krumbacher, Geschichte der byzantinischen Litteratur von Justinian bis zum Ende des oströmischen Reiches (527–1453), 2nd ed., Handbuch der klassischen Altertums-Wissenschaft, ιx, Pt. 1 (Munich, 1897), 279, believed the work was published after 1185, as shown by the statement in Kinnamos, 53–54, but this does not seem a clear reference to Andronicus' usurpation, only to his repeated treacheries toward Manuel. Moravcsik, Byzantinoturcica, ι, 325, dates the composition to 1180–83, the lifetime of Alexius II.

19. Kinnamos, 4.

20. Ferdinand Chalandon, Jean II Comnène (1118–1143) et Manuel I Comnène (1143–1180), Les Comnènes: Etudes sur l'Empire byzantin au XIᵉ et XIIᵉ siècle, ιι (Paris, 1912; repr., New York, ca. 1960) [hereafter cited as Chalandon, ιι], xvi–xviii; on Kinnamos' hostility to Latins, see xx–xxii.

21. Nicetas, Hist. (see n. 1, above), 430–31. The subject under debate was the Gospel expression, "My Father is greater than I." Since Euthymius had earlier supported the heterodox view on this point (Kinnamos, 254–55), he probably restated this position, while Kinnamos would have defended the conventional orthodoxy he expresses in his history (251–57, esp. 256).

22. E. Miller, Catalogue des manuscrits grecs de la Bibliothèque de l'Escurial (Paris, 1848), 218; Krumbacher, Geschichte der byzantinischen Litteratur, 279, 281.

23. Neumann, Griechische Geschichtschreiber, 91–93, pointed out that there was no tradition of documentary accuracy in ancient history; Chalandon, ιι, xvi–xvii, joined in rejecting the texts of the documents allegedly quoted by Kinnamos, pointing out that where we have genuine surviving documents, as in the corre-

spondence of Manuel and Conrad III, it bears no relationship to what Kinnamos alleges was written. Only Moravcsik, *Byzantinoturcica,* I, 325–326, has supported the accuracy of Kinnamos' alleged documents as summations from a register. But his examples are nearly all manifest rhetorical creations by Kinnamos himself; only the papal documents (alluded to, not quoted, in Kinnamos, 220) can have any real validity.

24. Kinnamos, 5; see Nicetas, *Hist.,* 7.

25. Kinnamos, 20.

26. Ibid., 127, 129–30; Chalandon, II, 410. John Comnenus and Andronicus were bitter enemies. Note that John Comnenus was killed in 1176 at Myriokephalon, so Kinnamos must have listened to his recollections before then.

27. Kinnamos, 109–13, 136–69 (see above, n. 9), 257–59.

28. Anna Comnena, *Alexiad,* XIV, vii, 7 (ed. Leib, III, 175–76).

29. Kinnamos, 38–63.

30. Kinnamos, 67–83, 84–87. If Kinnamos did *not* participate in the Italian expedition, and if John Doukas was *not* his informant, a written narrative by a participant should confidently be hypothesized.

31. Kinnamos, 3–4, 163. Among other possible Herodotean usages would be Kinnamos, 42, line 23 (Herodotus, VII, 18), and Kinnamos, 139, line 3, contains the same thought ("darken the air with arrows") as Herodotus, VII, 226, but not in the same words.

32. Kinnamos, 121. Kinnamos' style in general seems to imitate that of Thucydides.

33. Ibid., 218; the reference is to Procopius, *De bello gothico,* I, 1; see Neumann, *Griechische Geschichtschreiber,* 86.

34. Kinnamos, 52, 280. Kinnamos, 232, line 20, seems to reflect Hesychius, *Lexicon,* ed. Kurt Latte, II (Copenhagen, 1966), 112.

35. On this Byzantine practice, see Herbert Hunger, "Die byzantinische Literatur der Komnenenzeit: Versuch einer Neubewertung," *Anzeiger der Phil.-Hist. Klasse der Österreichischen Akademie der Wissenschaft,* 105 (1968), 61–62. For the sake of clarity, these names have ordinarily been translated into their medieval equivalents: see Preface. A similar classical echo is the consistent designation of Roger II as the "tyrant" of Sicily (Kinnamos, 118, and elsewhere), which merely signified that his title to rule had not been recognized by Constantinople.

36. Chalandon, II, xvi; the same author's *Histoire de la domination normande en Italie et en Sicile* (Paris, 1907; repr., New York, 1960), II, 253 n. 4.

37. Kinnamos, 26–28; see below, Book I, n. 30.

38. Kinnamos, 30, 58–59, 67–68, 76–80, 172–75, and many other places. On the question of the genuineness of the documents quoted, see the discussion in n. 23 above.

39. Kinnamos, 46–58 (esp. 55–56), 143–45, 246.

40. See above, n. 17.

41. Kinnamos, 265–69; Nicetas, *Hist.*, 187–89. For examples of panegyric to Manuel, see Kinnamos, 42–43, 47, 56, 61, 99–100, etc. Neumann, *Griechische Geschichtschreiber*, 99–101, offers a particularly good discussion.

42. Michael Psellos, *Chronographie, ou Histoire d'un siècle de Byzance (976–1077)*, ed. and trans. Emile Renauld, Collection byzantine publiée sous le patronage de l'Association Guillaume Budé, II (Paris, 1928), 172–85; Michael Attaleiates, *Historia*, ed. Immanuel Bekker, Corpus scriptorum historiae byzantinae (Bonn, 1853), 3–6, 216–29; Nicephorus Bryennios, *Commentarii*, ed. Augustus Meineke, Corpus scriptorum historiae byzantinae (Bonn, 1836); for Anna Comnena, see n. 1, above.

43. A number of 12th-cent. court orations are to be found in W. Regel, ed., *Fontes rerum byzantinarum*, I, fasc. 1–2 (all pub.) (Petrograd, 1892–1917); see my own translation of an oration by Nicephorus Chrysoberges to Alexius IV, in "A Byzantine Plan for the Fourth Crusade," *Speculum*, 43 (1968), 462–75. For Nicetas' orations, see the new edition: Nicetas Choniates, *Orationes et epistulae*, ed. Ioannes Aloysius van Dieten, Corpus fontium historiae byzantinae, III (Berlin, 1972 [pub. 1973]).

44. See in particular Kinnamos, 192; Neumann, *Griechische Geschichtschreiber*, 98–99, a particularly good discussion; Moravcsik, *Byzantinoturcica*, I, 326, places excessive trust in Kinnamos' claims of objectivity.

45. Kinnamos, 121–22. This confused chronology reappears at pp. 125–26, where again the necessity of explaining the fatal destiny of Andronicus leads the historian into rapid temporal and topical shifts. Neumann, *Griechische Geschichtschreiber*, 85–88, discusses the composition.

46. Moravcsik, *Byzantinoturcica*, I, 325.

47. Kinnamos, 236, 261; other back-references without corresponding texts are to Manuel, oft-mentioned as John's youngest son (21), but really only once before; to Andronicus as having received an extended account already (61), while he has only been alluded to among the unnamed sons of Isaac (53–54); to Suleimān's having been in command at Kalograia (66); to a certain Sotas (95); and to subsidies paid by Manuel to Kilidj Arslan (291). This is the list furnished by Neumann, *Griechische Geschichtschreiber*, 80, augmented by the case of Kilidj Arslan, which he had not noted. Neumann, 81, also mentions that Kinnamos fails to fulfill a promise (Kinnamos, 10) to record the rebuilding of Zeugminon, although he alludes to the event.

48. For the view that the existing Kinnamos text is an abridgment, see Neumann, *Griechische Geschichtschreiber,* 80–84, who originated the hypothesis; Krumbacher, *Geschichte der byzantinischen Litteratur,* 279–80; Chalandon, II, xiv–xv. The opposite view was put forward (I think successfully) by V. Grecu, "Nicétas Choniatès a-t-il connu l'Histoire de Jean Cinnamos?" *Revue des Etudes Byzantines,* 7 (1949), 202–03; Moravcsik, *Byzantinoturcica,* I, 325, states both views and leaves the question open. Epitomes exist for Anna Comnena's *Alexiad* (see edition by Leib, I, clxxi–clxxv), and for Nicetas Choniates' *History:* the B version partially published at the base of the text of the Bonn edition, and the simplified version by [Theodore Scutariotes,] in K. N. Sathas, Μεσαιωνικὴ Βιβλιοθήκη (*Bibliotheca graeca medii aevi*), VII (Venice and Paris, 1894). Leib, I, clxxiv, notes that Anna Comnena's epitomator made senseless excisions which destroy the meaning of the text; such is never the case in Kinnamos' history.

49. Nicetas, *Hist.,* 7.

50. Grecu, "Nicétas Choniatès," 194–204; A. P. Kazhdan, "Eshche raz o Kinname i Nikite Khoniate," *Byzantinoslavica,* 24 (1963), 4–31, which is a detailed comparison of the two authors' treatment of the reign of John II (pp. 6–23), and a brief review of some aspects of Manuel's reign (pp. 23–27).

51. Psellos, *Chronographie,* ed. Renauld, I (Paris, 1926), lxi–lxii; Anna Comnena, *Alexiad,* ed. Leib, I, clxiii–clxxi.

52. The 13th-cent. manuscript of Kinnamos is designated *Vaticanus graecus* 163 (fol. 221ʳ–268ᵛ); for its being in Constantinople in 1453, see the marginal note published by Neumann, *Griechische Geschichtschreiber,* 101–02. The best discussion of the history of the text, with a stemma of manuscripts and editions, is Gyula Moravcsik, "Συμβολαὶ εἰς τὴν χειρόγραφον παράδοσιν τῆς Ἐπιτομῆς Ἰωάννου τοῦ Κιννάμου," in his *Studies Byzantina* (Amsterdam, 1967), 293–96. The variants from *Vat. gr.* 163 for the sections of Kinnamos touching on Hungarian affairs were published by Ferenc Babos, *Adalékok Kinnamos Szövegtörténetéhez: Symbolae ad historiam textus Cinnami,* Magyar-görök Tanulmánok: Οὑγγποελληνικαὶ μελέται, 26 (Budapest, 1944), 6–13, and have been utilized for the present translation. The first edition is: Ioannis Cinnami, *De Ṛebus Gestis Imperat. Constantinop. Ioannis & Manuelis, Comnenorum Historiar. Libri IV,* Cornelius Tollius, Primus edidit, vertit, castigavit, Trajecti ad Rhenum [i.e., Utrecht], 1652; note that this edition was in four books (Books II, III, and IV begin where the present Books II, III, and IV do, so that the last book is extremely long). A Latin translation accompanied it, but a new one was made by Du Cange, and it is essentially his translation which is given in the Bonn edition; Du Cange divided the text into six books, the Bonn editor, into seven, but the divisions are not at the same points. The MS gives only two books, the modern Book I (John's reign), and the modern Book II as the entire remainder (Manuel's reign), but does have a paragraph mark or an ornamental stripe at the points where the Bonn editor's other books commence (Neumann, *Griechische Geschichtschreiber,* 82–84).

Du Cange's edition, Paris, 1670, in the Paris Corpus of Byzantine historians, was reprinted in Venice in 1729 in the Venice Corpus. Meineke's edition (see n. 1, above) was reprinted in J.-P. Migne, ed., *Patrologiae cursus completus,* Series graeca, Vol. 133 (Paris, 1864), col. 309–677. Fritz Hörmann, *Beiträge zur Syntax des Johannes Kinnamos,* diss. Munich, 1937 (Munich, 1938), discusses Kinnamos' grammar as a prelude to what proved an abortive new edition.

Even before Tollius' edition, the existence of Kinnamos' work was known; the title page of P. Poussines' edition of Anna Comnena reads in part as follows: *Annae Comnenae Porphyrogenitae Caesarissae Alexias . . . Notae mox opportunius edentur, unà cum Sinnamo Continuatore Annae . . .* (Paris, 1651), and on folio T. ij^r appeared the statement, "Hanc Alexiadem continuauit *Ioannes Sinnamus Regius Grammaticus;* quae nunc lucem aspexit e Codice Vaticano 319. cum Versione & Notis P. Possini." The projected publication was evidently forestalled by the appearance of Tollius' text.

There is a general, rather uncritical study of Kinnamos as a historian by M. M. Freĭdenberg, "Trud Ioanna Kinnama kak istoricheskiĭ istochnik," *Vizantiĭskiĭ Vremennik,* 16 (1959), 29–51; the bulk of it (pp. 30–47) analyzes Kinnamos' account of Byzantine relations with the Slavic states, Hungary, and Western Europe (except for the Italian cities); pp. 47–50 relate to Kinnamos' interests in military affairs. Peter Wirth, "Zur Frage nach dem authentischen Titel von Johannes Kinnamos' Geschichtswerk," *Byzantion,* 41 (1971), 375–77, points out that, in addition to the lengthy title given at the beginning of the MS (Kinnamos, 3), there are the titles given to the only two books attested by the manuscript, "Histories" and "Roman History." The long title, he thinks, might go back only to a scribe or epitomator, but which of the two other names Kinnamos applied to his whole work remains unknown.

New editions of Kinnamos have repeatedly been projected, most recently by B. Schartau, in XIVe Congrès international des études byzantines, Bucarest, 6–12 September 1971, *Résumés—Communications* (Bucharest, 1971), 196–98, and by P. Wirth. I have been privileged by some communications from Dr. Wirth.

Since these notes were composed, a French translation of Kinnamos has been published: Jean Kinnamos, *Chronique,* trans. J[acqueline] Rosenblum, Publications de la Faculté des lettres et des sciences humaines de Nice, 10 (n.p. [Paris], 1972). The translation is occasionally defective: e.g., in Book I, Ch. 1 (Kinnamos, 4–5), John Comnenus is made out to have rebelled against Nicephorus Botaneiates, and the last sentence in the chapter has been misunderstood (Rosenblum, p. 18). The annotation is incomplete and often inaccurate: Laodikeia on the Lykos, mentioned in Book I, Ch. 2, is identified as "Lattakieh" (Rosenblum, p. 199), a mistake for Syrian Laodikeia, now Latakia. Mlle Rosenblum's introduction takes a different view of Kinnamos' trustworthiness from the one expressed here (Rosenblum, pp. 7–9). See the review by D. Stiernon, *Revue des études byzantines,* 32 (1974), 407–09.

BOOK I

1. Nicephorus Bryennios, Alexius I's son-in-law, commenced a biography of him; it was revised and completed by his wife, Anna Comnena.

2. Moravcsik, *Byzantinoturcica* (see above, Introduction, n. 4), II, 70–71. Ἰωάννης should evidently be corrected to Ἰωάννην.

3. Moravcsik, "Συμβολαί" (see above, Introduction, n. 52), 295. On this campaign, see Chalandon, II (see above, Introduction, n. 20), 46; Claude Cahen, *Pre-Ottoman Turkey: A General Survey of the Material and Spiritual Culture and History, c. 1071–1330*, trans. J. Jones-Williams (New York, 1968), 92–93; Speros Vryonis, Jr., *The Decline of Medieval Hellenism in Asia Minor and the Process of Islamization from the Eleventh Through the Fifteenth Century*, Publications of the Center for Medieval and Renaissance Studies, U.C.L.A., No. 4 (Berkeley, Calif., 1971), 117–19. On Laodikeia, see W. M. Ramsay, *The Historical Geography of Asia Minor*, Royal Geographical Society, Supplementary Papers, IV (London, 1890), 134–35; W. M. Ramsay, *The Cities and Bishoprics of Phrygia: Being an Essay of the Local History of Phrygia from the Earliest Times to the Turkish Conquest* (Oxford, 1895–97), I, Pt. 1, 32–71; on the Kapros River, 35: "the river of Serai-Keui," i.e., Sarayköy, but recent maps call it the Kadiköy Dere.

4. On Sozopolis, see Ramsay, *Historical Geography*, 400–01; Vryonis, *Asia Minor*, 154–68.

5. An unknown location near Attaleia/Antalya: Ramsay, *Historical Geography*, 381, 420; Peter Wirth, "Zur asiatischen Toponymie im Geschichtswerk des Johannes Kinnamos," *Byzantinische Forschungen*, 3 (1968 [publ. 1971]), 251–52.

6. A Turkic people who had occupied much of the Ukraine, Moldavia, and Wallachia since the 10th cent. In 1091 they had been severely defeated by Alexius I, acting in cooperation with the Cumans (Polovtzi), who subsequently occupied the same regions: Moravcsik, *Byzantinoturcica*, I, 87–90; Constantine Porphyrogennetos, *De administrando imperio*, Vol. II, Commentary, ed. R. J. H. Jenkins (London, 1962), 12–14, 142–45. On this campaign, 1121–22, see Chalandon, II, 48–51.

7. On the Anglo-Saxons, who made up the chief part of the Varangian Guard from early in Alexius I's reign, see A. A. Vasiliev, "The Opening Stages of the Anglo-Saxon Immigration to Byzantium in the Eleventh Century," *Annales de l'Institut Kondakov (Seminarium Kondakovianum)*, 9 (1937), 39–70; Richard M. Dawkins, "The Later History of the Varangian Guard: Some Notes," *Journal of Roman Studies*, 37 (1947), 39–46 (see rev. by V. Laurent, *Revue des Etudes Byzantines*, 6 [1948], 114); Armin Hohlweg, *Beiträge zur Verwaltungsgeschichte des oströmischen Reiches unter den Komnenen*, diss. Munich, 1962, Miscellanea byzantina monacensia, 1 (Munich, 1965), 46–50.

8. So Chalandon, II, 51, dates these engagements.

9. Kinnamos is confused about the genealogy of the Hungarian kings. See table in the Appendix, based on that in Gyula Moravcsik, *Byzantium and the Magyars*, trans. Mihály Szegedy-Maszák, Miklós Szenczi, and Zsigmond Ritoók (Amsterdam, 1970). Álmos and István II were uncle and nephew; neither descended from László I.
On the text of this passage, see Moravcsik, "Σνμβολαί," 295.

10. R. Janin, *Les Églises et les monastères,* La Géographie ecclésiastique de l'Empire byzantin, Part I, Tome III (Paris, 1953), 529–38 (modern Zeyrek Kilise Cami).

11. Located on the Danube, three miles northwest of Belgrade; modern Yugoslav Zemun appears in Kinnamos as Zeugme or Zeugminon, in Nicetas, *Hist.*, 25, as Zeugminon, in Hungarian as Zimony, and in German as Semlin. See Jovanka Kalić, "Zemun u XII veku," *Zbornik radova Vizantološkog instituta,* 13 (1971), 27–56 (esp. 32–50).

12. Chalandon, II, 56–62; Moravcsik, *Byzantium and the Magyars,* 78–79.

13. Moravcsik, *Byzantinoturcica,* II, 59, 158.

14. On this campaign, see Chalandon, II, 81–87; Claude Cahen, "The Turks in Iran and Anatolia Before the Mongol Invasions," *The Later Crusades, 1189–1311,* ed. Robert Lee Wolff and Harry W. Hazard, A History of the Crusades, ed. Kenneth M. Setton, II, 2nd ed. (Madison, Wis., 1969), 677; Vryonis, *Asia Minor,* 119, 162.

15. Gümüshtigin Ghāzī (ca. 1105–34/35), leader of the Dānishmendid dynasty: Cahen, "Turks in Iran and Anatolia," 676; Cahen, *Pre-Ottoman Turkey,* 94–95; Chalandon, II, 87–89.

16. Mas'ūd, 1116–55, of the Seljuk (Selchük) dynasty, opponents of the Dānishmendids.

17. Apparently the valley of the Rhyndakos, the modern Orhaneli River.

18. Leon or Levon I, 1129–37: Chalandon, II, 107–12; Sirarpie Der Nersessian, "The Kingdom of Cilician Armenia," *The Later Crusades* (see above, n. 14), 636–37.

19. Bohemond II, 1126–30: Chalandon, II, 121–39; Robert L. Nicholson, "The Growth of the Latin States, 1118–1144," *The First Hundred Years,* ed. Marshall W. Baldwin, A History of the Crusades, ed. Kenneth M. Setton, I, 2nd ed. (Madison, Wis., 1969), 431–32, 436–39; Claude Cahen, *La Syrie du nord à l'époque des croisades et la Principauté franque d'Antioche,* Institut français de Damas, Bibliothèque orientale, I (Paris, 1940), 349–50, 357–61.

20. This is a fiction of Kinnamos; Raymond of Poitou was purposely summoned

by king Fulk of Jerusalem to marry Constance: Nicholson, "Latin States," 434, 436–38. Raymond of Poitou was prince of Antioch from 1136 to 1149.

21. This campaign and the siege of Shaizar in 1138 mark a high point of Byzantine intervention in the Crusading States; Kinnamos exaggerates the extent of John's success, especially in the siege: Chalandon, II, 130–46; Nicholson, "Latin States," 439–40; Cahen, *Syrie du nord,* 359–63; Wirth, "Zur asiatischen Toponymie," 252.

22. Chalandon, II, 175–79; Vryonis, *Asia Minor,* 119–20, considers this failure the beginning of the end for the Comnenian reconquest of Anatolia.

23. Ramsay, *Historical Geography,* 359, 389; I have corrected the MS reading "Pasgouse" on the basis of Wirth, "Zur asiatischen Toponymie," 253. On Sozopolis/Uluborlu, see Kinnamos, 6; on the campaign, see Chalandon, II, 180–83; Vryonis, *Asia Minor,* 120, 215.

24. An exaggeration; the distance is "over sixty miles" by road: Ramsay, *Historical Geography,* 389.

25. Alexius was born in 1106, crowned co-emperor in 1122 (after John's victory over the Petchenegs), and died in 1142; he married a Russian princess, and left a daughter: Chalandon, II, 12–13. Alexius' portrait, as co-emperor, survives in the south gallery of Hagia Sophia: Thomas Whittemore, *The Mosaics of Haghia Sophia at Istanbul: Third Preliminary Report, Work Done in 1935–1938: The Imperial Portraits of the South Gallery* (Boston, 1942), 7, 26–28, and plate facing p. 21.

26. Purple boots were in Byzantine usage the prerogative and special mark of the emperor; a sebastokrator (Manuel's rank) was entitled to blue boots: Louis Bréhier, *Le Monde byzantin,* L'évolution de l'humanité, XXXIIbis (Paris, 1949), II, 12.

27. The co-emperor Alexius died in 1142 at Attaleia; Andronicus the sebastokrator, the second son, died while taking his brother's body back to Constantinople by sea; he was accompanied on this mission by the third brother, Isaac the sebastokrator, who remained in the capital: Chalandon, II, 12–14, 182–83.

28. This word, evidently signifying "membrane" or something similar, is not found in the lexica of Du Cange, Liddell-Scott-Jones, Sophocles, or Demetrakos.

29. The ancient custom of reclining while dining continued among the Byzantines: Louis Bréhier, *Le Monde byzantin,* L'évolution de l'humanité, XXXII[ter] (Paris, 1950), III, 52.

30. The actual circumstances of John II's death were quite different: he was apparently murdered, possibly by the Latin mercenaries in the army, who disliked his aggressive policy toward Antioch and the other Crusading States. They favored Manuel, who was known to be partial to Westerners and to Western chi-

valric culture. The discovery of the true circumstances, from several contemporary rhetorical compositions, is the achievement of Robert Browning, "The Death of John II Comnenus," *Byzantion,* 31 (1961), 228–35.

Note that John II actually reigned 24 years, 7 months, 25 days (15 Aug. 1118–8 Apr. 1143): Kazhdan, "Eshche raz," 23.

BOOK II

1. Antioch had been regained by the Byzantines from the Arabs in 969; the Turks took it in 1085 from Philaretos, once a lieutenant of Romanus IV Diogenes; he had established himself as an independent ruler after Romanus' downfall. When the First Crusade seized it in 1098, Bohemond refused to acknowledge Byzantine overlordship. Alexius I had vainly struggled to achieve this; John II had in 1138 momentarily imposed himself, when Raymond did homage: Chalandon, II, 119–50, 183–90; Cahen, *Syrie du nord,* 357–68.

2. On the route (through Attaleia and Chonai/Honaz), see Chalandon, II, 198–99. On dromonds, triremes, and biremes, repeatedly mentioned by Kinnamos, see Hélène Ahrweiler, *Byzance et la Mer: La Marine de guerre, la politique et les institutions maritimes de Byzance aux VIIe–XVe siècles,* Bibliothèque byzantine, Etudes, 5 (Paris, 1966), 410–18, esp. 418: "Le bateau à voiles est en effet l'une des unités principales des flottes impériales du XIIe siècle. Le tonnage des bâtiments byzantins s'est alors considérablement accru, les unités de guerre sont maintenant des bâtiments ronds et lourds, ils continuent cependant à être désignés comme *dromons* et surtout comme *chélandia,* terms indiquant à ce moment le navire de guerre en général sans aucune précision spécifique."

3. The senate was then an advisory body of officials.

4. This Isaac Comnenus the sebastokrator, after initially enjoying the trust and confidence of his brother John II, turned against him; from 1130 to 1138 he wandered the Near East, striving to create a league against John. His exile at Herakleia Pontika apparently dates from soon after his return and reconciliation with John. In 1140, during the siege of Nea Kaisareia, his son John went over to the Turks, turned Muslim, and married a daughter of the sultan of Ikonion. Isaac's other son, Andronicus, continued the family tradition of opposition to the ruling Comneni. He figures largely in the histories of Kinnamos and Nicetas Choniates; in 1182 he effectively deposed Manuel's son Alexius II and ruled as Andronicus I. From him descend the so-called Grand Comneni, emperors of Trebizond. Chalandon, II, 17–18, 83–85, 152–53, 179–80, 195, etc.

5. Patriarch Leo Styppes had died in Jan. 1143; Manuel's first patriarch, Michael II Kourkouas Oxites, held office from July 1143 to March 1146: V. Grumel, *La Chronologie,* Traité d'études byzantines, I (Paris, 1958), 436; Chalandon, II, 196, 199–200; Peter Wirth, "Leon Styppes oder Styppeiotes?" *Byzantinische Forschungen,* 3 (1968 [publ. 1971]), 254–55.

6. Chalandon, II, 239–41; Nicholson, "Latin States," 445–47.

7. Evidently a Turk in Byzantine service; Moravcsik, *Byzantinoturcica*, II, 257.

8. A classical byword for easy spoil: Liddell-Scott-Jones, s.v.

9. The Byzantine term is λίζιος, adapted from Old French *liege;* it is used by Anna Comnena and later authors to designate western Europeans who had become imperial vassals. See Jadran Ferluga, "La Ligesse dans l'Empire byzantin: Contribution à l'étude de la féodalité à Byzance," *Zbornik radova Vizantološkog Instituta,* 7 (1961), 97–123.

10. Kinnamos' chronology is here somewhat erroneous. The negotiations for Manuel's engagement were managed by John II between 1140 and 1142; seemingly it was in the latter year that Bertha of Sulzbach (renamed Irene, in accord with Byzantine custom) arrived in Constantinople. She was sister-in-law to the German emperor Conrad III; her birth evidently madē her seem unsuitable to Manuel when he unexpectedly became emperor, and only pressure from Conrad and need for alliance with Germany brought about the marriage, in January 1146: Chalandon, II, 169–72, 209–12, 259–62.

11. That is, the death (1142) of co-emperor Alexius, which caused his wife to enter a convent.

12. The date of this expedition to re-fortify the Bithynian frontiers is vague, but prior to Manuel's attack on Ikonion in 1146: Chalandon, II, 247–48; Vryonis, *Asia Minor,* 120, 187–88. On Melangeia-Malagina, see Ramsay, *Historical Geography,* 202–09, and map facing p. 178.

13. John Roger was a Norman of unknown background and lineage, who married John II's eldest daughter, Maria. For his attempted coup in 1143 he recruited prince Robert of Capua, who was in Constantinople as an envoy of Conrad III: Chalandon, II, 11–12, 197–98; Chalandon, *Domination normande* (see above, Introduction, n. 36), II, 126–29 (I have adopted the textual correction suggested on p. 127, n. 4).

14. The fort of Lopadion, where the modern Orhaneli River leaves the Apolyont Gölü, figures repeatedly in 12th-cent. history: Ramsay, *Historical Geography,* 160 (Uluabat is the modern spelling of Ulubad).

15. Prakana, in Cilicia Tracheia, lay almost due west of Seleukeia/Silifke: Ramsay, *Historical Geography,* 364, and map facing p. 330, is to be corrected by W. M. Calder and George E. Bean, *A Classical Map of Asia Minor,* published by the British Instiute of Archaeology at Ankara (London, 1958), reference square Hg.

16. Apparently located between Melangeia and Nikaia/Iznik: Ramsay, *Historical Geography,* 201–02; Vryonis, *Asia Minor,* 21, 31, and map facing p. 14.

17. Evidently the road to Kotiaion/Kütahya; the route led to Akroenos/Afyonkarahisar, Philomilion/Akşehir, and Ikonion/Konya: Ramsay, *Historical Geography,* 199. On this campaign against Ikonion (1146), see Chalandon, II, 248–57.

18. The Kaystros or Cayster valley (modern Küçükmenderes): Ramsay, *Historical Geography*, 130, and map facing p. 104.

19. The second son of Gümüshtigin Ghāzī ibn Dānishmend, and emir of Sebasteia/Sivas, 1140/42–64: Cahen, "Turks in Iran and Anatolia," 677–78; Cahen, *Pre-Ottoman Turkey*, 96–97, 100–01.

20. Moravcsik, *Byzantinoturcica*, ii, 337.

21. Neither Ramsay, *Historical Geography*, 359, nor Moravcsik, *Byzantinoturcica*, ii, 69, have any identification to suggest.

22. Adrianople or Hadrianopolis was on the route between Philomilion and Ikonion, south of modern Cavuşçugölü: Ramsay, *Historical Geography*, 140; Calder and Bean, *Asia Minor*, reference square Fe. Ramsay, *Historical Geography*, 359, identifies Gaïta as Aghait, now Akait, southeast of Akşehir: this suggests that Kinnamos has confused the sequence of stopping places.

23. Ramsay, *Historical Geography*, 359; the location is apparently a pass through the Ala Dağ, west of Ikonion/Konya. Kaballa is possibly an abandoned fort atop Takali Dağ (also called Gevele Dağ) eight miles west-north-west of Konya; see notes to Calder and Bean, *Asia Minor*, reference square Gf. Medieval Ikonion was on an oval mound, perhaps a third of a mile long and seventy-five feet high, in an otherwise level plain.

24. An important domestic official: Bréhier, *Monde byzantin*, ii, 148. Chouroup is not discussed by Moravcsik, but the name is possibly Turkish.

25. Not word of the Second Crusade, but news of the Turkish allies' gathering to the sultan's banner probably turned Manuel back: Chalandon, ii, 254–55.

26. On the hypothetical family of rulers, see Franz Dölger, "Die 'Familie der Könige' im Mittelalter," *Byzanz und die europäische Staatenwelt* (Ettal, 1953), 34–69.

27. Evidently Muḥammad, 1134/35–1140/42. Since the eleventh century the Dānishmendid family of Cappadocia had been the chief Turkish rivals of the Seljuks established at Ikonion. After Muḥammad's death, however, the principality was divided between his son Dhū-n-Nūn at Kaisareia/Kayseri (1140/42–64), and Muḥammad's two brothers, Yaghi-Basan at Sebasteia/Sivas (1140/42–64) and 'Ain-ad-Daulah at Melitene/Malatya (1140/42–52). These princes and their sons became pawns in power struggles between the Seljuks of Ikonion, the Byzantines, and Nūr-ad-Dīn. See Cahen, *Pre-Ottoman Turkey*, 91–110.

28. Not precisely identified, but one of several passes west of Ikonion: Ramsay, *Historical Geography*, 359.

29. These might have included Manuel Anemas (married to Theodora), Stephen Kontostephanos (Anna), and Theodore Batatzes (Eudokia); probably John Roger was still in custody, although he was at some date restored to favor.

30. Perhaps a brother of Constantine Angelus, husband of Manuel's aunt Theodora: G. Ostrogorsky, "Der Aufstieg des Geschlechts der Angeloi," *Zur byzantinische Geschichte: Ausgewählte kleine Schriften* (Darmstadt, 1973), 168–69.

31. Commander of the armies, second only to the emperor. John Axouchos was a former Turkish captive reared alongside John II, whose trusted minister he became. Axouchos was a leading supporter of Manuel in the difficult outset of his reign; he was chief of Manuel's advance representatives to the capital, and by his ability bloodlessly suppressed the conspiracies (real or potential) of Manuel's brother Isaac and of the caesar John Roger.

32. Moravcsik, *Byzantinoturcica*, II, 256–57.

33. John Comnenus was eldest son of Manuel's older brother Andronicus; he was a favorite of Manuel, and is often mentioned by Kinnamos. The title of protosebastos was one of the highest in the Comnenian scheme: Hohlweg, *Beiträge*, 36–38.

34. The text of the sentence is confused; I have followed the editor's suggestion.

35. Probably Basil Tzikandyles Goudelios: Chalandon, II, 648.

36. Moravcsik, *Byzantinoturcica*, II, 331, has no suggestion.

37. On the Gabras family, see Claude Cahen, "Une Famille byzantine au service des Seldjuqides d'Asie Mineure," *Polychronion: Festschrift Franz Dölger zum 75. Geburtstag,* ed. Peter Wirth (Heidelberg, 1966), 145–49; Anthony Bryer, "A Byzantine Family: The Gabrades, *c.* 979-*c.* 1653," *University of Birmingham Historical Journal,* 12 (1970), 164–87 (Bryer's No. 6, pp. 179–80); Vryonis, *Asia Minor,* 231–32.

38. Literally, "Rhomaïs," evidently a rhetorical variant of "R(h)omania," which by the 12th cent. was in official Byzantine use to designate the empire: Robert Lee Wolff, "Romania: The Latin Empire of Constantinople," *Speculum,* 23 (1948), 5–8.

39. This is the correct reading of the manuscript: Wirth, "Zur asiatischen Toponymie," 253. The ancient name was Lake Karalis, of which "Skleros" is thought to have been a medieval corruption; it is now Beyşehir Gölü: Ramsay, *Historical Geography,* 359, 389. Rather than return the way he had approached Ikonion, Manuel withdrew nearly due west, through the Ala Dağ, and made for the upper valley of the Maeander.

40. On this important evidence of Turkomen pressure westward, into the Maeander valley, see Vryonis, *Asia Minor,* 121, 147, 189; Moravcsik, *Byzantinoturcica,* II, 259, has no suggestion to identify Rama(n).

41. Son of John II's brother Isaac the sebastokrator: see above, n. 4.

42. This clearly refers to the region from Apameia/Dinar to Soublaion/Choma/Homa and further west: Ramsey, *Historical Geography,* 79, 434; Ramsay,

Cites and Bishoprics (see above, Book I, n. 3), I, Pt. 2, 454, and map facing p. 353.

43. Actually, both the name and the site were older: it is on the north coast of Bithynia, just outside the Astakenos Gulf: Ramsay, *Historical Geography,* 187; Calder and Bean, *Asia Minor,* reference square Dc.

44. Kosmas II Attikos was patriarch of Constantinople from April 1146 to 26 February 1147.

45. Nephon was thus propagating a Bogomil dualism, whereby the Divinity of the Old Testament was alleged to be the Evil Principle: Hans-Georg Beck, *Kirche und theologische Literatur im byzantinischen Reich,* Handbuch der Altertumswissenschaft, Abt. XII, Teil II, Band I (Munich, 1959), 661; D. Obolensky, *The Bogomils* (Oxford, 1948), 221–22.

46. Moravcsik, *Byzantinoturcica,* II, 285; on the fight at Kalograia, see Kinnamos, 40. On these negotiations, see Chalandon, II, 257–58.

47. On the Second Crusade and the Byzantine Empire, see Chalandon, II, 262–315; Virginia G. Berry, "The Second Crusade," *The First Hundred Years* (see above, Book I, n. 19), 463–503; on western plans to seize Constantinople, see Sibyll Kindlimann, *Die Eroberung von Konstantinopel als politische Forderung des Westens im Hochmittelalter: Studien zur Entwicklung der Idee eines lateinischen Kaiserreichs in Byzanz,* Geist und Werk der Zeiten, 20 (Zurich, 1969), esp. 149–68.

48. On Alexander of Conversano, Count of Gravina, who became a leading diplomat in John II's and Manuel's service, see Chalandon, II, 170, 226–27, 270, and index; Chalandon, *Domination normande,* II, 27–29, and index; Paolo Lamma, *Comneni e Staufer: Ricerche sui rapporti fra Bisanzio e l'occidente nel secolo XII,* Istituto storico italiano per il Medio Evo, Studi storici, 14/18 and 22/25, 2 vols. (Rome, 1955–57), indices of each vol., s.v. "Gravina."

49. An exaggeration: Berry ventures no estimate, but Steven Runciman, *A History of the Crusades,* II (Cambridge, Eng., 1952), 259, suggests "nearly twenty thousand" for the German force.

50. This is a literary usage, in no way reflecting official nomenclature.

51. The *chartoularios* was chief of the archive office in the treasury department: Bréhier, *Monde byzantin,* II, 257. This individual would seem to have been the *chartoularios* Basil Tzintziloukes: Chalandon, II, 196, 273, n. 3. Michael Palaiologos was a cousin of Manuel, and later commanded a force in Italy: Chalandon, II, 218–19.

52. See above, Kinnamos, 33.

53. The future Frederick I Barbarossa; Kinnamos' estimate of him is based on his later prolonged opposition to Manuel and the Byzantine Empire.

54. See Kinnamos, 56, and n. 35 above.

55. Near modern Bahşayiş in Thrace, west of Istanbul: Constantin Jos. Jireček, *Die Heerstrasse von Belgrad nach Constantinopel und die Balkanpässe: Eine historische-geographische Studie* (Prague, 1877; repr. Amsterdam, 1967), 102.

56. On the park and palace of the Outer Philopation, see R. Janin, *Constantinople byzantine: Développement urbain et répertoire topographique*, 2nd ed., Archives de l'Orient chrétien, 4A (Paris, 1964), 143–45, 452–53. The statement by Kinnamos involves punning etymologies; *"philopatein"* could mean "enjoy frequenting;" *"phyllopatein,"* "walk on leaves."

57. Janin, *Constantinople byzantine*, 465–66; this passage is further evidence for the existence of a bridge over the Golden Horn outside the city wall, just west of Blachernai, in the modern Eyüp district: see my *Byzantium Confronts the West*, 237–38 and nn.

58. A section of Üsküdar (Scutari): Janin, *Constantinople byzantine*, 495–96.

59. Commander of the Varangian Guard: Hohlweg, *Beiträge*, 49–50.

60. Identity uncertain: Moravcsik, *Byzantinoturcica*, ii, 181; Vryonis, *Asia Minor*, 121, 188.

61. Kinnamos always regards the Blachernai Palace (situated at the western extremity of Constantinople) as south of the city: Kinnamos, 171–72, 207. A number of famous relics were kept at Blachernai: Janin, *Eglises et monastères*, 169–79.

62. Franco-Byzantine relations were actually more strained than Kinnamos states: Berry, "Second Crusade," 489–92.

63. Patriarch Nicholas IV Mouzalon, Dec. 1147–Mar./Apr. 1151.

64. Theodotos II, elected between Mar./Apr. 1151 and Apr. 1152; died between Oct. 1153 and Oct. 1154, having held office two-and-a-half years.

65. Vladislav II of Bohemia, 1140–74 (but he was not crowned king until 1158), and Boleslav IV of Poland, 1146–73.

66. L. Oeconomos, "Remarques sur trois passages de trois historiens grecs du Moyen Age," *Byzantion*, 20 (1950), 180–82, and H. Grégoire's note on p. 183; I have adopted Grégoire's suggestion.

67. Actually, only to Ephesos at this time (Dec. 1147): Berry, "Second Crusade," 497–98. Conrad's actual reason for temporarily returning to Constantinople was illness.

68. On Conrad's meeting with Manuel near Thessalonica, and his subsequent second stay in Constantinople, see Chalandon, ii, 326–28; Berry, "Second Crusade," 510–11. The purpose of the treaty alluded to by Kinnamos was a joint attack on Roger II of Sicily. Chalandon, ii, 326–27 (esp. 327, n. 2) accepts Kin-

namos' allegation that Conrad pledged to return "Italy" (i.e., Apulia and Calabria), once conquered, to Manuel. Lamma, *Comneni e Staufer*, I, 90–93, is dubious. It was at this time that Henry of Austria wedded the emperor's niece, Theodora; see Kinnamos, 236, 261. On this Theodora's identity, see my *Byzantium Confronts the West*, 34, n. 9 (p. 322–23).

69. Berry, "Second Crusade," 511; Chalandon, II, 330–32.

70. Frederick I Barbarossa, 1152–90.

71. Actually, sons of Henry V's sister Agnes, who married duke Frederick of Swabia.

72. Lothar II, 1125–37.

BOOK III

1. Roger II was count of Sicily from 1105.

2. Duke William of Apulia, 1111–27, was a grandson of Robert Guiscard. The story of a loan and mortgage on Apulia is a fiction; William died without an heir, and Roger II speedily moved to appropriate his domain: Chalandon, *Domination normande*, I, 321–26, 380–89.

3. Roger II was opposed by both Pope Honorius II, 1124–30, and Innocent II, 1130–43. Roger supported the anti-pope Anacletus II, 1130–38.

4. See Chalandon, *Domination normande*, II, 69–70.

5. Roger II had first been recognized as king by the anti-pope Anacletus II in 1130. On the capture of Pope Innocent II in 1139 and his subsequent acceptance of Roger as king, see Chalandon, *Domination normande*, II, 89–91.

6. On this exchange, see Chalandon, *Domination normande*, II, 129.

7. Ibid., II, 135–37; Chalandon, II, 317–20.

8. Perhaps modern Zimnicea, Romania: Chalandon, II, 324, n. 2; on this campaign, see 323–25. In regard to this place, P. Ş. Năsturel, "Valaques, Coumans et Byzantines sous le règne de Manuel Comnène," *Byzantina*, I (1969), 169–75, suggests the late-medieval place-name Holevnic (modern Turnu-Măgurele).

9. So Moravcsik, *Byzantinoturcica*, II, 305–06; for another interpretation, see Chalandon, II, 325, n. 1. Năsturel, "Valaques," 175, identifies the site as the hill of Măgura Aranului, near the Teleorman River.

10. The citadel at Kerkyra is a rocky peninsula. On the siege, see Chalandon, II, 325–33; Chalandon, *Domination normande*, II, 137–45.

11. Pervoslav Uroš II, ca. 1131–60 (briefly dispossesssed ca. 1155).

12. Chalandon, II, 333–34.

13. Chalandon, II, 384–86, believes that on his return from Kerkyra (autumn 1149), Manuel marched from Valona/Avlona/Vlonë through Pelagonia to the Vardar and Morava valleys; Rhason/Ražanj is near the Morava, north of Niš. Constantin Jireček, *Geschichte der Serben,* Allgemeine Staatengeschichte, Abt. I, No. 38, Vol. I (Gotha, 1911), 246–47, has little to contribute on these campaigns.

14. Manuel's uncle by marriage, the progenitor of the Angeli dynasty.

15. Galitza was allegedly at the mouth of the Morava: K. v. Spruner, ed., *Spruner-Menke Hand-Atlas für die Geschichte des Mittelalters und der neueren Zeit,* 3rd ed., ed. Th. Menke (Gotha, 1880), Map No. 84; Jireček, *Serben,* 247, n. 3, however, suggests a location in south-central Yugoslavia, consistent with his identification of Rhason as Ras (modern Novi Pazar), and Chalandon, II, 385, n. 4, places Galitza on Mt. Golija, north of Novi Pazar. Nikava is unidentified; Chalandon, II, 385 and n. 4, thinks it the Nišava valley. That the entire campaign was in the Nišava and Morava valleys seems probable.

16. Identification uncertain; Chalandon, II, 388, n. 1, cites several possibilities. On this campaign, see Chalandon, II, 387–91. Moravcsik's opinion (*Byzantium and the Magyars,* 80) that Kinnamos participated in this campaign is scarcely acceptable; he could have been only six or seven years old at the time.

17. Géza II, 1141–62. Kinnamos is confused about the genealogy: Uroš I of Serbia's daughter Helen married Béla II the Blind of Hungary; her brother Beloš or Bela became very influential at the Hungarian court; Chalandon, II, 74–75, 384–85, 399.

18. See above, Book II, n. 33.

19. Evidently a scribal error for the Drymon/Drina: Chalandon, II, 389, n. 1.

20. An upper tributary of the Drina.

21. Perhaps Sjenica, on the Uvac River, west of Novi Pazar: Chalandon, II, 389.

22. The Chalisioi were probably refugee Jewish Khazars: Moravcsik, *Byzantinoturcica,* II, 338–39; D. M. Dunlop, "The Khazars," *The Dark Ages: Jews in Christian Europe 711–1096,* ed. Cecil Roth and I. H. Levine, The World History of the Jewish People, Ser. II, Vol. II (n.p. [New Brunswick, N.J.], 1966), 356.

23. Dj. Sp. Radojičić, "Kinamov Γουρδέσης," *Zbornik radova Vizantološkog instituta,* 8, Pt. 1 (1963), 255–59, provides documentary and inscriptional evidence for this person.

24. Allegedly John Doukas Kamateros: Demetrios I. Polemis, *The Doukai: A Contribution to Byzantine Prosopography,* University of London Historical Studies, XXII (London, 1968), 127–30 (No. 99). P. Karlin-Hayter, "99. Jean Doukas," *Byzantion,* 42 (1972), 259–65, suggests that Polemis has conflated six or

seven individuals; she is not, however, ready to state which of Manuel's close relatives this particular individual was.

25. Donald M. Nicol, *The Byzantine Family of Kantakouzenos* (*Cantacuzenus*) *ca. 1100–1460: A Genealogical and Prosopographical Study*, Dumbarton Oaks Studies, XI (Washington, D.C., 1968), 4 (No. 2).

26. So Moravcsik, *Byzantinoturcica*, II, 85. Bakchinos' identity is disputed: he was not the grand župan of Serbia proper (who was Pervoslav Uroš II), but probably was the leader of the Hungarian contingent: Moravcsik, *Byzantinoturcica*, II, 85; Chalandon, II, 390, n. 2; Jireček, *Serben, 248, n. 2.*

27. Just as Géza II and the Serbs were allied, so the Byzantines were linked to Vladimirko, prince of Galicia (1130–52): George Vernadsky, *Kievan Russia*, A History of Russia, II (New Haven, 1948), 217–18; Chalandon, II, 402–05; G. Vernadsky, "Relations byzantino-russes au XIIe siècle," *Byzantion,* 4 (1927/28), 273–76. Géza had just defeated and made peace with Vladimirko: Chalandon, II, 401–03.

28. Beloš or Bela was a son of Uroš I of Serbia (Rascia or Raška), and Géza II's maternal uncle: see above, n. 17, and Chalandon, II, 399, 405–07.

29. Chalandon, II, 406, suggests the mountains along the Timţş, now in western Romania.

30. He was a son of king Kálmán: see Appendix, and Chalandon, II, 62–63, 401, 406–07. His son was Constantine Kalamanos, who played a prominent role in Manuel's later years.

31. Maria, often called "Porphyrogenita," "Born-in-the-Purple," was born in March 1152: Chalandon, II, 212. On this Hungarian campaign, see Chalandon, II, 403–07; Moravcsik, *Byzantium and the Magyars,* 81.

32. Chalandon, *Domination normande,* II, 188–89; Chalandon, II, 347–48.

33. On this campaign, see Chalandon, II, 407–08; and, on Kinnamos' chronological slips, 408, n. 3.

34. The Byzantine year ended August 31; these events then fell in the summer of 1154: Chalandon, II, 348.

35. Chalandon, II, 408–09.

36. Der Nersessian, "Cilician Armenia," 638–39: this was Ţoros (or Thoros) II. Chalandon, II, 418–29.

37. Marshall W. Baldwin, "The Latin States under Baldwin III and Amalric I, 1143–1174," *The First Hundred Years* (see above, Book I, n. 19), 532–33.

38. Baldwin, "Latin States," 536; Chalandon, II, 426–27. To become a monk before dying was normal for a Byzantine.

39. Der Nersessian, "Cilician Armenia," 638–39; Chalandon, II, 426–28.

40. Chalandon, II, 408–09. Bitola in Yugoslavia is the modern center of the plain of Pelagonia. Chalandon II, 408–09, dates this incident to Manuel's 1153 stay at Pelagonia, but Kinnamos, a few lines further on, indicates that it was prior to Andronicus' first governorship in Cilicia (1152). Manuel was probably at Pelagonia in 1149 and 1150: Chalandon, II, 385, 387; see 408, n. 3, on the difficult chronology of this period.

41. Chalandon, II, 408–09; Babos, *Adalékok,* 9, gives an important correction to the text. Protosebastos was a rank in the court hierarchy (sebastokrators, protosebastoi, sebastoi, etc.), protovestiarios or chief chamberlain was an honorary position in the palace services. See Hohlweg, *Beiträge,* 34–40 (esp. 39–40).

42. Chalandon, II, 410; on the grand stratarches (an undefined, apparently honorary military title), see Hohlweg, *Beiträge,* 131.

43. This quarrel at Melangeia seemingly occurred during one of Manuel's early campaigns: he was at Melangeia in 1144 or 1145 (Kinnamos, 36), and passed close by (Pithekas) in 1146 (Kinnamos, 38). On the latter campaign, both his brother Isaac and his cousin Andronicus attended him (Kinnamos, 49, 61). Some names in the text have evidently suffered scribal corruption, and I have followed the emendations suggested by Chalandon, II, 215, n. 6. Polemis, *Doukai,* 113, n. 1, believes the John Doukas, cousin of the emperor, here mentioned, was John Doukas [Bryennios], son of Nicephorus Bryennios and Anna Comnena. But John Doukas [Kamateros] could equally well be meant, and John Doukas [Angelus] would also qualify. Karlin-Hayter, "99. Jean Doukas," 261, is unable to identify this person, but would reject John Doukas the future great heteriarch on grounds that he is not elsewhere called cousin of the emperor. John Doukas was presumably punished for raising his whip against a prince of the blood. Apparently out of pique, Isaac stole the seals. Andronicus was probably offended by the light penalty imposed on Isaac, and then infuriated by the favor showered on John Comnenus the protosebastos at Pelagonia. The incident is briefly discussed in Chalandon, II, 215.

44. This seems to have been Alexius Axouchos, son of the grand domestikos John Axouchos: see Kinnamos, 170, line 5, and Chalandon, II, 377–78.

45. Moravcsik, *Byzantinoturcica,* II, 140.

46. The dates can only be approximate, but Andronicus was in prison nine years and fled to Russia in autumn 1164: Chalandon, II, 220–21, 410–11, 482, 483, n. 2.

47. Perhaps Svilajnac on the Morava: Chalandon, II, 412. On this campaign, see Chalandon, II, 411–13; Moravcsik, *Byzantium and the Magyars,* 81–82.

48. Borić ruled from before 1154 to 1163.

49. On Basil Tzykandeles Goudelios, see Kinnamos, 56, 72, 77.

50. Probably Géza II's *brother* Stephen, later István (Stephen) IV: Chalandon, ii, 413, n. 1.

BOOK IV

1. Frederick I Barbarossa, 1152–90.

2. On this sequence of embassies, and the offers made, see Chalandon, ii, 343–50, esp. 344, n. 3, which examines the chronology in detail; Lamma, *Comneni e Staufer,* i, 137–47.

3. On Michael Palaiologos, see Kinnamos, 70, 82. John Doukas is possibly John Doukas [Kamateros]: Polemis, *Doukai,* 127–30 (No. 99), but Karlin-Hayter, "99. Jean Doukas," 262, considers this to be the future great heteriarch. On Alexander of Conversano, Count of Gravina, see Book ii, n. 48, above. See Chalandon, ii, 349.

4. Robert II of Bassonville, Count of Loritello, son of Roger II's sister: Chalandon, ii, 352, n. 5; Chalandon, *Domination normande,* ii, 182–83. Under William I, 1154–66, Robert led the barons' opposition to the low-born chief minister, Maio or Maione of Bari.

5. This word has been added to the text by the editor.

6. Chalandon, ii, 358, and Chalandon, *Domination normande,* ii, 191, 204–10, dates the events narrated here and following (Kinnamos, 137–46) to late August–September 1155. See Lamma, *Comneni e Staufer,* i, 149–231.

7. According to Chalandon, *Domination normande,* ii, 205–06, possibly Fano, ancient Flavia Fanestris, north of Ancona. Doukas, however, was moving from Ancona to Apulia, and the now-ruined site of San Flaviano, adjacent to the present town of Giulianova, at the mouth of the Tordino River, between Ancona and Pescara, would better suit the text. According to [*Murray's*] *Handbook for Travellers in Southern Italy and Sicily,* 9th ed. (London, 1892), i, 234, San Flaviano owed its name to the body of a saint brought from Constantinople in the Middle Ages. Chalandon, ii, 353, n. 4, was unable to locate this place in the directories available to him.

8. Chalandon, *Domination normande,* ii, 206, believes the Byzantine force had now entered the Bassonville lands.

9. Ibid., 209.

10. Hadrian IV, 1154–59. Chalandon, *Domination normande,* ii, 210–14; Chalandon, ii, 358–62.

11. In the text, Masagetoi; see Moravcsik, *Byzantinoturcica,* ii, 183, citing this passage.

12. On this relief force, see Chalandon, II, 363; Chalandon, *Domination normande,* II, 215–16, but by a slip he makes the Germanoi of the text into Germans instead of French. This John Angelus is probably John Doukas Angelus, son of Constantine Angelus and Manuel's aunt Theodora, but this expedition is not cited in the note on him by Polemis, *Doukai,* 87–88 (No. 40). This appearance of John, with the name Angelus, repeated in Kinnamos, 162 and 238, is omitted in his survey of references to John by Lucien Stiernon, "Les Origines du Despotat d'Epire: A propos d'un livre récent," *Revue des Etudes Byzantines,* 17 (1959), 102–17, who is thus able to write: "Nulle part JEAN, *fils* de Constantin Ange . . . ne porte le patronyme d'Ange ou de Comnène, mais celui de DOUKAS . . ." (p. 114). While the references by Kinnamos do not specify his relationship to the emperor, I know of no other John Angelus in this period, and Manuel's proclivity for using his relatives as army commanders is well known. Kinnamos doubtless calls him "Angelus" to distinguish him from the John Doukas who was commanding land forces in Italy.

13. Tonsured as a monk, the normal preparation for death.

14. The name given in the text is Polymilion; Chalandon, *Domination normande,* II, 217, identifies this as Polignano (on the east coast between Bari and Monopoli). But the village of Palagiano is close to Massafra and Mottola, the scene of Byzantine operations. Also, the fact that the Norman garrison of "Polymilion" fled to Taranto (not Monopoli or Brindisi, both still in Norman hands) suggests Palagiano, scarcely ten miles from Taranto.

15. This is a paraphrase of Procopius, *De bello gothico,* IV, 1, 11 (ed. Haury, II, 489), as Neumann, *Griechische Geschichtschreiber,* 96, pointed out.

16. Probably a Latin from the principality of Antioch, a mercenary in Byzantine service.

17. Archilochus, Frag. 55 (Diehl).

18. Probably Alezio, between Otranto and Gallipoli.

19. Keltoi in the text: see Kinnamos, 67 and 167. The bulk of the Byzantine army consisted of Norman rebels and mercenaries, not troops sent from the empire.

20. He had done a like feat at Marathon: Herodotus, VI, 114.

21. Alexius Comnenus [Bryennios], son of Anna Comnena.

22. Moravcsik, *Byzantinoturcica,* II, 243.

23. Chalandon, *Domination normande,* II, 229.

24. Chalandon, *Domination normande,* II, 248–54; Chalandon, II, 377–81.

25. Chalandon, *Domination normande,* II, 250, thinks this an accurate account of events in Rome in the summer of 1157.

26. Chalandon, II, 232–33; on Kinnamos' misconception of the location of Blachernai, see above, Book II, n. 61.

27. Perhaps Simon, illegitimate son of Roger II: Chalandon, *Domination normonde,* II, 307.

28. Kilidj Arslan II, 1155–92.

29. Unknown locations, apparently in Cilicia, south of Laranda/Karaman: Ramsay, *Historical Geography,* 369, 450.

30. Chalandon, II, 434–35. Oinaion/Ünye is on the Black Sea coast; Pauraë/Bafra is on the lower Halys/Kizil.

31. According to Chalandon, II, 640–41, the text is from the liturgy of Saints Basil and John Chrysostom: "You are He Who offers and Who is offered and Who receives."

32. Chalandon, II, 640–43; Beck, *Kirche und theologische Literatur,* 623–24.

33. Chalandon, II, 437–39; Baldwin, "Latin States," 539–41, 559–60.

34. Apparently the region of Laodikeia/Denizli: Ramsay, *Historical Geography,* 150–53, 382.

35. Kistramos and Longinias are unknown (Ramsay, *Historical Geography,* 348, 380, 382), but Anazarbos is 'Ain Zarbâ or Andvorza, an abandoned fortress sixteen miles south of Sis/Kozan. Tili or Til is modern Toprakkale, Arabic Tall-Hamdūn, on the Adana-Alexandretta railway line, just west of the pass between Cilicia and the plain of Alexandretta: J. Gottwald, "Die Burg Til im südöstlichen Kilikien," *Byzantinische Zeitschrift,* 40 (1940), 89–104 (esp. 96–97). Kinnamos seems to have disordered events slightly: the capture of Anazarbos and Tili probably followed that of Tarsus. On this campaign, see Chalandon, II, 441–45; Der Nersessian, "Cilician Armenia," 640–41; Baldwin, "Latin States," 543.

36. Probably John Comnenus and other captives taken in Cyprus and the Cilician wars.

37. On Reginald and Aimery of Limoges (Latin patriarch of Antioch, ca. 1139–96), see Cahen, *Syrie du nord,* 505–06; Baldwin, "Latin States," 540; Chalandon, II, 443.

38. Presumably Muḥammad (II), the Great Selchükid sultan of Persia, 1153–59: C. E. Bosworth, "The Political and Dynastic History of the Iranian World (A.D. 1000–1217)," *The Cambridge History of Iran,* V (Cambridge, Eng., 1968), 175–76.

39. The text here is corrupt; I have read παρά for περί.

40. Bréhier, *Monde byzantin,* II, 148.

41. By an error of the editor the number "21" has been repeated for chapters commencing on pp. 186 and 188.

42. Bertram of Toulouse, grandson of Raymond of Saint-Gilles, had been captured in 1149: Baldwin, "Latin States," 532, 545.

43. Bertrand of Blancfort, master of the Templars, had been captured in 1157: Baldwin, 539, 545.

44. Ramsay, *Historical Geography*, 382n. In 1158 Manuel had followed the coast from Attaleia/Antalya in Pamphylia; in 1159, he chose to return from Cilicia through the center of the plateau, by way of Laranda/Karaman and Kotiaion/Kütahya, a route which could have taken him near Ikonion.

45. On this campaign of 1158–59, see Chalandon, II, 435–56; Baldwin, "Latin States," 543–45; Der Nersessian, "Cilician Armenia," 640–41.

46. Chalandon, II, 457–59.

47. See Kinnamos, 63.

48. Augouste was perhaps an imperial estate on the Astakenos Gulf; Rhitzion was probably near Chalcedon: Ramsay, *Historical Geography*, 185–86. Possibly Manuel stayed near Constantinople, but did not enter it. He then turned south to Philadelphia/Alaşehir.

49. Dubious word.

50. Alternate translation, equally possible: "Reaching a certain village, Sarapata, called by the natives Mylonos. . . ." In the opinion of Ramsay, *Cities and Bishoprics*, I, Pt. 1, pp. 19, n. 1, and 341; Pt. 2, pp. 598, n. 4, 679, and 696, the name is Turkish-Greek, Mylonos or Mylon perhaps the original Greek name, Sarapata representing "Hissar-Abad," "Place-of-the-Castle." He suggests modern Sandikli (on the Glaukos/Kufi River, a northern tributary of the Maeander). The area was clearly in Turkish hands: Vryonis, *Asia Minor, 122, 190.*

51. Moravcsik, *Byzantinoturcica*, II, 285.

52. Abu-Bakr: ibid., 256–57; see Kinnamos, 48, 50.

53. At first glance, the "oft-mentioned John" would seem to be John Comnenus the protosebastos, but he was a nephew of the emperor, not a relative-in-law *(gambros)*: see L. Stiernon, "Notes de titulature et de prosopographie byzantines: Sébaste et gambros," *Revue des Etudes Byzantines*, 23 (1965), 222–43, esp. 223. Probably this is John Doukas, former Byzantine commander in Italy and future great heteriarch; he is identified in very similar language by Kinnamos, 260, line 24. This possible date in his career is not mentioned by Karlin-Hayter, "99. Jean Doukas." John Doukas is not elsewhere called a *gambros* of the emperor, and some other individual might be meant.

54. For Phileta as a late-Byzantine name of Phaselis (near modern Tekirova), on the Lycian coast southwest of Attaleia/Antalya, see Ramsay, *Historical Geography*, table facing p. 424; Ramsay, *Cities and Bishoprics*, I, Pt. 1, pp. 19, n. 2,

and 300. On these attacks, see Chalandon, II, 460–61; Vryonis, *Asia Minor,* 122, 189.

55. Evidently descendants or followers of Kogh Vasil, an Armenian who ruled Kesoun/Keysun (east of Marash/Maraş) at the time of the First Crusade. Kesoun formed part of the County of Edessa; in 1150, after the loss of its capital, the remnants of that county were ceded to Manuel Comnenus (Baldwin, "Latin States," 533–34). Possibly some of the Armenian inhabitants, using their former leader's name, remained in Byzantine service.

56. Chalandon, II, 459–60.

57. Kallipolis or Gallipoli, modern Gelibolu.

BOOK V

1. Kinnamos has here erred in his chronology: she died in early 1160, perhaps while Manuel was staying at Rhitzion (Kinnamos, 194): Chalandon, II, 211–12, 459. Part of John Kontostephanos' mission to Palestine, 1160–61, was to seek a bride for Manuel: Kinnamos, 199; Chalandon, II, 459, 517–19.

2. 31 May 1161. On this stage in Manuel's lengthy intervention in Hungarian affairs, see Chalandon, II, 469–73. For the genealogy and dates of the various rulers who follow, see Appendix I. The dating of these events is disputed; Moravcsik, *Byzantium and the Magyars,* 82–83 and appended genealogy, gives the reign of Géza II as 1141–62, László II as 1162–63, István IV as 1163, and István III as 1162–72. Chalandon gives the dates a year earlier, basing his data largely on western chroniclers.

3. According to Chalandon, II, 469–73, László II ruled 1161–62. On "Urum," "My Lord," see Moravcsik, *Byzantinoturcica,* II, 238; G. Ostrogorsky, "Urum-Despotes: Die Anfänge der Despoteswürde in Byzanz," *Byzantinische Zeitschrift,* 44 (1951), 448–60; repr. in his *Zur byzantinischen Geschichte,* 153–65.

4. Grumel, *Chronologie,* 390, believes Primislav (or Prvoslav) is another name for Uroš II; see Kinnamos, 113, on his earlier restoration by Manuel's decision.

5. Borislav Radojčić, "La Region de la Dendra de la Serbie au XIIᵉ siècle," *Balkan Studies,* 11 (1970), 249–60, is able to show that Dendra was Serbian territory, granted to Desa in 1155 by Manuel's judgment regarding the županate of Serbia, between Uroš II and Desa; he is, however, unable to give any more exact identification of the region than Kinnamos' expression here. Desa ruled ca. 1161–65. See Chalandon, II, 391–92 (but the identity of Desa and Stephen Nemanja, there asserted, is not generally accepted); Jireček, *Serben,* I, 250–52; Borislav Radojčić, "Prilog proučavanju vazalnih odnosa Srbije prema Vizantiji pedesetih i šezdecetih godina XII veka," *Zbornik radova Vizantološkog instituta,* 8, Pt. 2 (1964), 347–54.

6. Kilidj Arslan II, 1155–92. On this visit, see Chalandon, II, 462–66; Vryonis, *Asia Minor,* 122; Cahen, ''Turks in Iran and Anatolia,'' 678.

7. Patriarch Loukas Chrysoberges, 1157–70.

8. The reference is to the Byzantine disaster in 1176, at Myriokephalon. The earthquake mentioned in this section is not included in the lists by Grumel, *Chronologie,* 480, or Glanville Downy, ''Earthquakes at Constantinople and Vicinity, A.D. 342–1454,'' *Speculum,* 30 (1955), 600.

9. Again, the reference is to Blachernai Palace: see Book II, n. 61.

10. Chalandon, II, 517, renders this as Excubitor, chief of the interpreters.

11. Matth. 22:8.

12. The girl in question was Melisend, sister of Raymond III, count of Tripoli. The tale told by Kinnamos is a fiction: neither miraculous diseases nor (groundless) allegations of illegitimacy prevented the marriage. Rather, negotiations were prolonged for a year (1160–61) by Manuel, then broken off by him, because a more favorable match seemed possible in Antioch: Chalandon, II, 517–21; Baldwin, ''Latin States,'' 546.

13. Chief official of the city of Constantinople: Bréhier, *Monde byzantin,* II, 186–92.

14. Chalandon, II, 520–24; Baldwin, ''Latin States,'' 546–47.

15. Chalandon, II, 392–93 (who, however, errs in identifying Desa with Stephen Nemanja, and also in dating the event 1163: see 475, where Manuel's campaign is dated 1162); Jireček, *Serben,* 252; Grumel, *Chronologie,* 390; Radojčić, ''Vazalnikh,'' 347–54.

16. Chalandon, II, 474–76; the territory ceded as Béla's inheritance was ''Sirmion'' (i.e., the region between the Sava and the Danube) and Dalmatia: 475 and n. 3. On the title of Despotes, see Ostrogorsky, ''Urum-Despotes,'' 448–60.

17. Joscelin II of Edessa was captive 1150–59, and died in captivity: Baldwin, ''Latin States,'' 533; Robert Lawrence Nicholson, *Joscelyn III and the Fall of the Crusader States* (Leiden, 1973), 21.

18. Chalandon, II, 525, n. 2, says he was called this because his father had also been titled Kalamanos.

19. Hamilton A. R. Gibb, ''The Career of Nūr-ad-Dīn,'' *The First Hundred Years* (see above, Book I, n. 19), 524; Baldwin, ''Latin States,'' 551; Chalandon, II, 524–25; Nicholson, *Joscelyn III,* 33. Reginald of Châtillon, regent of Antioch, had been captured by Nūr-ad-Dīn in 1160 (Gibb, ''Nūr-ad-Dīn,'' 523; Baldwin, ''Latin States,'' 546); the captives in 1164 included Bohemond III, prince of Antioch; Raymond III, count of Tripoli; Joscelyn III, titular count of Edessa; and Hugh of Lusignan, as well as Kalamanos. Kinnamos has confused Reginald and

Bohemond. Toros of Armenia was also a member of the defeated coalition: Der Nersessian, "Cilician Armenia," 641.

20. On the locality, and the geographic difficulties posed by Kinnamos' reference to a crossing of the Sava (rather than of the Danube), see Chalandon, II, 477 and n. 2. The text, however, says that Manuel sat down opposite Titel; this could have meant on the south bank of the Danube, opposite the mouth of the Tisa (or Tisza); Titel is only a few miles upstream. The emperor's next stopping place, Petrikion, may be Petrovaradin, on the south bank of the Danube opposite Novi Sad; therafter, he reached Bač, north of the river; the three sites show a generally northwestward line of march. This agrees with Kinnamos, 221, who puts the crossing of the Danube in the subsequent part of the campaign.

21. Kinnamos, 68–69.

22. Frederick Barbarossa himself had balked at the requirement of serving as squire to the pope, but had had to yield to precedents: Ugo Balzani, "Frederick Barbarossa and the Lombard League," *The Cambridge Medieval History,* V (Cambridge, Eng., 1929), 419–20.

23. The allusion is somewhat mysterious, perhaps a reference to previous papal obedience to decrees of the Byzantine emperor ("someone else").

24. This tirade was inspired by Pope Alexander III's prolonged dispute with Frederick Barbarossa, during the course of which the pope at least discussed (in 1166) accepting Manuel as the single emperor of a united Roman Empire: Chalandon, II, 558–67. Eventually, after his defeat by the Lombard League, Frederick was reconciled with Alexander. On the political philosophy expressed in this passage, see Chalandon, II, 556–57.

25. Perhaps at Novi Sad.

26. On this Orthodox population, mentioned here and on Kinnamos, 221, see N. Oikonomides, "A propos des relations ecclésiastiques entre Byzance et la Hongrie au XIᵉ siècle: Le Métropolite de Turquie," *Revue des Etudes Sud-Est Européenes,* n.s., 9 (1971), 530.

27. See above, Book II, n. 9.

28. See above, Book II, n. 65.

29. On this campaign and negotiations, see Chalandon, II, 476–80, who gives some credit to Kinnamos' story of Manuel's relations with Vladislav II.

30. Bryer, "Gabrades" (cited above, Book II, n. 37), 180 (No. 7). He was married to Eudokia, daughter of Manuel's brother Andronicus: Chalandon, II, 480–81.

31. Chalandon, II, 526, n. 2 (for the chronology), 528–29; Der Nersessian, "Cilician Armenia," 640–41.

32. Probably a reference to Alexander III's flight from Rome to France, 1162; even in 1167, Frederick was able to occupy only the Leonine section of the city.

33. Ottaviano, anti-pope as Victor IV, 1159–64; Alexander III was pope from 1159 to 1181. On this conflict and on Manuel's role in the subvention of the Lombard League, see Chalandon, II, 572; Balzani, "Barbarossa and the Lombard League," 430–47.

34. Guardian and doorkeeper of the palace: Bréhier, *Monde byzantin*, II, 355.

35. Rostislav I Mstislavič, grand prince of Kiev, 1158–67; Primislav or Pervoslav is unidentified, but perhaps was prince of Volynia: Chalandon, II, 482; Vernadsky, *Kievan Russia* (see above, Book III, n. 27), 219–20.

36. This would seem to be a scribal error for Iaroslav.

37. This appears to be an accidental repetition of the previous reference to Rostislav; Kinnamos is not very well-informed on Russian affairs. The MS gives "Kiama" as the name of the city, but this is considered to be an error by Kinnamos or the scribe for "Kioba," i.e., Kiev.

38. Henry Jasomirgott, who was from 1156 duke of Austria; he had married Manuel's niece Theodora (daughter of Manuel's brother Andronicus) in 1148, at the time of Conrad III's residence in Constantinople during the Second Crusade.

39. Vladislav is unidentified; George might be George (or Iuri) Dolgoruky, prince of Suzdal and grand prince of Kiev, 1155–57: Chalandon, II, 482, n. 4.

40. Theodora, daughter of Manuel's brother Isaac.

41. After the capture of Reginald of Châtillon (1160), the people of Antioch had turned to Baldwin III, who assumed guardianship of the principality. In 1163, after Baldwin's death, the populace, with aid from Toros of Armenia, drove out Constance and established her son (by Raymond of Poitiers), Bohemond III, as prince. Amalric I's embassy to Manuel is thought to have occurred soon after his accession, but only in 1167 did Maria, daughter of John Comnenus the protosebastos, wed him: Baldwin, "Latin States," 546–47, 554.

42. Moravcsik, *Byzantinoturcica*, II, 141.

43. Chalandon, II, 483.

44. Probably Kama, east of Branitshevo.

45. Probably across the Sava: note that Manuel proceeds to attack Zeugminon/Zemun, on the south bank of the Danube. Since "all Sirmion" (i.e., the territory between the Sava and the Danube) was in Hungarian hands, this would equally be a crossing into hostile country, yet the enemy forces would be effectively divided by the Danube: Chalandon, II, 484.

46. Tentatively, I would here suggest a lacuna of a sentence or two in the text; Manuel is seen in one sentence with an injured leg, then, in the next, attacking

the walls of Zeugminon/Zemun. On the other hand, the discontinuity may be the result of the author's haste, evident in this rather disordered section of his history.

47. Moravcsik, "Συμβολαί," 295.

48. Polemis, *Doukai,* 190 (No. 220), as a "Doukas of unknown family background." He suggests he may be Andronicus Doukas Angelus, father of Isaac II and Alexius III (p. 86, his No. 39), but this person would in 1165 have been rather elderly to be behaving in so impetuous a fashion.

49. See Kinnamos, 107.

50. Chalandon, II, 484–85.

BOOK VI

1. Chalandon, II, 221, 526, n. 2, 529–30.

2. Ramsay, *Cities and Bishoprics,* I, Pt. 1, 228 and n. 4.

3. John 14:28.

4. Euthymius Malakes, metropolitan of Neai Patrai, was a prominent theologian and author of the second half of the century; see his writings, Τὰ σωζόμενα, ed. Konstantinos G. Mpones [Bonis], 2 vols. (Athens, 1937–49).

5. The synodal decision came in 1166: Jean Gouillard, ed. and trans., "Le Synodikon de l'Orthodoxie," Centre de recherche d'histoire et civilisation byzantines, *Travaux et mémoires,* 2 (1967), 75–77; Chalandon, II, 564, 644–51; Beck, *Kirche und theologische Literatur,* 58, 622–23; the inscribed stones from Hagia Sophia have been recovered: C. Mango, "The Conciliar Edict of 1166," *Dumbarton Oaks Papers,* 17 (1963), 315–30.

6. Alexius II (emperor, 1180–83) was born 14 September 1169: Peter Wirth, "Wann wurde Kaiser Alexios II. Komnenos geboren?" *Byzantinische Zeitschrift,* 49 (1956), 65–67.

7. This revival of the debate, and the condemnation of John (Constantine) of Kerkyra and Eirenikos, occurred in 1169–71, under Patriarch Michael of Anchialos (1169–77): Gouillard, "Synodikon," 77–81; Chalandon, II, 651–52; Beck, *Kirche und theologische Literatur,* 623, 627.

8. Moravcsik, *Byzantinoturcica,* II, 118.

9. Chalandon, II, 486–87.

10. Ibid., 487; Moravcsik, *Byzantium and the Magyars,* 83–85. These campaigns are analyzed in Năsturel, "Valaques" (see above, Book III, n. 8), 177–86.

11. I.e., accept Manuel as emperor. The year 1166 marked the peak of Manuel's negotiations for the western throne (see Kinnamos, 218–20); one of the causes of their collapse was, as Kinnamos notes below, Manuel's refusal to reside in Rome.

12. Moravcsik, "Συμβολαί," 295.

13. Janin, *Constantinople byzantine*, 443: Aphameia or Apameia, a village with an imperial villa, northwest of Hebdomon and north of San Stefano/Yesilkoi, perhaps modern Bosnaviran.

14. Ibid., 496: Samandira and adjacent Alemdaği, ca. 16 miles east of Üsküdar.

15. Polemis, *Doukai*, 192–93 (No. 226): Constantine Doukas or Makrodoukas, who later figured prominently in the reign of Andronicus I.

16. Chalandon, ii, 219–20; Nicetas, *Hist.*, 187–88, maintains that the accusation against the protostrator was false, the work of hostile courtiers. He names Isaac Aaron as his chief opponent.

17. According to Babos, *Adalékok*, 13, MS *Vat. gr.* 163 leaves a short gap here; the editor, Meineke, suggests that the name of John Kontostephanos (see below) has dropped out of the text.

18. This battle occurred on 8 July 1167: Chalandon, ii, 488–90; Moravcsik, *Byzantium and the Magyars*, 85–89.

19. Janin, *Constantinople byzantine*, 215, 465, is unable to offer an exact identification, but suggests the vicinity of Eyüp. Eustathius of Thessalonica addressed an oration to Manuel on the water shortage in Constantinople, ed. W. Regel, *Fontes* (see Introduction, n. 43, above), i, 126–31; the editor (xvi–xvii) dates the shortage to the winter of 1168 and Manuel's construction to 1169, but on what grounds are unclear. The oration was definitely prior to 1174, when Eustathius was appointed to the see of Myra.

20. Chalandon, ii, 611–12; Franz Dölger, *Regesten der Kaiserurkunden des oströmischen Reiches von 565–1453*, Corpus der griechischen Urkunden des Mittelalters und der neueren Zeit, Reihe A, Abt. i, Teil 2 (Munich, 1925), No. 1476 (dated shortly after 8 July 1167, solely on the basis of its position in the text of Kinnamos; Kinnamos, however, is here giving a non-chronological review of some important civil acts of the emperor); A. P. Kazhdan, "Odin netochno istolkovannyĭ passazh v 'Istorii' Ioanna Kinnama," *Revue des Etudes Sud-Est Européenes*, 7 (1969), 469–73.

21. J. and P. Zepos, ed., *Jus graecoromanum*, i (Athens, 1931), 381–85; Dölger, *Regesten*, No. 1419; N. Svoronos, "Les Privilèges de l'Eglise à l'époque des Comnènes: Un Rescrit inédit de Manuel Iᵉʳ Comnène," Centre de recherche d'histoire et civilisation byzantines, *Travaux et mémoires*, 1 (1965), 330–33 (No. 4 of his series), 375–76.

22. Zepos, *Jus*, i, 397–402; Dölger, *Regesten*, No. 1466.

23. Chalandon, ii, 204 and n. 2; Beck, *Kirche und theologische Literatur*, 662; Janin, *Les Eglises et les monastères*, 530.

24. Perhaps Tinnis, a mistake for Pelusium (modern al-Faramā'), captured at this time.

25. While this account makes numerous factual errors and distortions, it vividly reflects the hostility which sprang up between the Palestinian and Byzantine commanders during this expedition: Chalandon, II, 536–45; Baldwin, "Latin States," 556–58.

26. Chalandon, II, 546–50; Baldwin, "Latin States," 558–60.

27. Libanius, *Or.* XI, 38 (ed. R. Foerster, I, 449). Except in the northern Adriatic, tides are unknown in the Mediterranean and, evidently, were unfamiliar to Kinnamos.

28. Horatio F. Brown, "The Venetians and the Venetian Quarter in Constantinople to the Close of the Twelfth Century," *Journal of Hellenic Studies,* 40 (1920), 75, says, "An *Embolum,* it seems, was a place where merchants stored and sold their goods and generally transacted business. . . . It was a building with an open loggia running round it and was of the nature of an Exchange-house rather than of a bazaar. But the word *Embolum* soon acquired a secondary and wider meaning and came to be applied to the whole quarter; '*in Embolo Peramatis*' means in the quarter and district of the Ferry. We find the word *Embolani* signifying the Pisans dwelling in the Pisan Quarter."

29. Chalandon, II, 156–58.

30. The text of this sentence is corrupt; the translation is based on the suggestions in the editor's notes.

31. Chalandon, II, 582, 584–91; H. Kretschmayr, *Geschichte von Venedig, Allgemeine Staatengeschichte,* Abt. 1, No. 35, Vol. I (Gotha, 1905; repr. Aalen, 1964), 254–62. The "second blow" was perhaps the Venetians' defeat at Ancona (Kinnamos, 289).

32. In 1173, Mleh seized Tarsus, Adana, and Mopsuestia from the Byzantines, and captured Constantine Kalamanos, then in his second term as governor: Chalandon, II, 526, n. 2, 531–33; Der Nersessian, "Cilician Armenia," 642–43. Mleh was murdered by his soldiers in 1174.

33. Chalandon, II, 596.

34. Stephen Nemanja had been grand župan since 1168, and eagerly attacked Byzantine Dalmatia: Jireček, *Serben,* I, 258–61.

35. The real reason for the termination of Béla's engagement to Maria Porphyrogenita was the birth of Manuel's son, who was proclaimed co-emperor in 1172. Béla's bride was Anne, daughter of Reginald of Châtillon, and thus half-sister to the empress. A Byzantine army assisted Béla III to obtain his throne: Chalandon, II, 491–92.

36. Jireček, *Serben*, I, 261–62.

37. The ruler of Ankyra and Galatia at this time was probably Shāhan-Shāh, restored by pressure of Nūr-ad-Dīn on Kilidj Arslan. The latter was compelled to yield to Nūr-ad-Dīn in 1173, and restore the Dānishmendid heir to Sebasteia/Sivas. The alliance was destroyed by the deaths of Nūr-ad-Dīn and Mleh in 1174, which left Kilidj Arslan free to expand his realm at the expense of lesser princes: Chalandon, II, 494–98, 501; Gibb, "Nūr-ad-Dīn," 527; Cahen, "Turks in Iran and Anatolia," 678–79.

38. Chalandon, II, 597; Lamma, *Comneni e Staufer,* II, 244–53; Paolo Lamma, *Oriente e occidente nell' alto medioevo,* Medioevo e umanesimo, 5 (Padua, 1968), 383–94; Peter Schreiner, "Der Dux von Dalmatien und die Belagerung Anconas im Jahre 1173. Zur Italien- und Balkanpolitik Manuels I.," *Byzantion,* 41 (1971), 285–311 (includes German translations of this passage and of Nicetas' account of the siege).

39. Moravcsik, *Byzantinoturcica,* II, 339.

40. At the death of Nūr-ad-Dīn, 1174, Shāhan-Shāh and the Dānishmendid heir, Dhū-n-Nūn, fled to Manuel: Chalandon, II, 498.

41. Baldwin, "Latin States," 561.

42. The *a secretis* were notaries; the *protoasecretis,* probably referred to here, was director of the imperial chancery: Bréhier, *Monde byzantin,* II, 167.

BOOK VII

1. Late 1174 or early 1175: Chalandon, II, 502.

2. Nicol, *Kantakouzenos,* 4–5 (Nos. 2 and 3).

3. Ramsay, *Historical Geography,* 212–213 (he considers the fish inedible); Vryonis, *Asia Minor,* 123, 153 (with a translation of this passage). The caesar in question must have been Nicephorus Melissenos, who received his title at the outset of Alexius I's reign. P. Wirth, "Kaiser Manuel I. Komnenos und die Ostgrenze. Rückeroberung und Wiederaufbau der Festung Dorylaion," *Byzantinische Zeitschrift,* 55 (1962), 21–29, compares the accounts of Kinnamos, Nicetas, Eustathius (in an unpublished oration), and Euthymius Malakes on this event.

4. Chalandon, II, 502–03, suggests that partisans of Shāhan-Shāh held the town, and that the latter had been sent from Dorylaion to join the Byzantine expedition.

5. Ibid., 502–04.

6. Moravcsik, *Byzantinoturcica,* II, 140.

7. Ramsay, *Cities and Bishoprics,* I, Pt. 1, 227–28: the plains are between the upper Büyükmenderes and the Acigöl; the modern place-name Lappa, mentioned by Ramsay, is no longer found on maps.

8. Ibid., 221–27 (esp. 224): Soublaion allegedly derives from ancient Siblianoi, and is also called by the Byzantines Choma (Nicetas, *Hist.*, 231), hence is equivalent to modern Homa, northwest of Dinar.

9. Bryer, "Gabrades," 180 (No. 9).

10. Chalandon, ii, 504–07, 550. No Byzantine attack was made on Egypt at this time; the attack on Nea Kaisareia by Andronicus Batatzes and the Dānishmendid Dhū-n-Nūn failed, because of disagreement of the two commanders, and Batatzes was slain. On the route Manuel followed in 1176, and the location of Myriokephalon, see W. M. Ramsay, "Preliminary Report to the Wilson Trustees on Exploration in Phrygia and Lycaonia," *Studies in the History and Art of the Eastern Provinces of the Roman Empire,* ed. W. M. Ramsay (Aberdeen, 1906), 235–38.

Index